One Lifetime, Many Lives

The Experience of Modern Hindu Hagiography

by
Robin Rinehart

Scholars Press
Atlanta, Georgia

One Lifetime, Many Lives
The Experience of Modern Hindu Hagiography

by
Robin Rinehart

Library of Congress Cataloging in Publication Data

Rinehart, Robin, 1964–
One lifetime, many lives : the experience of modern Hindu hagiography / by Robin Rinehart.
p. cm. — (AAR the religions ; no. 6)
Includes bibliographical references and index.
ISBN 0-7885-0555-6 (paper : alk. paper)
1. Rama Tirtha, Swami, 1873–1906. I. Title. II. Series.
BL1175.R254R56 1999
294.5'092—dc21
[B] 99-23116
CIP

Printed in the United States of America
on acid-free paper

Contents

Acknowledgements

It is a pleasure to thank the many people who have helped with the research and writing of this book. The officials of the Swami Rama Tirtha Mission in New Delhi welcomed me at their weekly *satsaṅg* sessions, allowed me to use the Mission library, and patiently answered many questions. I would especially like to thank the late Swami Amar Muni Maharaj, who served as head of the Mission until the early 1990s; the late Mrs. Mela Devi Malhotra, President of the Mission; Mr. Hari Rai Sachdev, Secretary of the Mission, and the Mission's members at both the Swami Rama Tirtha Nagar and Rani Bagh branches. The Swami Rama Tirtha Mission kindly granted permission to reproduce photographs of Swami Rama Tirtha, and the Swami Rama Tirtha Pratishthan in Lucknow gave permission to quote from Swami Rama Tirtha's works and the Pratishthan's other publications. Nina and Ashok Anand (and the *kutte log*) helped make me feel at home in India, as did my friends Jurie Kakoti, Rajeev Bhagat, and the Kapur family.

My earliest research in India on Swami Rama Tirtha was funded by a Junior Fellowship from the American Institute of Indian Studies, whose staff in New Delhi was invaluable. Subsequent research in India was supported by grants from the Lafayette Academic Research Committee, and the writing of the book was supported by a Lafayette College Junior Faculty Leave. While I was on leave in the spring of 1998, an affiliation with the Department of Philosophy and Religion at North Carolina State University provided library access.

The staffs of the Jawaharlal Nehru Library in New Delhi, the Oriental and India Office Collections of the British Library in London, the Tripsaver office at D.H. Hill Library at North Carolina State University, and the Interlibrary Loan office of Skillman Library at Lafayette College all provided cheerful, efficient assistance in locating books and other materials.

This work would not have been possible without many wonderful Hindu, Urdu, and Punjabi instructors: at the University of Washington, Jack Hawley, Michael C. Shapiro, Saroj Gupta, and Naseem Hines; at the American Institute of Indian Studies Hindi language school, Santwana Nigam, Vina Mehta, and Ranjana Daniels; at the University of Pennsylvania, Vijay Gambhir and Amrit Gahunia; and on the Berkeley Urdu Language Program in Pakistan, Qamar Jalil, Bushra Hamid, Arif Waqar, Mohammad Razzaq, and Mushtaq Ahmad.

Frank Conlon first encouraged me to study saints' biographies when I was an undergraduate at the University of Washington. At the University of Pennsylvania, Guy Welbon guided my earliest research on Swami Rama Tirtha, and Ann Matter helped broaden my knowledge of sainthood and hagiography in world religions. Whitney Sanford has been a supportive friend since our first year at Penn. My colleagues in the Religion department at Lafayette College have also been very helpful, especially Bob Cohn, who provided useful comments on early drafts of some sections of the book.

I would also like to thank the anonymous readers of the manuscript for their valuable suggestions; David Gilmartin; Paul Courtright, Editor of the Religions Series; Leigh C. Andersen, Assistant Publications Manager at Scholars Press, who guided me through the preparation of camera-ready copy; and Jason Fuller, who carefully proofread the text. Yvonne Osmun, secretary in the Religion department at Lafayette College, helped with many aspects of the production of the book, as did Sue Leopold, Tracy Logan, and the staff of Academic Computing Services at Lafayette College. George Panichas provided expert assistance in reproducing photographs.

Finally, my greatest thanks go to Tony K. Stewart, who encouraged me to develop and complete this project, gave insightful comments and suggestions on countless drafts of the manuscript, and was a constant source of support.

Abbreviations

BMR: *Bhārat ke Mahān Ṛṣi*

GMP: *Swami Rama Tirtha: Great Mystic Poet of the Modern India*

IWGR: *In Woods of God-Realization: The Complete Works of Swami Rama Tirtha*, vols. 1-7

KeR: *Kulliyāt-e-Rām*, vols. 1-3 (Urdu)

LSRT: *Life of Swami Rama Tirtha*

LTW: *Life, Teachings, and Writings of Swami Rama Tirtha*

RJC: *Rām Jīvan Citrāvalī* (Hindi)

RP: *Rām-patra* (Hindi)

RRT: *Ramanand to Ram Tirath*

RV: *Rām-varṣā* (Hindi)

SIS: *Some Indian Saints*

SKK: *Santõ kī Kahāniyā̃*

SSR: *The Story of Swami Rama: The Poet-Monk of India*

SRTM: Swami Rama Tirtha Mission

SRTP: Swami Rama Tirtha Pratishthan

TSI: *Ten Saints of India*

Note on Transliteration and Translation

The standard transliteration for Indic languages is used; the final mute *a* in Hindi and Urdu words has been dropped. Diacritics are not used for the names of places and institutions. When they first occur in the text, names of people and deities are given in their typical Anglicized version with full diacritics in brackets, and without diacritics thereafter (e.g. Krishna [*Kṛṣṇa*]). Other terms from Indic languages are given with diacritics. In the appendix and bibliography, authors' names and titles of Hindi and Urdu texts are given with full diacritics. In cases in which a person uses an English spelling of his or her name which does not follow standard transliteration, the person's own English spelling is used (e.g. Ayodhia Nath for Ayodhya Nath [Ayodhyā Nāth]). All quotations preserve the exact spelling of the text. When comparing Hindi, Urdu, and English texts, inconsistencies are unfortunately inevitable, although every effort has been made to standardize spellings.

Although Swami Rama Tirtha [*Swāmī Rāma Tīrtha*] and his followers typically spell his name in English with the final inherent "*a*" in both "Rama" and "Tirtha," the final "*a*" in "Rama" is usually not pronounced, and "Tirtha" is pronounced something like "Tee-rut" (rendered in some texts as "Tirath").

All translations from Hindi and Urdu are the author's unless otherwise noted.

Swami Rama Tirtha. Courtesy of the Swami Rama Tirtha Mission

1
The Experience of Hindu Hagiography

Sometime in the year 1901, a young Hindu man from Lahore named Tirath Ram [Tīrath Rām] took vows of renunciation, leaving behind his life as a mathematics professor, husband and father. Even before he took those vows, casting his Brāhmaṇ's sacred thread into the Ganges river, Tirath Ram had already achieved some fame in his native province of Punjab, first through his passionate speeches advocating worship of the god Krishna [Kṛṣṇa], and later through lectures and published essays in which he explored the monistic philosophy of Advaita Vedānta. As a renunciant, newly renamed Swami Rama Tirtha, he quickly attracted followers in the Punjab and northern India. A maharaja was so impressed with him that he sent him to Japan to represent Hinduism; from there, Swami Rama Tirtha traveled to the United States, where he spent nearly two years lecturing on what he considered the essence of Hinduism and indeed all religion, a philosophy he now termed "Practical Vedānta."[1] He was met with great acclaim when he returned to India in 1904; people thronged to the lectures and public appearances of this young Swami, just over thirty, who had championed India's cause abroad. But in 1906, less than two years after his triumphant return from America, Swami Rama Tirtha withdrew from public life and retired to the foothills of the Himalayas. Weary of constant public lectures and the adoration of the public, he sent away even his closest followers, and prepared to write a systematic exposition of his philosophy of Practical Vedānta. His plans were cut short when he drowned while bathing in the Ganges river in October, 1906.

Swami Rama Tirtha's sudden death at the age of thirty-three was a severe blow to his followers. Two of his closest disciples were Narayan Swami [Nārāyaṇ Swāmī], who had taken vows of renunciation at Swami Rama Tirtha's insistence, and Puran Singh[Pūraṇ Singh], a poet and engineer who first met the Swami in Japan. To them fell the task of organizing Swami Rama Tirtha's papers and few personal effects after he drowned. They wandered aimlessly in the area around Swami Rama Tirtha's hut as they tried to understand and find some meaning in the drowning of their beloved

Swami who had always told them that he could control death itself. Eventually, both men would endeavor to leave a record of the Swami's life so that others could learn about the man they had so loved. Puran Singh's *The Story of Swami Rama: The Poet Monk of India* (*SSR*) was first published in 1924; the original English text has been reprinted many times, and translated into Hindi as well. Around the same time that Singh's text was published, Narayan Swami wrote an untitled Urdu account of Swami Rama Tirtha's life, which was first published in 1935 as part of the Swami's collected works. These were just two among what would grow to be a body of over twenty-five accounts of the Swami's life in Hindi, Urdu, and English within less than a century.

In 1990, over eighty years after Swami Narayan and Puran Singh first tried to understand why Swami Rama Tirtha had drowned, a group of young uniformed schoolchildren stood before the audience at the weekly devotional meeting [*satsaṅg*] of the Swami Rama Tirtha Mission's headquarters in New Delhi. Students at the primary school operated by the Swami Rama Tirtha Educational Society, they had prepared a presentation on the life of Swami Rama Tirtha as part of the Mission's annual celebration of the Swami's birthday. In Hindi, the young students earnestly described Swami Rama Tirtha's trials and tribulations as a student and his role as an inspirational figure for citizens of independent India. Their stories of Swami Rama Tirtha are another part of the ongoing tradition established by Puran Singh and Narayan Swami many years before them—though they are perhaps not quite the same stories.

These many "lives" of Swami Rama Tirtha, the multiple accounts of his life, written and oral, provide an excellent opportunity for studying hagiography, one of the most popular genres of religious literature in India. The tradition of hagiography dates back centuries in India, with hagiographical accounts not just from Hinduism, but also Buddhism, Jainism, Sikhism, and Islam, including the Jātaka tales (stories of the Buddha's past lives), the *janam-sākhī* literature about Guru Nanak [Gurū Nānak], and the lives of Sufi *shaykhs* and *pīrs*,[2] as well as the accounts of the Tamil saints of the Śaiva and Vaiṣṇava devotional movements, the legendary stories of the life of the great Advaita Vedānta philosopher Sankara [Śaṅkara], and the stories of the medieval *sant*s and *bhakta*s such as Kabir [Kabīr], Surdas [Sūrdās], and Mirabai [Mīrābāī]. The genre continues to thrive both in the regional languages of India as well as English, from comic book accounts of saints' lives geared towards children (e.g. the popular *Amar Citra Katha* series) to lengthy studies of the lives of saints past and present, and hagiographical collections recounting the lives of many saints.

While hagiographies are a treasure-trove of information about saints, the study of hagiography has often been frustrating for scholars seeking historical facts, for despite their mutual concern with the lives of saints, hagiographers' aims are much different than those of the scholar constructing a critical historical biography. Where some scholars seek the facts that will constitute a factual account of the saint's life, the hagiographer has often blended those facts into an intricate mix of myth and legend. Although the challenging task of separating the historical elements from the mythical in the mix has been the goal of many scholars, the mix of myth and history itself is central to the purposes of hagiography, and tells us a great deal about how the followers of a saint construct and preserve his or her memory. It is also important to note that while not everything that a hagiography reports may be historically accurate, the blending of myth and history itself within a hagiographical tradition takes on a historical dimension as the portrayal of the saint changes over time. Tracing the development of the hagiographical tradition surrounding Swami Rama Tirtha allows us to investigate the dynamics of this blending of myth and history with a precision not always possible for earlier traditions. Unlike medieval Hindu hagiographies which are often difficult to date and may contain only brief accounts of saints' lives, in the Swami Rama Tirtha tradition there is a larger body of information against which to compare that provided by hagiographies. The corpus of Swami Rama Tirtha's work (essays, letters, lectures, poems etc.) is clearly established, so we are not troubled by questions of textual authenticity when we examine how hagiographers have used his writings.[3] We know the identities of nearly all the hagiographers, and the exact dates of almost all their texts, as well as the larger historical context of India in the late nineteenth and twentieth centuries, making it possible to identify the specific historical situations hagiographers address as they concoct their blends of myth and history. Swami Rama Tirtha became relatively well-known during his own lifetime in a particular region of India (in Swami Rama Tirtha's case, the Punjab and north India), and had a small community of followers which has preserved his memory, and as such, the hagiographical tradition surrounding him is typical of many such traditions around saints throughout India. The wealth of information available about Swami Rama Tirtha—the hagiographies about him and his own writings, coupled with the accessibility of the recent past—helps us to illumine the nature of hagiography itself, an often maligned and misunderstood genre of religious literature.

The Definition and Study of Hagiography

The most common application of the term hagiography (literally, "sacred writing") has been to writings about the lives of saints.[4] Both "saint" and "hagiography" are terms that require some clarification. While the designation "saint" was first applied to particular figures in Christianity, it is now used in a much wider context across religious traditions to refer to those people whom the members of a particular religion deem to exemplify their highest ideals. The saint has achieved something that most ordinary people cannot; nonetheless, the saint's achievement of the religion's highest ideals makes him a worthy figure for imitation. Richard Kieckhefer and George D. Bond (1988: viii), in considering this tension between the saint's imitability versus his or her "utter distinctness from normal humanity," conclude that the term "saint" may best be applied across religious traditions to individuals "who come to be both imitated and venerated."[5] Such a broad-based definition is valuable, for it allows us to recognize a general category across religious traditions, yet leaves room to analyze the specific nature of what each tradition considers worthy of imitation and veneration, and the concomitant tension between imitability and veneration.[6] In this study, we are applying the designation "saint" to Swami Rama Tirtha, a Hindu. As we shall learn, his followers believed that he was in certain ways a worthy exemplar but that at the same time he had attained a level of spiritual achievement far beyond the range of the ordinary person, thereby illustrating the central tension in sainthood between imitability and inimitability. Nonetheless, there is no one word in either Hindi or Urdu which corresponds directly to "saint." The range of related terms and titles is vast: in Hindi, Swami Rama Tirtha is variously referred to as a *guru* (teacher), an *avatār* (divine descent), a *paramahaṃs* (supreme liberated spirit), a *sannyāsī* (renunciant), and in Urdu he is also called a *faqīr* (ascetic; one who lives in poverty).[7] Yet despite the wide range of terms available in Indian languages, most of the hagiographers who have written about the Swami in English identify him simply as a "saint" (or even "supersaint").[8] In Hindu hagiographies composed in or translated into English, "saint" is the most commonly used designation for figures known by the Hindi and Urdu titles above.[9] The present-day followers of Swami Rama Tirtha themselves call him a "saint" when they speak of him in English; their use of the term encompasses all the Hindi and Urdu terms above, with the general connotation of someone especially holy, a man whose spiritual attainments were far beyond those of the ordinary person. Because the Swami's own followers consider the term "saint" appropriate for him, it will serve our purposes as well.

Just as "saint" was first used in the context of Christianity, "hagiography" too first designated writings about the lives of Christian saints, but has since been applied to a far wider range of writings from different religious traditions. There are sometimes negative connotations associated with the term which derive from critical assessments of hagiography as a largely fictional and therefore unreliable style of biographical writing. Indeed in popular usage, "hagiography" has come to refer to a glowing, completely uncritical description of a person. As a result, some scholars have preferred to abandon the term hagiography altogether in favor of "sacred biography" in order to escape the negative associations with hagiography.[10] Frank E. Reynolds and Donald Capps, however, in their introduction to *The Biographical Process*, make a helpful distinction between sacred biography and hagiography. Sacred biography they define as "those accounts written by followers or devotees of a founder or religious savior," and hagiography, "the lives of saints, mystic prophets, kings and other charismatic religious figures" (Reynolds and Capps 1976: 3-4).[11] The benefit of this distinction is that it allows us to distinguish the significant difference between accounts of the lives of founders (such as Jesus and the Buddha) which establish a new religious ideal, and the lives of saints (e.g. Swami Rama Tirtha) which in some way exemplify an already existing ideal. The rhetorical strategies involved in creating a new religious ideal versus portraying someone as an exemplification of an already existing ideal may differ dramatically. Since much of our focus will be on the ways in which Swami Rama Tirtha's followers have understood him to exemplify various pre-existing ideals, we shall follow Reynolds' and Capps' distinction between sacred biography and hagiography, designating the accounts of Swami Rama Tirtha's life as hagiographies rather than sacred biographies. A further complication in terminology is that whereas Indian authors writing in English often use the term "saint," they tend to use the term "biography" rather than hagiography to designate their writings about saints' lives.[12] However, those texts that devotees term "biographies" are in fact better understood as hagiographies because their strategies and goals differ significantly from those of the critical biographer. Like many hagiographies, those written about Swami Rama Tirtha would not fare well if judged by the variously conceived standards of critical historical biographies; for example, they are not based on extensive research or investigation, and often include historically inaccurate reports and stories of fantastic miracles. Many of the negative associations with the genre of hagiography in fact result from the application of the standards of critical historical biographies (according to which miracles and the like must be rejected) to hagiographical texts.

Early studies of Christian hagiography were often highly critical of the genre because of its apparent lack of regard for historical accuracy and uncritical acceptance of miracles and other wonders. Such criticism of hagiography came both from scholars seeking historical information amidst the tangled mythical web of hagiographical narrative,[13] and from apologists within the Christian tradition itself who sought to establish the historical basis for the widespread worship of saints. Hippolyte Delehaye's 1907 study, *The Legends of the Saints: An Introduction to Hagiography*, illustrates the latter approach well. Delehaye, a Bollandist monk, assessed hagiography from the position of an insider working towards the definitive account of the lives of officially canonized saints of the Roman Catholic church (the Bollandists' massive *Acta Sanctorum*, begun by Jean Bolland in the seventeenth century). Delehaye defined a "hagiographic document" as a text concerning the life of a saint which should be "of a religious character and aim at edification. The term may only be applied therefore to writings inspired by devotion to the saints and intended to promote it" (Delehaye 1907: 2). Delehaye's basic definition of hagiography is helpful, and we shall return to it; however, his approach to the study of hagiography was based primarily upon his application of the criterion of historical verifiability or plausibility. A quick glance at the topic headings of the second chapter of Delehaye's book reveals his estimation of hagiography: "Unconscious distortion of truth by the individual—by the people—Level of popular intelligence—Tendency to simplification—Ignorance—Substitution of the abstract form for the individual type—Poverty of invention—The borrowing and transmission of legendary themes" and so forth (Delehaye 1907: xiii). Delehaye's position as an apologist suggests that we must read his assessments of the Christian saints' lives very carefully; nonetheless, his chapter headings are instructive because they capture so clearly many of the negative views of the genre. Hagiographies, then, in the reckoning of Delehaye and many others since, tend to distort the truth (by which Delehaye presumably meant historical truth), and either cater to or are the product of a relatively unsophisticated audience; they are therefore simplistic and unimaginative, and shamelessly borrow from the lives and legends of other saints. Delehaye and many other scholars have thus sifted through hagiographies searching for historical "facts," discarding the mythical and legendary material that seemingly obscured historical truth.[14] While Delehaye's approach is of course dated, similar attitudes persist in more recent studies of hagiography though they may not be so baldly stated. Heffernan, for example, has shown that much of the contemporary understanding of medieval Christian hagiography has been shaped by the emphasis on positivist historiography which grew out of the Enlightenment response to hagiographical literature (1988: 54).[15] For many, hagiography was in effect a substandard genre of historical writing. However, as Heffernan points out, and as Delehaye had earlier noted, the primary function of hagiography is instructional, not historiographical—it aims for religious edification, not historical documentation.

Because the goals of hagiographers are so different from those of the historian, ongoing hagiographical traditions concerning the life of one saint often develop in directions that take them farther and farther afield from the original life as it was actually lived (bios). The later hagiographical documents within a tradition are often replete with stereotypical descriptions, mythical imagery, and tales that seem to have been lifted wholesale from the lives of other saints to the extent that there is virtually no trace of the original historical figure, making such documents of virtually no use to the historically-minded scholar.[16] Because texts from the later stages of a hagiographical tradition may rely so heavily upon myth (rather than "history"), these texts are often neglected in favor of those deemed to have some salvageable historical data. Lost in such assessments of hagiography, however, is serious attention to the conventions of the genre itself and an understanding of why hagiographical traditions follow this pattern of development. In her study of Christian hagiography as a genre, Alexandra Hennessey Olsen (1980) notes that we must understand hagiographies not simply as biographical accounts, but as didactic and polemical texts. Thus all the elements in a hagiography (e.g. miracle stories) are part of an overall narrative structure which serves the text's polemical purposes. Olsen also points out that scholars combing through hagiographies for historical data may miss the fact that hagiographers often have a sense of humor, and that "the lighter side of the cult of the saints" may well be responsible for some of the patently fictitious incidents in hagiographies (1980: 408).[17] Miraculous events and seemingly fictitious tales often are an integral part of the hagiographer's rhetorical strategy.

The study of Indian hagiography has in many ways paralleled the study of Christian hagiography, with similarly negative characterizations of the "legendary" and "mythical" nature of hagiographical reporting of historical figures. This is particularly true in cases in which hagiographical materials are the only extant sources of information on important religious leaders. Yet sifting through hagiographical (or sacred biographical) material to extract historical facts may yield very little information. For example, in his study of the life of Guru Nanak, the founder of Sikhism, W.H. McLeod worked through the voluminous *janam-sākhī* literature about Guru Nanak and was able to extract less than a single page of material which he found historically plausible (1968: 146).[18] Such approaches privilege the scholar's "historically accurate" account over the memories of the saint's followers. Yet the ongoing hagiographical tradition itself constitutes a kind of history—the history of how the saint's followers have chosen to remember him or her. Recognizing this, other scholars have moved beyond the strictly "historical" approach to hagiography, acknowledging what Reynolds and Capps identified as the "mythohistoric character" of sacred biography and hagiography, its tendency to blend historical information with mythical and legendary images (1976: 1). From this standpoint, the mythical and legendary components of Indian hagiographies serve not simply as sources of historically plausible data, but also as a useful source of information on the political, social, and religious concerns of the communities who produced and read them. For example, as the hagiographical tradition surrounding the poet Kabir developed, the story that Kabir was born to Hindu parents (not Muslim, as his name suggests) and was initiated by the Brāhmaṇ *guru* Ramananda [Rāmānanda] became increasingly popular. Whether or not these stories accurately record the parentage and initiation of the historical figure Kabir, they do show that in the centuries after Kabir's death, many of his followers found it important to connect him to a specifically Hindu ancestry and lineage of initiation.[19] In his study of some of the hagiographies of Kabir, David N. Lorenzen argued that "the legends take the form of stories that the members of the community tell about and for themselves. They are reflexive commentaries that define the imagined shared past of the community, its historical identity, as well as normalize its religious, social, moral, political and even economic values" (Lorenzen 1991: 4). Thus when hagiographical traditions record mythical or legendary information, they nonetheless reveal what are indeed historical facts—not necessarily about the historical figure of the saint, but about the situation of the community the hagiographer addresses.

Hagiography and Myth

When we examine such mythical imagery in hagiography, it becomes clear that hagiographers seem to draw from a stock set of motifs and patterns as they construct their texts. Scholars working with Indian hagiographies cannot help but notice the recurrence of common mythological themes and motifs, and many have presented what they find to be typical life patterns for Indian saints. A.K. Ramanujan (1982), for example, charted typical patterns found in the lives of female saints in south India.[20] Charles S. J. White (1974) has suggested that there is a "distinctive developmental structure" in the life history of Indian saints.[21] William Jackson (1992) has identified twelve motifs in the hagiographical tradition that developed around the musician-saint Tyagaraja [Tyāgarāja](1767-1847), motifs which may be found in other Indian hagiographical traditions as well.[22] Rupert Snell (1996: 12) noted typical formulae in hagiographies from different regions and languages.[23] Similarly, Lorenzen (1995) chronicled a basic pattern in the lives of *nirguṇī* saints (those who worship a god without attributes), noting that the basic pattern resembles the archetypal life stories of the hero as presented by Otto Rank, Lord Raglan, and Alan Dundes.[24] Others, too, have found motifs that are not unique to Indian hagiography; in his study of the biography of Dadu Dayal [Dādū Dayāl], Winand Callewaert (1988: 11) remarked on the similarities between literary devices used in Dadu Dayal's biography and those found in Christian hagiography.[25]

The existence of recurring themes and motifs in Indian hagiography and other religious traditions as well has given rise to all manner of speculation about possible ways of explaining their sources; some have linked these motifs to the various constructions of the hero-pattern delineated by Otto Rank, Lord Raglan, and Joseph Campbell, each of whom proposed a universal pattern in the life of heroic individuals.[26] While identifying the source of such motifs is not our concern here, it is important to note that such attempts are problematic; they often hypothesize a common source for life patterns and motifs (e.g. the collective unconscious, the storehouse of folk memory). Metaphorical constructs such as the idea of a "storehouse" of memories and images from which hagiographers draw suggest that there is a complete set of mythical images governed by some as yet undiscovered law of selection and organization. Yet this "storehouse" cannot be conclusively characterized or proven, nor can we set out the mechanisms through which it might operate. A further disadvantage in focusing on a common source for mythological motifs is that it may lead us to disregard other equally important aspects of these motifs and their use in different times and places. The idea of a common source (whether it be universal or tradition-specific) detracts focus from both the creativity of the individual hagiographer, and the specific context of each hagiographical tradition.[27] Additionally, while many scholars have identified patterns in the lives of Indian saints and saints in general, the patterns that they have extrapolated from their readings of different saints' lives vary widely, suggesting that even if there are universal patterns, there are many, not simply one.[28]

The situation within the Hindu tradition is particularly complex, for whereas a majority of the hagiographical models in Christianity relate in some way to the paradigmatic acts of Jesus or other biblical figures,[29] the hagiographical models of Hinduism may derive from any number of sources, from the acts of the many gods and goddesses to the lives of other saints. There are as yet many unanswered questions about the range of patterns available within the Hindu tradition and their use and applicability within different time periods, different regions, different languages, different social groups, etc. While patterns and motifs undoubtedly recur within Hinduism and across religious traditions, at some point, hagiographers and/or the saint's community of followers have made specific choices about which patterns and motifs to use and which to avoid. Their telling of a saint's life may in fact incorporate fragments of several different patterns, and different accounts of the same saint's life may use different patterns. In this study, therefore, we will focus on the different ways in which patterns and motifs are used and the different contexts in which they appear, rather than trying to account for their recurrence. Through paying attention to the differences in the ways in which hagiographers select certain motifs and not others, and the ways in which a life may reflect parts of one pattern and parts of another, we learn more about the hagiographer's art. Charting the differences in motifs and patterns within a single hagiographical tradition allows us to come to a greater understanding of exactly how hagiographers mix myth and history together to create the "mythohistoric" character of hagiography (e.g. how they relate specific historical incidents to larger mythic models) and can aid us in understanding the historical development of such traditions.[30] For example, some of the earliest hagiographies of Swami Rama Tirtha contain "stock" images of him as a saint, as do some of the later hagiographies—but they are not the same stock images. Attributing those changes to the appropriation of different patterns is a useful way of describing what happens, but it cannot help us analyze how and why it happens. To understand why the images change, we must examine these varying uses of myth within their specific historical contexts.

The Experience of Sainthood: Satsaṅg with Swami Rama Tirtha

Analyses of hagiographical images which stress the role of mythical imagery and common patterns and motifs may intentionally or otherwise give precedence to the ahistorical, timeless nature of myth. Yet every hagiography, however much it makes the individual saint into a "type," is in some way firmly rooted in a particular community, a particular time, and a particular place. One of the advantages of following the development of a recent hagiographical tradition such as that of Swami Rama Tirtha is that it is possible to identify those particulars of time and place, permitting us to investigate the nature of the interaction of those historical particularities with the imagery of myth. As we shall learn in chapter five, while the later hagiographers of Swami Rama Tirtha increasingly resort to mythical imagery in their portrayals of him, they present the story of his life as being directly relevant to their own historical situation, not in some ahistorical, timeless context. This is reflected in the language of the texts as well; while the earliest hagiographies were mainly in English, the more recent hagiographies are predominantly in Hindi, which indicates the hagiographers' choices about their intended audiences, as well as their larger concern with Indian nationalism (Hindi being the national language of India) and its relation to Swami Rama Tirtha. The later hagiographers also demonstrate an awareness of the fact that some of their readers might find stories of miracles difficult to accept; while this does not stop them from reporting such stories, they often present them along with arguments designed to assuage the doubts of a twentieth-century, "scientifically" oriented audience.[31] To answer questions about how specific historical circumstances may have governed the hagiographer's selection of materials (and even the language of the text), the hagiographer's appropriation and modification of typical patterns, and how the interaction between myth and history has changed over time, requires that we focus not only on the life of the saint but also the life of the community which recognizes and remembers the saint. It is in the interaction between saint and followers that images of sainthood are constructed.

One role which saints share across different religious traditions is that of mediator. The Christian saint, the Muslim *pīr*, the Hindu *guru*—all may intercede with the divine on behalf of their followers.[32] The saint's close relationship with the divine world beyond is the source of the inherent tension in sainthood mentioned above—as one who is especially close to divinity (or, in the case of Hindu figures such as Swami Rama Tirtha, who understands himself as some form of divinity itself), the saint may exemplify ideals to which all may aspire—yet at the same time, the saint's exalted status is worthy of veneration, and in that sense may seem inimitable to followers. In the Swami Rama Tirtha hagiographical tradition, this tension is revealed in sharp contrast in the writings of the Swami himself, who saw himself primarily as an exemplar and not an object of veneration, and in the writings of his followers, who saw him as primarily worthy of veneration, and therefore essentially inimitable (a subject explored further in chapter four). Ultimately, it was the followers' construction of Swami Rama Tirtha as an object of veneration which would come to dominate, not the Swami's own self-presentation, and the hagiographies demonstrate this clearly. While the saint mediates between the follower and the world of divinity beyond, hagiographers (followers who tell the life of a saint) also serve as mediators, creating a bridge between the saint and his followers through their texts.[33] This bridge is especially crucial for followers when the saint is no longer living, for the hagiography may become one of the few means by which followers may recall and relive the saint's presence.[34] The role of hagiographers as mediators (and recruiters) is in fact a crucial and sometimes overlooked aspect of the study of hagiography. While we may not always have much biographical information about particular hagiographers, even without such details, the hagiographies themselves serve as evidence of the hagiographers' rhetorical strategies. Their strategies are governed by their first and foremost goal of inspiring devotion to the saint (and often institutions in the saint's name) who is their subject.

It is the original followers of the saint who first recognize and confer upon him his saintly status, and it is they who create and preserve his memory once he is gone. In their study of saints in Western Christianity, Donald Weinstein and Rudolph M. Bell (1982: 9) acknowledged the crucial distinction between "the saint as historical person and as construct, the creation of other people's perceptions and expectations." Similarly, in his study of the "sanctification" of Mahatma Gandhi (who was himself reluctant to be characterized as such), Mark Juergensmeyer (1987: 188) noted that "saintliness, like beauty, exists largely in the eye of the beholder, and the point of view is as interesting as the object of attention." The exchange between the saint and his followers who perceive him as such is a fundamental part of sainthood, and is therefore a fundamental part of hagiography as well. Hagiography (the story of the saint's life) must chronicle the ways in which followers experienced the saint as a saint. The evidence from the Swami Rama Tirtha hagiographies suggests that as a result, hagiography is not simply an account of the life of a saint, but is also an account of the exchange between the saint and followers that led to the saint's recognition as a saint. Accounts of the experiences that Swami Rama Tirtha's followers had in his presence are a crucial part of the rhetorical strategy of all of Swami Rama Tirtha's hagiographers. It is in this area, perhaps, that hagiography diverges most sharply from various forms of biographical writing, with biography focusing on the writing of the life (bios), and hagiography emphasizing that about the saint's life that led to his recognition as a saint, i.e. the "sacred" or "holy" (hagios).[35] This challenges the hagiographer to describe something which may not be fully expressible in language, and one of the ways hagiographers attempt this is through trying to explain the effect that the saint had on them or on others. For example, Puran Singh, one of the Swami's first hagiographers, began his account not with the Swami's early life, but with page after page of descriptions of the effect that the Swami had on others:

> The effect of his presence was marvellous, his joy was infectious, his ideas still more so . . . To see him was to begin, as it were, one's life anew. (*SSR*: 3)

When Puran Singh tried to convey what was most meaningful about Swami Rama Tirtha, he provided not biographical details, but an account of his memory of what it was like to be in the Swami's presence, and this would become a constant refrain throughout the hagiographical tradition. Because the follower's experience of the saint is itself such a fundamental part of sainthood, when hagiographers write about a saint's life, they do much more than assemble and organize biographical information.

When we speak of followers' "experiences" of a saint, we are addressing what followers themselves often call *satsaṅg*, or "association with the good."[36] In modern Hindi, being in the presence of a saint is often designated as *satsaṅg*. It may also refer to a gathering of the saint's followers; the weekly meetings of the Swami Rama Tirtha Mission, for example, are called "*satsaṅgs*." Being in the presence of a saint (or good people in general) in and of itself is understood to have a positive, transforming effect.[37] As many have noted, the concept of "experience" is complex; here, we shall use it not only in reference to the initial experience of being in Swami Rama Tirtha's presence, but also its subsequent physical, emotional, intellectual, moral, and spiritual effects.[38] The term "experience" thus encompasses both the initial event itself, and its ongoing interpretation.[39] Furthermore, an experience and its interpretation may themselves constitute "experience" in the form of a body of knowledge or understanding gained as a result of various experiences; in this sense, experience may serve as a guide for making decisions about how to conduct one's life, and how to understand the world. People may always add to their store of experience; new experiences may color their memories and interpretations of earlier experiences. A person's store of experience is thus constantly revised. For example, when followers of Swami Rama Tirtha initially had certain kinds of experiences in his presence, their pre-existing body of experience (e.g. ideas about what a saint is supposed to be like) helped them to decide how to understand what their experience of Swami Rama Tirtha meant; their interpretations of those initial experiences shaped their interpretations of later experiences in the Swami's presence. When such experiences are reported to others, as when a hagiographer tells about an experience in Swami Rama Tirtha's presence, the report itself may become the basis for a new experience for the reader of the hagiography. The ongoing reporting and interpretation of experiences in all the senses described above is a critical element in the development of the Swami Rama Tirtha hagiographical tradition.

Indeed the Swami Rama Tirtha hagiographical tradition is not simply about the life of Swami Rama Tirtha; it is just as much (if not more) about his followers' experiences of that life, whether experienced directly or mediated through other means, such as hagiographies. If we understand hagiography to fulfill both these functions—recording a life and recording others' experiences of that life—it adds a new dimension to our understanding of hagiographical traditions. Taking into account the role that hagiographers' reporting of the experience of being in Swami Rama Tirtha's presence has played in the development of the hagiographical tradition allows us not only to describe the changes that take place in the hagiographies' portrayals of Swami Rama Tirtha, but also to explain why those changes have taken place as the tradition has adapted to the changing concerns of the Swami's devotees.

After Swami Rama Tirtha died in 1906, hagiographies became a valuable tool for solidifying the existing community of devotees and attracting new devotees. In its function as a kind of propaganda, hagiography must have an effective rhetorical strategy to convince readers (or listeners, in those cases in which hagiographies are read aloud) of the sanctity of its subject. As a result, hagiographers must take into account the interests and expectations of their intended audience when they craft their rhetorical strategies; naturally, such interests and expectations change over time. When hagiographers make an individual into a type, when they seem to "borrow" stories from the lives of other saints, when they report incredible miracles, or engineer face-to-face meetings between saints who lived in different centuries, we must ask why hagiographers tell these tales and how they contribute to the hagiographers' rhetorical strategies, asking questions about historical accuracy and verifiability only when they illuminate those strategies.[40]

While the earliest hagiographers writing about Swami Rama Tirtha emphasized many of the "facts" of his life, focusing more on the Swami as an individual than an exemplification of an ideal, the later hagiographies move away from specific biographical facts towards a portrayal that draws heavily on mythical images and traditional models, a trend that has been noted in other recent Hindu hagiographical traditions as well.[41] To begin our analysis of the Swami Rama Tirtha hagiographies, chapter two, "The Many Lives of Swami Rama Tirtha" is an introduction to the basic narrative account of the Swami's life found in virtually all the hagiographies about him, highlighting those aspects of his life which hagiographers have found important; the chapter concludes with a brief introduction to the most important hagiographies and their authors. Chapter three, "Positivism and Poetry: The First Phase of the Hagiographical Tradition," is an examination of the three most important of the early hagiographies, concentrating on their presentations of Swami Rama Tirtha's death at the age of thirty-three. How would these first hagiographers, all of whom had some direct contact with the Swami, make use of the "facts" about his life? How would they exploit the authority inherent in their own personal experience of Swami Rama Tirtha? What interpretive frameworks governed their portrayals of the Swami and their explanations of his actions? Which text would be most successful, and why? There is a spirited debate among these three hagiographers about how best to present the Swami's life, and much of that debate revolves around the role that the hagiographer's experience of Swami Rama Tirtha should play in the text.

Chapter four, "Fragments for an Autohagiography? Swami Rama Tirtha Writes the Story of His Life" is an analysis of the Swami's scattered autobiographical writings. Taken together, these writings suggest that the Swami attempted to provide for his followers an interpretive framework with which to present and understand his life, writings which effectively became "autohagiography." How did his hagiographers make use of that material? To what extent was Swami Rama Tirtha able to influence the ways in which he would be remembered? His "autohagiographical" writings were an attempt to chronicle his own spiritual experience, which was of course necessarily different from his followers' experience of him, and that difference helps to account for the signficant divergence between Swami Rama Tirtha's self-presentation, and his followers' presentation of him.

Chapter five, "From Bare Facts to Myth: Swami Rama Tirtha as *Avatār*" is a study of the most important of the recent hagiographies of Swami Rama Tirtha, the 1989 Hindi text *Rām Jīvan Citrāvalī* [illustrated life of Rama]. In this text published by the Swami Rama Tirtha Pratishthan, (which was established by Swami Rama Tirtha's followers to preserve his work), Swami Rama Tirtha is portrayed as an *avatār* of Krishna who performed many miracles and inspired the devotion of the world's most important political and religious leaders. Here, the Swami assumes the characteristics of other Hindu saints and even gods, and emerges as a character very different from the Swami of the earliest hagiographies. *Rām Jīvan Citrāvalī* adds new details to earlier stories of incidents in the Swami's life, and reports incidents for which there is no earlier basis. Yet the text is not based upon any new research into Swami Rama Tirtha's life. How are we to understand this mythicization of the Swami? How does it relate to the concerns of the Swami's followers in the late twentieth century? While it might seem that "myth" dominates "history" in this phase of the hagiographical tradition, the mythical dimension of *Rām Jīvan Citrāvalī* is in fact strongly grounded in specific historical concerns, and also reflects the changing nature of followers' experiences of Swami Rama Tirtha eighty years after his death.

Chapter six, "Many Saints, One Agenda: Hagiographical Collections," moves beyond the Swami Rama Tirtha hagiographical tradition to consider another form of hagiography, the collection, through an analysis of a representative sample of Hindi and English collections of saints' lives (several of which include accounts of Swami Rama Tirtha). Such collections often include a seemingly bewildering array of saints from different regions, times, sects, and even different religious traditions. In hagiographical collections, the concept of followers' experiences of saints is also important, but in a somewhat different way than in single-saint hagiographies; in collections, experiences serve not as a confirmation of sainthood (as they do in the Swami Rama Tirtha hagiographies), but rather as confirmations of the collection author's particular agenda.

Finally, chapter seven, "Swami Rama Tirtha as Poet, Nationalist, and Supersaint: Reflections on the Role of Experience in Hagiography," considers two important themes in the Swami Rama Tirtha hagiographical tradition: the Swami's status as a poet, and as an Indian nationalist. While the early evidence suggests that the Swami was neither much of a poet nor a nationalist (by his own admission), the later tradition glorifies him as a "poet-apostle" and even as the architect of independent India. This radical shift in the Swami's image may best be understood when we take into account the centrality of experience in the Swami's hagiographical tradition, for it is followers' experiences of him as a poet and nationalist that have transformed him not only into a model poet and nationalist, but also a member of a larger, universal community of "supersaints."

2

The Many Lives of Swami Rama Tirtha

The hagiographies about Swami Rama Tirtha all address in some way the life of a single historical figure who lived from 1873-1906, and at the most basic level, the "facts" and the outline of the Swami's life are the same in each hagiography. Yet although the hagiographies work with the same basic material, there are dramatic differences between the earliest hagiographies and the most recent ones, differences which center around the type of image that the same set of facts is used to construct, and the ways in which the facts may be embellished and recast in different interpretive frameworks. In subsequent chapters, we will consider how different hagiographers work with these "facts" to portray specific incidents in the life of Swami Rama Tirtha; in this chapter we will learn the basic story the Swami's life and the primary set of facts with which his hagiographers will work. Our goal is not to create a critical historical biography of the Swami; rather, it is to construct a narrative of the events deemed most important by his hagiographers, highlighting areas of particular interest or controversy.[1] To construct our story, in addition to occasional quotes from the Swami's own writings,[2] we will rely primarily on three of the earliest hagiographies of Swami Rama Tirtha: Puran Singh's 1924 *The Story of Swami Rama: The Poet Monk of India* (*SSR*), Narayan Swami's untitled, undated Urdu account printed as a part of the original three-volume Urdu collection of the Swami's works, *Kulliyāt-e-Rām* (*KeR*), and Brijnath Sharga's [Brajnāth Śarga] 1935 *Life of Swami Rama Tirtha* (*LSRT*).[3] Both Narayan Swami and Brijnath Sharga expressed an abiding regard for "facts," and in that sense, their texts are especially helpful in constructing the Swami's basic story. The "truth" of those facts is not our primary concern (though there is little reason to doubt most of them); rather, what is most important about these facts for our purposes is that they are the facts that hagiographers themselves selected as the most important and therefore worthy of recording. This means that there are some parts of the story that are incredibly detailed, and other parts where there are gaps; in many places, there is information whose significance is not immediately clear.

In one way or another, virtually all subsequent hagiographers would build upon the set of facts Puran Singh, Narayan Swami, and Brijnath Sharga assembled, developments which we will consider in more detail in subsequent chapters. The Swami's story is here arranged chronologically and divided into just two sections: Swami Rama Tirtha's life before he became a renunciant, and after. In later chapters, we will discover how Swami Rama Tirtha and his hagiographers divided his life into a series of phases. Our story concludes with a brief discussion of the organizations dedicated to Swami Rama Tirtha's memory, and an introduction to the texts in the Swami Rama Tirtha hagiographical tradition.

Tirath Ram

In the small Punjab village of Muraliwala (now in Pakistan), Hiranand [Hīrānand] and his wife, members of the Gosain [*gosvāmī*] Brāhmaṇ caste, welcomed a son in October, 1873. It was the time of the festival of Diwālī, when homes are decorated with lights to celebrate the return of Ram [Rām] to his kingdom of Ayodhya, and welcome Lakshmi [Lakṣmī], the goddess of wealth and prosperity. Hirananda and his wife named their son Tirath Ram. Like virtually all Hindu parents, they had their son's horoscope cast; some remember that the astrologer forecast that either the child or his mother might die. Tirath Ram's mother in fact died sometime soon after his birth.[4] Hiranand, who earned a modest living as a priest, asked his sister to come live with the family and look after his children. Tirath Ram and his brothers and sisters were raised by their aunt and grandmother; Tirath Ram would later remember that he had been weaned not on his mother's milk, but on cow's milk.

Much later, Hiranand would recall that his young son was fond of hearing the religious stories recited at the village temple, preferring the tales of the exploits of the gods and goddesses to candy or toys. Hiranand also remembered his son's fondness for school. Tirath Ram was sent to the village mosque for his first education, where he learned to read and write Urdu and Persian. A talented student, he quickly mastered the curriculum available in his village. Hiranand then sent him to the nearby town of Gujranwala for further schooling. As was then typical, Tirath Ram's family had arranged his engagement when he was still a toddler, and held his wedding ceremony when he was ten. It would be many years, however, before his wife would come to live with him.

When Hiranand sent his son to Gujranwala, he placed him in the care of Dhanna Ram [Dhanna Rām], a family friend. Dhanna Ram was by all accounts a rather unusual man, known affectionately to many of his friends as "Rabb-jī" or "God." A wrestler and lifelong bachelor, Dhanna Ram made his living training other wrestlers and running a metalware business. He was known for various ascetic practices, such as retaining his urine for long periods of time, wearing a bulky coat in summer, and light clothes in the cold winter.[5] To Tirath Ram, he became something of a father-figure, and for many years Tirath Ram would seek Dhanna Ram's permission and approval for virtually everything he did, writing him postcards when he could not see him in person.

Tirath Ram thrived in his Gujranwala school run by Christian missionaries, and discovered a special aptitude for mathematics and science. There was apparently some contention with Tirath Ram's father about the career path that he would choose; Tirath Ram wanted to continue his education in college, while his father wanted him to begin working and contribute to the family finances. Dhanna Ram apparently supported Tirath Ram's desire to attend college, and in 1888, at the age of fifteen, Tirath Ram enrolled in Forman Christian College in the city of Lahore. Lahore (now in Pakistan) was the capital of the province of British Punjab, and the center of a variety of religious and political activities. While living in Lahore, Tirath Ram became involved in those activities, but also maintained his close relationship with Dhanna Ram in Gujranwala, writing frequent cards and letters. (Dhanna Ram kept all those letters, and they were later published, providing a wealth of information for his hagiographers.[6]) In his letters, Tirath Ram kept Dhanna Ram apprised of virtually everything he did, from what he ate to the titles of books he had read and how long he spent studying each day. Tirath Ram continued to excel at his studies, placing twenty-fifth in the entire province of Punjab in his Intermediate examination in 1890.

Tirath Ram was desperately poor, living on a meager scholarship as he worked towards an undergraduate degree in mathematics at Forman Christian College.[7] He sent most of his money both to his father and Dhanna Ram, and often had to take out loans from friends so that he could eat. Though he would have been able to live relatively well in the college hostel, Tirath Ram preferred to live alone in tiny rented rooms in the old, walled city of Lahore. According to his letters, in his years as a student, he was robbed several times, had the walls of one room collapse during the monsoon, and often came home to find snakes slithering across his possessions.[8] His friends and officials of his college worried about his living conditions and suspected they contributed to his chronic poor health.

Tirath Ram's letters to Dhanna Ram, along with the reminiscences of people who knew him at the time, suggest that there continued to be tension between Tirath Ram and his father. According to some of the early hagiographies, Hiranand's father was so angry with his son for continuing his education rather than finding work that he sent Tirath Ram's wife to live with him in Lahore even though he had neither room for her nor the means to support her. However, Tirath Ram's first priority was his education, and he earned his bachelor's degree in mathematics in 1893. Against his family's wishes, he enrolled at Government College in Lahore later that year to begin work on a master's degree in mathematics. He now received a relatively generous scholarship stipend, but his family increasingly demanded more and more of his money. He often did not even have enough money to send a postcard to Dhanna Ram.

Tirath Ram's letters indicate (and all his hagiographers agree) that as he progressed in his studies, he became more and more involved in spiritual activities. Many of his letters to Dhanna Ram chart his fervent longing for a vision of the god Krishna, a longing so intense that he would often collapse in tears. By 1894, he considered himself sufficiently advanced in his knowledge of Krishna that he gently began advising his teacher Dhanna Ram on the proper devotional attitude.[9] At the same time, he worked hard at his studies, and passed the examination for his masters degree with flying colors in April, 1895.

Tirath Ram likely could have secured a government job, but wanted to become a teacher. He made several unsuccessful attempts to secure scholarships for further studies in England. Pressured by his family to earn money, he worked as a tutor in Lahore, but had to return to Muraliwala for several months to recuperate from a debilitating illness. When he returned to Lahore in the summer of 1895, he continued to look for work, and also became involved in the activities of the Lahore Sanantana Dharma Sabha [society for the eternal *dharma*], which was an organization dedicated to preserving what it considered the true Hindu tradition against the onslaught of reform and revival groups then active in the Punjab such as the Arya Samaj, which sought to make drastic changes in typical Punjabi religious practice and belief.[10] Soon after he became involved with the Lahore chapter, Tirath Ram secured a job teaching at Mission College in the Punjab town of Sialkot. There Tirath Ram joined the local chapter of the Sanatana Dharma Sabha, and began to give lectures on Krishna-devotion. According to his letters, he quickly became a very popular teacher, but continued to struggle with poor health. After less than a year in Sialkot, he happily accepted an offer to return to Forman Mission College in Lahore as a professor of Mathematics, and began his new job there early in 1896.

One of his first projects in his new position was to write a short pamphlet in English called "How to Excel in Mathematics" (*IWGR* 4:329-336), in which he advised students to practice "high thinking and plain living." He deemed the working of difficult problems a kind of "intense meditation," a "perfect yoga where the mind becomes one with the subject" (*IWGR* 4: 335-336).

Mathematics and devotion to Krishna remained his two favorite pursuits; Tirath Ram also returned to his work with the Lahore chapter of the Sanatana Dharma Sabha, continuing to lecture on the joys of devotion to Krishna.[11] In his letters to Dhanna Ram, he wrote of reading the *Bhagavad Gītā* regularly and taking long walks along the Ravi river where he would gaze at dark storm clouds and imagine them to be manifestations of Krishna, his dark lord. His devotional fervor was so intense that he would often end his public lectures with tears streaming down his face, and he began to earn the reputation of a serious devotee and gifted lecturer. Chapters of the Sanatana Dharma Sabha throughout the Punjab invited him to speak. In the summer of 1896, his devotion more fervent than ever, he went on a pilgrimage to Mathura and Brindavan, retracing the steps of his beloved Krishna in the land where the god had frolicked as a child.

Sometime that same year, a young man named Narayan Das [Nārāyaṇ Dās] attended some of Tirath Ram's lectures in the city of Amritsar a short distance from Lahore. Though not a member of the Arya Samaj, Narayan Das admired the argumentative style that its founder Swami Dayananda Saraswati [Swāmī Dayānanda Saraswatī] had adopted in *Satyārth Prakāś* (*KeR* 2:205), and had not expected to be impressed by a young man lecturing under the auspices of the Sanatana Dharma Sabha. Yet something about Tirath Ram affected him deeply. He would eventually become Tirath Ram's chief disciple.[12]

Through his work with the Sanatana Dharma Sabha, Tirath Ram accepted the task of arranging the Lahore visit of Swami Madhva Tirtha [Swāmī Mādhva Tīrtha], then the leader of the Dwarka monastery in western India said to have been established by the great Advaita Vedānta philosopher Sankara. The two apparently got along well, and the Swami instructed young Tirath Ram in the monistic philosophy of Advaita Vedānta. When Swami Madhva Tirtha left Lahore, Tirath Ram began to read English translations of Vedānta philosophical texts. He had learned the Devanāgarī script and some basic Sanskrit in college, but always remained most comfortable with Urdu and English. Through his readings on Vedānta in English translation, Tirath Ram found himself increasingly attracted to the philosophy of Advaita Vedānta (non-dual Vedānta), which asserts that each human has an imperishable spirit (*ātman*) which is a part of a larger, imperishable reality underlying all (*brahman*). His letters of 1896 and 1897 chronicle this shift from devotion to Krishna to a quest for realization of his *ātman* (considered in more detail in chapter four). He learned more about Vedānta when Swami Vivekananda [Swāmī Vivekānanda] visited Lahore in 1897; Swami Vivekananda espoused a philosophy of "Practical Vedānta" through which he sought to make Vedānta not simply an abstract philosophy accessible only to an elite few, but a part of everyday life.

As his enthusiasm for Vedānta grew, Tirath Ram continued to be troubled by poor health, and he often wrote to Dhanna Ram of various ailments. However, more and more he wrote of those ailments as somehow separate from his true sense of identity; his body was ill, but his spirit soared. Though he continued to teach at Forman Christian College, Tirath Ram began to dedicate more and more time to his spiritual pursuits, and started a small study group named the Advaitamrita Varshini Sabha [*advaitāmṛt varṣiṇī sabhā* or "society for the showering of the nectar of Advaita"], whose members included other local Vedānta enthusiasts as well as some renunciants. The Sabha met weekly at Tirath Ram's home.[13]

Indeed Tirath Ram found that he increasingly preferred the company of renunciants, and rather than visiting his home village, he spent the summer vacation of 1898 traveling through the Himalayas, consulting with renunciants and practicing meditation as he sat on the banks of the Ganges river. His letters reveal a changing sense of identity as he distanced himself more and more from his family and career in the Punjab. Later, he would write several essays chronicling this phase of his life.[14] Tirath Ram's family grew worried that Tirath Ram was contemplating taking vows of renunciation, an unusual move for a man only twenty-five years old. They had come to depend upon his professor's salary, and wrote to him often, requesting that he return home immediately. Even Dhanna Ram was worried, but to everyone's relief, Tirath Ram returned to Lahore in the fall and resumed his teaching responsibilities. Nonetheless, he spent more and more time absorbed in meditation, and it apparently began to affect his work. According to some accounts, he began to lecture about Krishna and Vedānta in his math classes, which the Christian officials of the college found troubling.[15] Perhaps at their suggestion, Tirath Ram resigned his position early in 1899, taking a less demanding, lower-paying position as a grader for Oriental College in Lahore.

That summer, Tirath Ram once again journeyed to the mountains, this time to Kashmir. He later wrote an essay about this trip in which he detailed his increasing sense of self-realization and his experience of his identity with the world around him.[16] Though he now described himself as utterly detached from his responsibilities in Lahore, he still returned there at the end of the summer. By then, Narayan Das had moved to Lahore with his family, and asked a mutual acquaintance to introduce him to the man whose lectures had so moved him earlier. Narayan Das had been visiting religious teachers of various persuasions, but was not satisfied with their responses to his questions. Tirath Ram, however, seemed to have compelling answers, and Narayan Das became his follower.[17] Soon, he and Tirath Ram were virtually inseparable.

Tirath Ram's letters to Dhanna Ram were now few and far between; most hagiographers agree that by that time Tirath Ram had surpassed his teacher in spiritual understanding. He still suffered from frequent sicknesses, and late that year, fell ill with fever so severe it left him unconscious. It was Narayan Das who nursed him back to health, and when he finally recovered, Tirath Ram told Narayan Das that his recovery had made him realize it was time to circulate his ideas more widely (a decision that would assume great significance in the hagiographical tradition). Tirath Ram enlisted Narayan Das and some other friends to begin a journal called *Alif* in which he could publish his essays describing his spiritual experiences. *Alif*, the first letter of the Persian alphabet, is represented by a single vertical stroke, and in Islamic mysticism often represents the whole of spiritual knowledge. In choosing "*alif*" as the name of his journal, Tirath Ram acknowledged his debt to the Persian and Urdu Sufi literature he had admired since childhood when he first attended school at his village mosque.[18]

As the publication of *Alif* got underway, Tirath Ram still chafed at the pressures of job and family in Lahore. Early in 1900, he suddenly left Lahore for a quick trip to the port city of Karachi to see the ocean. Though he quickly returned home, soon thereafter, when several issues of *Alif* had appeared, Tirath Ram decided he could no longer stand his life in Lahore. He led a procession of his wife and children,[19] Narayan Das, and other friends to the Lahore railway station, where they boarded a train northward to Hardwar, where Tirath Ram planned to lead them in full-time spiritual pursuits. From Hardwar, the party traveled to the mountain town of Tehri, where Tirath Ram instructed each of them to practice ceaseless meditation. He also told Narayan Das to throw all their money into the Ganges river, and Narayan reluctantly agreed. Fortunately, a local resident made arrangements for food and shelter for the group.

One night, Tirath Ram slipped away from his family and friends to make a solitary pilgrimage to Gangotri, the source of the Ganges river. Tirath Ram's sudden disappearance was apparently quite troubling to his wife, and when Tirath Ram finally returned after several days, she asked that she and their children be allowed to return home. Tirath Ram concurred, and had Narayan Das escort them back to Tirath Ram's family in Muraliwala. It was the last time Tirath Ram would see his wife for many years. After several months, likely sometime early in 1901, Tirath Ram decided to take vows of renunciation. Like Swami Vivekananda, he did not undergo the traditional rite, which is conducted by a renunciant [*sannyāsī*], but instead initiated himself, taking the name Swami Rama Tirtha.[20]

Swami Rama Tirtha

Living in Tehri, the now saffron-clad Swami Rama Tirtha began to attract the attention of local residents. The adulation of the public was something that would always trouble him, and when he first experienced it, his immediate response was to flee higher into the mountains. Sometimes he would make these journeys alone; other times, Narayan Das and other acquaintances would accompany him. He made one climb to the top of Mt. Sumeru, accompanied by local mountaineers. Such journeys occupied most of the year 1901; at the end of the year, he returned to the plains of the Punjab and the United Provinces, where he began to receive invitations to give public addresses. In late 1901 and early 1902, he lectured at Mathura and Faizabad on the topics of reform and *karma* (*IWGR* 4:246-302). He also returned to the topic of his earlier love, the god Krishna, in a lecture entitled "Mysteries of Krishna Lila or His Life Incidents" (*IWGR* 6:92-123). When he gave these lectures, he was in the early stages of developing a philosophy he would eventually term "Practical Vedānta." His references in these lectures were far-ranging, from Sufi poets to the Vedas to the New Testament. In his lecture on the life of Krishna, he argued that the culmination of Krishna-devotion was the pursuit of Advaita Vedānta, an idea he would later develop further. Narayan Das continued to travel with him much of the time (though he had a wife and child of his own), and soon after Swami Rama Tirtha's speeches in Mathura in February, 1902, Swami Rama Tirtha asked him to take vows of renunciation and travel to the western province of Sind to teach Vedānta.

Narayan Das was by his own account completely opposed to the idea. He had no desire to become a renunciant, nor did he want to leave Swami Rama Tirtha to teach Vedānta in some distant land. Reluctantly, however, he acceded to the Swami's request, and took vows of renunciation in Lucknow in February, 1902, thereafter to be known as Narayan Swami (*KeR* 2: 250-252). Just a few days later, the two swamis parted company at a train station, Narayan Swami traveling on to the province of Sind (now in Pakistan), Swami Rama Tirtha returning to the Himalayan foothills, and eventually Tehri.

The Tehri region was then under the rule of the Maharaja Kirti Shah [Kīrti Śāh], who took it upon himself to meet the Swami who was becoming so well-known in his kingdom. Impressed by Swami Rama Tirtha's developing theory of Practical Vedānta, he visited regularly, and met Narayan Swami as well when he rejoined Swami Rama Tirtha in May, 1902 after his adventures in Sind. Later that summer, the Maharaja read a newspaper article which announced a religion conference to be held in Japan. The Maharaja decided that Swami Rama Tirtha would be a worthy representative of Hinduism, and made arrangements for him and Narayan Swami to sail to Japan in August. Their ship left from Calcutta at the end of the month; they stopped for about a week in Hong Kong, and then sailed on to Yokohama, arriving in September, 1902.

When the two swamis arrived in Japan, they discovered that the Indian newspaper reports had been in error, and there was to be no conference on religions. Nonetheless, they traveled on to Tokyo, where they were taken in by the Indo-Japanese club, whose secretary was a young Sikh student from the Punjab named Puran Singh. Puran Singh, who would later write one of the first hagiographies of Swami Rama Tirtha, was immediately entranced by the Swami from his native province. He arranged for Swami Rama Tirtha to give lectures in Tokyo, one of which was entitled, "The Secret of Success" (*IWGR* 1:114-121). In this lecture, the Swami presented seven principles of success: work, self-sacrifice, self-forgetfulness, universal love, cheerfulness, fearlessness, and self-reliance. He told the audience:

> The religion that Rama brings to Japan is virtually the same as was brought centuries ago by Buddha's followers, but the same religion requires to be dealt with from an entirely different standpoint to suit it to the needs of the present age. It requires to be blazoned forth in the light of Western Science and Philosophy. (*IWGR* 1:121)

The Swami was beginning to express ideas that would remain fundamental to his Practical Vedānta, particularly the notion that religion had to suit contemporary needs and be in accordance with scientific discovery. Swami Rama Tirtha was then apparently interested in how Indians before him had represented their religion in foreign countries; he was thrilled when Puran Singh brought him a copy of the proceedings of the 1893 World's Parliament of Religions in Chicago, where Swami Vivekananda had spoken of his own version of Practical Vedānta (*SSR*: 114).

While in Tokyo, Swami Rama Tirtha met professors of Sanskrit, Theosophists from Australia, the members of an Indian circus performing in Tokyo, and countless others. Puran Singh was his guide; he remained utterly enchanted by the Swami and himself would soon take vows of renunciation. While Puran Singh would stay on to complete his studies in Japan, Swami Rama Tirtha took advantage of the opportunity to travel on to the United States with the Indian circus, which had chartered a ship for its journey there. Swami Rama Tirtha despatched Narayan Swami to Hong Kong and southeast Asia to spread the word of Vedānta; from there he traveled to Africa and London.

Sometime in October, 1902, Swami Rama Tirtha arrived at the port of Seattle, Washington.[21] All the hagiographies are vague about his subsequent activities in the United States; most concur that he spent most of his time in San

Francisco and Shasta Springs, California, occasionally traveling to cities throughout the country to give public addresses. He managed to attract a number of ardent admirers who carefully transcribed many of his lectures, which would come to constitute the fullest exposition of the Swami's Practical Vedānta. While in America, he read novels, poetry, scientific treatises, and the works of western philosophers. He admired America's economic success and concluded that Americans unconsciously practiced his Practical Vedānta.

The Swami's vision of a Practical Vedānta began to take full shape in his American lectures. It was to encompass Indian philosophy and religion, as well as the discoveries of science, and Swami Rama Tirtha proclaimed it the essential religion of all humanity. He argued that Practical Vedānta was not a matter of faith, but of individual experience, and that anyone could arrive at its truths in the same way he had. It was the philosophy that was to unite religion and science, east and west, erasing all conflicts among different faiths and nations. These lectures attracted a fair amount of media attention, and the Swami's American admirers carefully saved newspaper articles about him along with their transcriptions of his lectures. They also saved the letters that the Swami wrote to them.[22] The transcriptions of the Swami's American lectures would eventually make up the first three volumes of the Swami's collected works, entitled *In Woods of God-Realization*. There is one other incident of note to the Swami's hagiographers from his American stay: while Swami Rama Tirtha was staying in Shasta Springs, President Theodore Roosevelt's train passed through the town, an incident which would be increasingly glorified in the hagiographical tradition.

After spending nearly two years in the United States, Swami Rama Tirtha began his homeward journey to India. He sailed on a German ship, and stopped in Egypt en route, where he lectured in Persian at a Cairo mosque.[23] In December, 1904, his ship docked at Bombay, where he was met by his old acquaintance Swami Shivagunacharya [Swāmī Śivaguṇācārya], who took him to his *āśram* in Mathura. Perhaps at Swami Shivagunacharya's urging, Swami Rama Tirtha began to give public lectures in which he spoke not only of Vedānta, but also its application to politics and the burgeoning Indian independence movement. There were apparently many among the Swami's admirers who thought that he should establish a formal organization to promulgate his views, but he was reluctant, maintaining that such organizations were doomed to failure because their members would focus on "hero-worship" of the organization's founder rather than their own spiritual progress. Instead, the Swami argued, people should adopt the practice of Practical Vedānta on their own.

After a brief stay in Mathura, Swami Rama Tirtha traveled to the town of Pushkar in Rajasthan. Why he left Mathura, and what exactly he was thinking in these days would become a topic of heated debate in the hagiographical tradition. In any case, he wrote to Narayan Swami, who had also returned to India, and asked him to join him in Pushkar. The two were reunited there late in 1905 or early in 1906, and Puran Singh (who had by then returned to India) joined them as well. From Pushkar, Swami Rama Tirtha continued to correspond with some of his American devotees; one of them even traveled to India to be with him. The Swami's letters from this time suggest that he felt the need to move away from public life, and why exactly he chose to do this would trouble his hagiographers later.

After several months in Pushkar, Swami Rama Tirtha and Narayan Swami went briefly to Jaipur, Rajasthan. Swami Rama Tirtha once more sent Narayan Swami on a mission to spread Vedānta, this time to Sind and Afghanistan. Swami Rama Tirtha spent the following summer alone in Darjeeling in the eastern state of Bengal. In a letter to an American devotee, he mentioned having written five books, but no record of them survives (*LSRT*: 327). By the end of the summer, he had returned to the United Provinces, and lectured in Faizabad, Ghazipur, and Lucknow (*IWGR* 4:58-169, 191-224). He was based at the home of a Lucknow devotee and met with admirers there daily; he also often spoke at high schools and colleges. It was then that a young man named Brijnath Sharga, who later wrote *Life of Swami Rama Tirtha*, first heard him speak. As Sharga recalls, he was then a student at Canning College, "and seldom missed an opportunity of keeping company with Rama. . . He insisted on students taking regular exercise and dedicating themselves to the service of the motherland (*LSRT*: 332)."

Sometime in October, 1905, the Swami left Lucknow and traveled to Hardwar. In poor health yet again, he sent a telegram to Narayan Swami in Sind, asking that he come to look after him as he convalesced. Narayan arranged for Swami Rama Tirtha's medical treatment, and his condition improved. Swami Rama Tirtha then went to Muzaffarnagar, sending Narayan Swami to Lucknow. After a brief stay in Muzaffarnagar, Swami Rama Tirtha summoned Narayan Swami yet again, and the two traveled to Hardwar. They spent some time with other swamis, and then decided to build small huts outside the town of Rishikesh. In Hardwar, some pandits had told Swami Rama Tirtha that he was not likely to reach many young Indians with his message if he continued to write primarily in English; when he and Narayan Swami settled outside Rishikesh, Swami Rama Tirtha took up the study of Sanksrit grammar in earnest.

By February, 1906, Swami Rama Tirtha announced that he wished to move to an even more secluded place, so he and Narayan Swami journeyed to a place called Vasishtha Ashram (at an elevation of at least 12,000 feet) about fifty miles north of the town of Tehri. Swami Rama Tirtha now declined all speaking invitations, and sent Narayan Swami in his stead. While lecturing in Lucknow, Narayan Swami received word that Swami Rama Tirtha had fallen ill. He returned to Vasishtha Ashram sometime in May, 1906 where he too soon fell ill. The two swamis concluded that the location did not suit them, and continued to wander through Tehri, searching for a suitable place to live. In the meantime, Puran Singh and some other admirers of the Swami arrived for a visit. When the entire party continued to suffer from various digestive problems, they convinced Swami Rama Tirtha that they should all move to yet another location where there was better food. In September, 1906, when Puran Singh left to return to his job, Swami Rama Tirtha bade farewell to him in a manner that suggested the two would not meet again; an American admirer reported receiving a letter expressing a similar sentiment around the same time.

Swami Rama Tirtha now decided to settle near the town of Tehri; the Maharaja arranged for a cook to provide the Swami's meals, and also had plans to construct huts for both Swami Rama Tirtha and Narayan Swami. Announcing his intention to work full-time on a major statement of his thought, Swami Rama Tirtha instructed Narayan Swami to keep at least a mile away from him, visiting only when summoned. In the middle of October, Narayan Swami received a message asking him to visit Swami Rama Tirtha the next Sunday to collect what he had written, but the day before their scheduled meeting, he received word that his beloved Swami had drowned while bathing in a tributary of the Ganges river. The Swami's cook was the only one present when he died, and he would later tell Narayan Swami just what he had seen. The exact circumstances and causes of the Swami's death at the tragically young age of thirty-three would become the source of great speculation.

Preserving Swami Rama Tirtha's Memory

Swami Rama Tirtha always had misgivings about formal organizations, and thus never established one despite the requests of his followers. This did not mean, however, that his memory would die (he still has followers today) in part because of the work done by Narayan Swami and Puran Singh after the Swami's unexpected death. Narayan Swami and Puran Singh went through the Swami's belongings and discovered the transcriptions of his American lectures (which he had apparently kept hidden) as well as other writings. Narayan Swami entrusted the Swami's papers to Puran Singh, who agreed to arrange for their publication. When Puran Singh could not secure the necessary financing, he returned the papers to Narayan Swami. Narayan Swami by then had some followers of his own, and he enlisted the aid of one of them, a man named Master Amir Chand [Amīr Cand], in publishing Swami Rama Tirtha's works. Amir Chand had been on the verge of converting to Christianity when he heard Narayan Swami speak about Swami Rama Tirtha and became an instant admirer. In 1909, he supplied the funds for the publication of some of Swami Rama Tirtha's works. The first volume sold out quickly, and further volumes were planned. In the meantime, Amir Chand was charged with conspiracy in a bombing attempt against the British Viceroy Lord Hardinge, and many of his papers, including perhaps some of Swami Rama Tirtha's lectures, were confiscated by British intelligence officers.[24]

Narayan Swami also came under suspicion because of his connection with Amir Chand and the publication of Swami Rama's further works had to be delayed. While waiting for the situation to calm, Narayan Swami moved to Dehradun and dedicated himself to writing a three-volume commentary on the *Bhagavad Gītā*. Later, some admirers of his in Lucknow provided the funds for the publication of the commentary, and Narayan began to spend more and more time there in the city where he had become a *sannyāsī*. Despite his *guru*'s suspicions about the utility of reform organizations, Narayan Swami became an active religious and social reformer in Lucknow, where he founded the Oudh Seva Samiti, whose aim was to train young men for social service, and also helped found the United Provinces Dharma Rakshana Sabha, which sought to reform the administration of temples in the province. Still, he never abandoned his hope that Swami Rama Tirtha's works could be published and preserved, and finally in 1919, he helped found the Swami Rama Tirtha Publication League, which he continued to supervise until his death in Lahore in 1937 (SRTP 1965: 23-29). The Publication League was renamed the Swami Rama Tirtha Pratishthan (hereafter cited as SRTP) after India became independent in 1947; the Hindi word *pratiṣṭhān* means "establishment" or "institution." The SRTP is still based in Lucknow, and prints not only Swami Rama Tirtha's compositions, but works by his admirers as well. The Swami's collected works include the transcriptions of his American lectures, the essays that he wrote for the journal *Alif*, transcriptions of some of his Indian lectures, letters to his devotees, some of his poetry, and selections from his notebooks.[25] Since Narayan Swami's death in 1937, the SRTP has been led by devotees of Narayan Swami, including Rameshwar Sahay Sinha [Rāmeśwar Sahāy Sinha], Din

Dayalu [Dīn Dayālu], and Ayodhia Nath [Ayodhyā Nāth] (who died in 1991), each of whom later wrote about Swami Rama Tirtha (SRTP 1991: 25).

In addition to Narayan Swami, there were several other *sannyāsīs* who considered themselves Swami Rama Tirtha's disciples, including Swami Govindananda [Swāmī Govindānanda] (1862-1938), who initiated a disciple named Swami Hari Om Ji [Swāmī Hari Oṃ Jī] (1912-1955) and asked him to dedicate his life to spreading the teachings of Swami Rama Tirtha (*KeR 2*:355). Swami Hari Om Ji spent some years in the Himalayas in study and meditation, and then, honoring his guru's request, began sponsoring events dedicated to the preservation of Swami Rama Tirtha's message. From 1941-1946, he presided over yearly Vedānta conferences in Amritsar, which attracted *sannyāsīs* from all over India (SRTM 1991: 4-5). In 1945, he founded a school in the village of Muraliwala where Swami Rama Tirtha was born, but it had to be closed after the partition of India in 1947 when Muraliwala became a part of Pakistan. Determined to create a lasting memorial to the Swami he had never met, in 1948, Swami Hari Om Ji established the Swami Rama Tirtha Mission Ashram in the town of Rajpur, about nine miles from Mussoorie (SRTM 1977: 1-2). The Swami Rama Tirtha Mission was formally founded and registered in 1948 in Delhi (although an informal Rama Society was apparently formed in 1936, the official registration of the society took place only after India became independent). Soon thereafter, Hari Om Ji inaugurated branches in Amritsar, Shiv Puri (Madhya Pradesh), Gwalior, Delhi, Meerut, Aligarh, Calcutta, Bombay, Raikot, Bangalore, and other locations, many of which are still in operation. The purpose of the Mission is "to study, attain, impart and promote the Vedantic principles of the Eternal Universal Religion of Monism and Comparative Theology in their widest form as propounded, practised and preached by the universally reputed Paramahans Swami Rama Tirtha for the establishment of Universal Unity, Brotherhood, Love, Peace; and for the attainment of True and Supreme Happiness of mankind by the realization of the Self and reconciling the whole Self with the welfare of the whole universe without distinction of caste, creed, colour, community, nationality, sex, and without limitation of time or space; and creating in them the spirit of catholicity, tolerance, for-bearance, charity, and fearlessness . . . to maintain that the Fundamental Principles of all the religions of the Universe are based on Truth and to live in peace and fellowship with the followers of all religions" (SRTM n.d.: 2-3).

Swami Hari Om Ji was the first head of the Mission, and served until his death in 1955. Swami Govind Prakashji [Swāmī Govind Prakāśjī] then led the Mission until 1977. Swami Amar Muni Maharaj [Swāmī Amar Muni Mahāraj] next took over, and served until his death in 1992. The Swami Rama Tirtha

Mission and Swami Rama Tirtha Pratishthan often work together though they are not formally connected; the Mission, for example, serves as a distributor of the Pratishthan's publications. The Mission branches maintain libraries containing the works of Swami Rama Tirtha and other religious figures. The Mission is also involved in social service, and sponsors Ayurvedic health clinics in poor areas. Most recently, one of the Mission's primary goals has been the promotion of education. In 1987, New Delhi devotees of the Swami founded the Swami Rama Tirtha National Education Society for the purpose of founding schools to provide elementary education and instill students with a sense of Vedantic patriotism. The Society has established an elementary school in a particulary impoverished area of New Delhi, described in a pamphlet as "a modern English-Hindi medium school, started with missionary zeal to give meaningful, interesting and also enjoyable education to our Young Buds—the future of our nation, for their all-round development, physical, mental and spiritual—to enable them to grow as useful, brave, dedicated and daring future citizens. The institution is to inculcate the ideas of humanism, discipline, self-reliance and the search of truth. We believe all humans are equal."

In addition to their social projects. the various branches of the Swami Rama Tirtha Mission hold regular gatherings (*satsaṅgs*) at which members read from the *Bhagavad Gītā*, sing devotional songs (*bhajans*), and discuss Swami Rama Tirtha's teachings. The head of the Mission visits the different branches throughout the year, and Swamis affiliated with the Mission give discourses weekly. The Mission celebrates Swami Rama Tirtha's birthday each year, and also commemorates the deaths of the Mission's other leaders. The *āśram* in Rajpur holds a Vedānta meeting (*sammelan*) each June and Mission members may visit the *āśram* throughout the year.

In addition to the Swami Rama Tirtha Pratishthan and the Swami Rama Tirtha Mission, there are several unaffiliated organizations dedicated to Swami Rama Tirtha (such as the Ram Tirtha Kendra in Saharanpur, Uttar Pradesh[26]), and there are also a fair number of people throughout India who know something about Swami Rama Tirtha and consider themselves devotees to some degree or another, though they may not be affiliated with a formal organization in his name. Many of those who become devotees of Swami Rama Tirtha first learn about him through reading his works, or through reading hagiographies. The composition and circulation of texts describing Swami Rama Tirtha's life has played a major role in maintaining his following. Indeed there are far more hagiographies than there are texts considering the Swami's teachings.

The Swami Rama Tirtha Hagiographical Tradition

Since Swami Rama Tirtha died in 1906, there have been no fewer than twenty-five hagiographies about him written in English, Urdu, and Hindi. It is possible to identify three stages of development in the hagiographical tradition: an initial phase in which direct followers of the Swami wrote about his life, a second phase (with relatively few texts) which reflects and critiques what were apparently oral traditions circulating about Swami Rama Tirtha, and most recently a third phase in which the Swami's hagiographers have sought to place him within a larger framework of Indian history and mythology.[27] These phases closely resemble the stages William Jackson identified in his study of the hagiographical tradition surrounding the south Indian poet Tyagaraja (1767-1847), suggesting that there are typical patterns of development in recent Indian hagiographical traditions.[28] The most important texts from each of the three phases are briefly described below; the appendix contains a complete annotated listing of the hagiographies.

Phase One: The Earliest Hagiographies

Many of the earliest hagiographies about Swami Rama Tirtha were written by people who had known him personally. In these earliest texts, written in the first thirty years after the Swami died, the hagiographers were particularly concerned with recording as much detail as possible about the Swami's life. Most of these hagiographies rely heavily on the primary material of the Swami's letters and lectures, and while there are hints of some of the mythical images that would later emerge in the hagiographical tradition, at this stage, it is a concern for "bios" rather than myth which dominates. One of the earliest accounts of Swami Rama Tirtha's life, *Swami Rama Tirath: A Sketch of His Life and Teachings*, was published by an anonymous author in Madras in 1912 as part of the series "Biographies of Eminent Indians." The author's account of the Swami's life is very brief; it apparently did not circulate widely (at least among Swami Rama Tirtha's followers) since none of the later hagiographies makes reference to it. Indeed, when Shripad Rama Sharma [Śrīpad Rāma Śarma] published *Swami Rama Tirtha: The Poet Apostle of Practical Vedanta* in 1921, he believed that he was writing the first biography of the Swami. Sharma's text also apparently did not circulate widely, though it is available in the library of the New Delhi headquarters of the Swami Rama Tirtha Mission. Sharma's account of the Swami's life is also relatively brief (eighty-seven pages), and contains essentially the same material as the 1912 anonymous hagiography. Neither of these texts would be as important as those written by three men who knew Swami Rama Tirtha personally.

In 1924, Puran Singh published *The Story of Swami Rama: The Poet Monk of India* (*SSR*). It was to become the most influential of the earliest hagiographies, and is still regularly reprinted by the Swami Rama Tirtha Pratishthan both in its original English, and in a Hindi translation (under the title *Swāmī Rām Tīrth Jīvan Kathā,* translated by Din Dayalu). Singh had earlier written a brief "life-sketch" of Swami Rama Tirtha for the first edition of *In Woods of God-Realization.* Sometime in this same period, Narayan Swami composed an untitled Urdu version of Swami Rama Tirtha's life, and it was published in the second volume of the Urdu collection of works by and about Swami Rama Tirtha entitled *Kulliyāt-e-Rām* (*KeR*). Narayan Swami's work was never published separately, nor was it translated into any other languages. Narayan Swami was unhappy both with his own account and with Puran Singh's, and he therefore drafted Brijnath Sharga to compose *Life of Swami Rama Tirtha* (*LSRT*), which was published in 1935. Puran Singh's, Narayan Swami's, and Brijnath Sharga's texts are the most important texts from the earliest phase of the hagiographical tradition—they became the foundation for the later hagiographies—and they are considered in chapter three.

Phase Two: Skepticism and Reassessment

Curiously, there are very few hagiographies that survived and still circulate from the 1940s or 1950s, and it was apparently not until the early 1960s that people began writing new hagiographies about Swami Rama Tirtha. Because of the more than two-decade break, the texts from this second phase reflect the new perspective of independent India, and the desire to record the history of the nationalist movement and its heroes. In the texts from this phase, there is a relatively equal balance between focus on Swami Rama Tirtha as a historical figure and portrayal of him in mythic terms. In the 1961 publication *Swami Rama Tirtha,* S.R. Sharma (not the same author as that of the *Swami Rama Tirtha: The Poet Apostle of Practical Vedanta,* published in 1921) highlighted the Swami's patriotism and nationalism, and directly challenged Puran Singh's earlier characterization of the Swami as indifferent to Indian nationalism. Alternatively, D.R. Sood's 1970 *Swami Ram Tirth,* published in English and Urdu (1974) by the National Book Trust, suggested that while the Swami did not play a major role in political or national activities, he nonetheless proclaimed a message of universal brotherhood which made him a worthy inclusion in the Trust's National Biography Series. Sharma and Sood each challenged what were apparently oral traditions circulating about Swami Rama Tirtha which proclaimed him a healer and performer of miracles. Both authors (Sood in particular) adopted a relatively skeptical approach to some of the more grandiose claims being made about Swami Rama Tirtha. While Sharma portrayed the Swami as a great nationalist, and Sood argued that he was not, the issue of nationalism and patriotism would from this point on remain a central concern.

Phase Three: Mythicization

After Sharma's and Sood's entries of the late 1960s and early 1970s, there was a flurry of interest in Swami Rama Tirtha, which may have in part been spurred by the celebration of the Swami's birth centenary in 1973, when the Government of India sponsored festivals and released a commemorative stamp. This resurgence of interest brought a number of new hagiographies, primarily in Hindi, which heralded Swami Rama Tirtha as a great saint and nationalist who played a significant role in the Indian independence movement. While the first phase evidenced strong concern for the "bios" of Swami Rama Tirtha (with only a hint of the mythicization to come), and the second phase exhibited a relatively even balance between the two, in this third phase, myth clearly takes precedence over "bios." From the 1970s to the present, various authors have proclaimed Swami Rama Tirtha as one of the greatest Indian saints, on a par with other great saints such as Sankara and Swami Vivekananda, and poets such as Tulsidas [Tulsīdās]. The authors of these texts urged young Indians to learn about Swami Rama Tirtha and heed his message which they believed to be sorely needed in modern India.[29] The texts of this phase exhibit the typical tendency of hagiographies from the later stages of a tradition to "mythologize" their subject, a trend considered in chapter five. In addition to these texts which deal exclusively with Swami Rama Tirtha, a number of hagiographical collections which address the lives of multiple saints include accounts of him as well, considered in chapter six.

Other Hagiographies

There are several other hagiographies of Swami Rama Tirtha which, while not easily categorized, are worth noting. Hari Prasad Shastri's [Hari Prasād Śāstrī] undated (though probably written sometime before 1950) *Scientist and Mahatma: An Account of the Life of Rama Tirtha and Translations from his*

Writings is unusual in part because Shastri was highly critical of both Narayan Swami and Puran Singh, whom Swami Rama Tirtha's followers remember as two of his closest devotees. Despite his title, Shastri did not focus on Swami Rama Tirtha's interests in both science and spirituality, but instead emphasized what he understood to have been the critical role that he played in the final years of the Swami's life. Shastri clearly did not care for many of the other people in Swami Rama Tirtha's immediate circle; he accused Dhanna Ram of "enslaving [Tirath Ram's] mentality," believed that Narayan Swami's interest in Swami Rama Tirtha was only for gaining "worldly advantage," and bluntly described Puran Singh as "mentally imbalanced" and "hardly a man" (Shastri n.d.: 19, 33-34, 37). Shastri's text was published in London by the Shanti Sadan, but was never printed in India, which is not surprising, given that it is so harshly critical of the very figures whom the Swami Rama Tirtha Pratishthan reveres. Nonetheless, the text is available in the Swami Rama Tirtha Mission library in New Delhi. However, none of the other hagiographies of Swami Rama Tirtha makes any reference to it, and none of the Swami's followers whom I met had ever read it. In 1982, the Shanti Sadan in London published another text about Swami Rama Tirtha, A.J. Alston's *Yoga and the Supreme Bliss: Songs of Enlightenment by Swami Rama Tirtha*, and it was soon reprinted by an Indian publisher. Alston's text includes a brief introduction to the Swami's life (the only account which refers to Shastri's text), and English translations of his Urdu poems. Alston's text is distributed by the Swami Rama Tirtha Mission.

There is another set of Urdu and Hindi texts by Kedarnath Prabhakar [Kedarnāth Prabhākar], who is associated with the Ram Tirtha Kendra in Saharanpur, Uttar Pradesh. Prabhakar's family were originally from Gujranwala, the town where Swami Rama Tirtha attended high school, and they knew Dhanna Ram and many of Swami Rama Tirtha's relatives. Prabhakar terms Swami Rama Tirtha the "saint of our era" [*yugsant*], and his account of the Swami's life in the Hindi *Yugsant Rāmtīrth* begins not with his birth in 1873, but with an intriguing account of his past lives in previous eras, information Prabhakar attributed to an ancient handwritten Sanksrit manuscript entitled *Kapālī Saṃhitā* (Prabhakar 1984: 29). Prabhakar's family and friends related a number of interesting reminiscences about Swami Rama Tirtha; his works, however, stand independent from the larger Swami Rama Tirtha hagiographical tradition. He makes little reference to other hagiographies, and more recent hagiographies do not refer to his works.

3

Positivism versus Poetry

The First Phase of the Hagiographical Tradition

Among the texts from the first phase of the Swami Rama Tirtha hagiographical tradition, the three most important are Narayan Swami's untitled Urdu account (in *KeR*), Puran Singh's *The Story of Swami Rama* (*SSR*), and Brijnath Sharga's *Life of Swami Rama Tirtha* (*LSRT*). Puran Singh's *SSR* has been the most popular of all the hagiographies—it is regularly reprinted both in English and Hindi translation, and frequently referred to in later hagiographies. In contrast, Narayan Swami's Urdu text and Sharga's *Life of Swami Rama Tirtha* have long been out of print.[1] That Puran Singh's *SSR* has been the most important of the hagiographies is especially interesting given that Narayan Swami, Swami Rama Tirtha's closest disciple, was highly critical of Puran Singh's presentation of the Swami. Indeed it was his dissatisfaction with Puran Singh's *SSR*, as well as with his own effort, that led Narayan Swami to commission Brijnath Sharga to write *LSRT*, which Narayan Swami hoped would become the definitive account of Swami Rama Tirtha's life. Although Narayan Swami's and Sharga's accounts of the Swami's life have not circulated as widely as Puran Singh's has, both texts are critical for understanding what was at stake in the earliest stage of the hagiographical tradition, and why Puran Singh's *SSR* should have become the most popular and frequently cited text in the hagiographical tradition.

Narayan Swami and Puran Singh were both close disciples of Swami Rama Tirtha; Brijnath Sharga heard Swami Rama Tirtha lecture and later became a follower of Narayan Swami, and thus each author could bring the authority of direct personal knowledge of Swami Rama Tirtha to his effort. The incorporation of personal experience into the hagiographies became one of the central issues in this first stage of the hagiographical tradition. Narayan Swami strongly believed that including personal experience, particularly personal opinions about Swami Rama Tirtha's actions, was completely unacceptable in composing an account of Swami Rama Tirtha's life. Using the then-popular idiom of positivism, he argued that only an objective, purely "factual" narrative was acceptable—which in part led him to reject his own account of the Swami's life (because he doubted his own "objectivity"), and draft Sharga, whose relationship with Swami Rama Tirtha was not so close, to write a definitive text. Puran Singh, in contrast, made his own experiences with Swami Rama Tirtha a central part of his *SSR*. Ultimately, this "subjectivism" was a crucial factor in the success of his hagiography; while Narayan Swami and Brijnath Sharga tried to use positivist historiography to chronicle the Swami's life, their texts never found as large an audience as *SSR*. Fortunately for our purposes, all three authors described their methods and goals in their works, and an examination of their statements about their intentions, as well as an analysis of the nature of their hagiographies themselves helps illumine what made Puran Singh's text the most popular even though Swami Rama Tirtha's closest disciple rejected it.

Narayan Swami, Puran Singh, Brijnath Sharga, and Their Texts

Narayan Swami, who first met Tirath Ram in Lahore (*KeR*: 204-206), took vows of renunciation (*sannyās*) in 1902, and is still remembered as the chief disciple of Swami Rama Tirtha.[2] His untitled Urdu account of Swami Rama Tirtha's life was published as part of the three-volume Urdu collection of works by and about Swami Rama Tirtha entitled *Kullīyāt-e-Rām*. Puran Singh was studying in Japan when Swami Rama Tirtha and Narayan Swami visited there for several weeks in 1902. He immediately became an ardent devotee of the Swami, and even briefly took vows of renunciation. However, when he later returned to India, his family pressured him to marry and pursue a career, although he still spent much time with Swami Rama Tirtha after the Swami had returned from the United States. Puran Singh went on to achieve fame in his own right as a Punjabi poet and writer; his *Story of Swami Rama* was published in 1924, and he died in 1931.[3] Brijnath Sharga, a Lucknow advocate and landholder, had been impressed by Swami Rama Tirtha when he heard him lecture in Lucknow in 1905 (*LSRT*: 332), and he later became a disciple of Narayan Swami. Since Sharga had already written a biography of M.K. Gandhi, Narayan Swami thought him the ideal candidate to write about Swami Rama Tirtha, although Sharga was reluctant to take on the task. When he finally consented, Narayan Swami loaned him the Swami's letters, writings, and all the other information available to him. Sharga found that at first he was so engrossed by the primary materials that he couldn't imagine writing. Finally, during the hottest days of a Lucknow summer, he began "almost involuntarily blackening sheet after sheet of paper," inspired by both Narayan Swami and Swami Rama Tirtha (*LSRT*: xi). When he was done, Narayan Swami carefully checked and edited Sharga's text himself, and Sharga's *Life of Swami Rama Tirtha* was published in 1935.

The resource material available to Narayan Swami, Puran Singh and Sharga was considerable: hundreds of letters that Tirath Ram wrote while a student, dozens of transcribed lectures, Swami Rama's autobiographical writings for his journal *Alif*, newspaper articles from India and abroad, his correspondence with Indian and American devotees, the reminiscences of other followers and Swami Rama Tirtha's former family, and of course the hagiographers' own experiences with him. For each author, selecting and organizing that information presented a real challenge. Neither Singh nor Narayan Swami, nor even Sharga, had sufficient distance, either personally or from the vantage point of time passed, to present a broad picture of Swami Rama Tirtha's legacy and historical significance (a task which later hagiographers would assume). But their efforts were nonetheless crucial because they had the opportunity to create the first records of Swami Rama Tirtha's life so that others could learn about him. Puran Singh began by abandoning any hope of creating an "authentic history," choosing instead to emphasize the nature of his personal relationship with the Swami. Narayan Swami made the opposite choice, trying his best to leave himself and his impressions out of the story, presenting "facts" which taken together would presumably lead readers to the inexorable conclusion that Swami Rama Tirtha was a man of the highest spiritual achievement. Concluding that he had failed in that effort, he instructed Sharga to take the same approach.

Organization and Style

The sources of information and the organizational structure of each text, as well as each author's approach to using his own firsthand experience of the Swami are important, for they reveal much about the authors' approach to presenting and interpreting the life of the Swami. In this earliest phase of the hagiographical tradition, the authors marshalled an enormous amount of factual information about Swami Rama Tirtha's life, filling their texts with countless names, dates, and lengthy quotes from various works by Swami Rama Tirtha. In many instances, they also quoted one another.

Of all the hagiographers of Swami Rama Tirtha, only Narayan Swami conducted serious research into the Swami's life. He traveled to Swami Rama Tirtha's family village to interview his father and went to Gujranwala to coax Dhanna Ram to allow him to reproduce the letters that Swami Rama Tirtha had sent him. To present the information he had collected, Narayan Swami arranged his text chronologically with extensive quotes from the Swami's letters and other writings. Although he devoted a great deal of space in his text to the period of Tirath Ram's life when they met in Lahore, even for those periods of Swami Rama Tirtha's life when Narayan Swami was with him and had firsthand knowledge of what happened, Narayan Swami used Swami Rama Tirtha's writings as much as possible (rather than relating his own memories), at one point quoting over one hundred twenty pages of Tirath Ram's essays with no commentary of his own (*KeR* 2:81-201). On those rare occasions in his text when he tried to convey the effect that the Swami had on him or the role that he himself played in certain events, he struggled to find adequate words. Of his first meeting with Tirath Ram he could only write, "it is not within the powers of the pen to describe the deep wound on Narayan's heart that came from [his] intoxicating *darśan* (*KeR* 2:205)."[4] Though he was an eyewitness to much of what happened in Swami Rama Tirtha's life, Narayan Swami himself is largely absent in his text. He believed that the material he presented would speak for itself, leading readers to conclude as he had that Swami Rama Tirtha was a great religious leader. From a stylistic perspective, Narayan Swami's Urdu prose is rather unimaginative, which makes the text disjointed and difficult to read; this too may have contributed to his decision to commission Sharga's text.

Although Narayan Swami included no prefatory material in his original Urdu text, his introductions to both Sharga and Singh's later works suggest that he relied so heavily upon the Swami's own writings because he believed this would make his text more objective. Yet the way Narayan Swami contextualized this unedited primary material from Swami Rama Tirtha's writings makes clear that in fact he wished to suggest a specific pattern of development from the moment of Tirath Ram's birth in 1873 until his death in 1906. Narayan Swami's narration of Tirath Ram's illness in 1899 illuminates his underlying interpretive strategy. Tirath Ram, then teaching in Lahore, was gravely ill with fever and late one night fell unconscious. Narayan sat by his side nursing him, fearing for his life. Finally the fever broke, and Tirath Ram awakened to announce to Narayan, "India's fortune may soon awaken, now that health has shown its face to Rama once more. My mind is full of countless issues and opinions. Who knows, maybe I've recovered so that these issues and opinions should be put in writing" (*KeR* 2:207). In his narrative, Narayan explained that this was the beginning of Tirath Ram's conscious sense of his mission, when he realized that his thoughts were worth sharing with others and that he had a significant role to play in India's future.

This was a crucial episode in Narayan Swami's text, for he used it to demonstrate that even before Tirath Ram became a renunciant, he had a firm sense of his mission in life as a religious leader. Clearly, the reader's interpretation of all of Tirath Ram's previous actions—and his future actions as a swami—is meant to hinge upon this sense of mission. Narayan Swami's portrayal of Tirath Ram's early life (based on his conversations with Hiranand after Swami Rama Tirtha's death) hinted at such a future (e.g. his fondness for hearing religious stories at the village temple, his increasingly intense devotion to Krishna as a student). Tirath Ram's actions after he awakened from his fever—his vows of renunciation, world travels, and retirement to the Himalayas—Narayan Swami presented as predictable, indeed almost inevitable developments in the life of a man who was destined from the very moment of his birth to become a great religious leader. Yet there is a strange disjunction between Narayan Swami's narrative structure and the nature of the writings of Swami Rama Tirtha which he quoted. Swami Rama Tirtha's writings both before and after he became a renunciant suggest a man very uncertain about the religious leadership role that was being thrust upon him, whereas Narayan Swami clearly believed that Swami Rama Tirtha always knew exactly what he was doing, even when his recorded statements and writings seemed to suggest otherwise.

In contrast to Narayan Swami's chronological organization, Puran Singh's *SSR* is arranged so that the primary emphasis is on Swami Rama Tirtha's life as a renunciant. In the first two chapters entitled "The Monk Himself," Singh related anecdotes about Swami Rama's travels and tried to convey something of the Swami's personality. Chapters three and four, "The Fruits in His Basket: His Fundamental Thoughts" and "The Fragrance that Sustained Him" were reserved for quotes from Swami Rama Tirtha's writings as well as from the writings of other thinkers he admired, along with Puran Singh's commentary. Chapter five, "What He Said," was devoted to further quotations and commentary. It was only later in the text, in chapters six through fifteen, that Puran Singh wrote more or less chronologically his version of the story of Swami Rama's life. The book concludes with a chapter of Swami Rama Tirtha's letters, two chapters on Swami Rama Tirtha's thoughts on India, a selection of Swami Rama's poetry, Singh's concluding reflections, and an appendix with newspaper articles from the United States about Swami Rama Tirtha's death.

The opening sentence of *SSR* suggests what was most important about the Swami to Puran Singh: "we all met him first as a monk, and it is best to present him as a monk, before one proceeds more intimately with the story of his early life" (*SSR*: 1). Thus for Singh his relationship with Swami Rama Tirtha was central; he first met the Swami as a monk, and therefore he believed that his readers should first meet him in that guise as well. The details about Swami Rama Tirtha's childhood and early life were not nearly as important as the relationship he had with his followers once he had become a monk. In highlighting that theme of relationship—the monk as perceived by his followers—Singh liberally sprinkled his narrative with his own comments. Unlike Narayan Swami, he suggested no particular pattern of development in Swami Rama Tirtha's life; his text reads more like a series of loosely connected vignettes. In placing the most emphasis on Swami Rama Tirtha's life as a renunciant, Singh focused especially on his own and others' experiences with Swami Rama Tirtha. Many of his anecdotes chronicle other people's reactions to the Swami's lectures, poems, and other writings, or Singh's report of how other people felt in Swami Rama Tirtha's presence. Singh's emphasis on people's relationships with Swami Rama Tirtha suggests that he believed that this aspect of the Swami's life would be of greatest interest to the reader. Throughout the text, he emphasized his own inability to convey fully the powerful effect that Swami Rama Tirtha had on him and others. Nonetheless, his lively, poetic prose manages to suggest something of the reaction that Swami Rama Tirtha evoked in him. In Singh's portrayal, the Swami himself emerges as a quietly dynamic, deeply spiritual man troubled by chronic illness, and racked with doubts about his purpose in life (a very different portrayal from that of Narayan Swami).

Sharga, like Narayan Swami, chose to employ a chronological style of organization in his *Life of Swami Rama Tirtha*, which is divided into the chapters "Birth and Early Training," "At the University," "In the School of Love," "On Heights of Wisdom," "Face to Face with Reality," "Supreme Sacrifice," "In the Land of the Rising Sun," "In the Land of Dollars," "Back Home," and finally, "The Last Pilgrimage." There are several additional chapters on the activities of Swami Rama Tirtha's followers after his death. The chapter titles alone make clear the sense of development Sharga saw in the Swami's life—he moved from a secular education to a spiritual education culminating in self-realization, embarked on an international teaching tour, returned home triumphant, and finally retired to the mountains. Following Narayan Swami's account, Sharga presented the early events in Tirath Ram's life as foreshadowings of his future as a religious leader. Sharga too quoted liberally from the Swami's letters and writings, and also established a precedent for future hagiographers by frequently quoting both Narayan Swami and Puran Singh as authorities. Sharga's quotations from Swami Rama Tirtha's writings, though there are many, are not as extensive as Narayan Swami's, and Sharga's English prose is more graceful than Narayan Swami's plodding Urdu.

Narayan Swami and Sharga in particular believed that abundant information was the most important part of writing a reliable account of the Swami's life. Both presented as much of the available information as possible without necessarily providing any context or commentary for it, although their overarching organizational structures suggest that this information was meant to be read in the context of their view of the Swami's inevitable development into a spiritual leader. In contrast, Puran Singh, whose text is the shortest of the three, was more discriminating in his selection of information as he attempted to create a more concise overall account of the Swami's life. Still, for all three, anything about Swami Rama Tirtha, no matter how trivial, was of interest and automatically considered worth recording, from his graphic descriptions of his digestive difficulties in letters to Dhanna Ram to his impressions of American women. Significantly, all three authors were essentially in agreement about the basic details of the life of Swami Rama Tirtha. Contention arose between Puran Singh and Narayan Swami on the matter of interpreting those details. In Narayan Swami's view, Sharga's *LSRT* settled the debates, but the continued popularity of Singh's *SSR* suggests otherwise.

The "Biographer's" Task

There is a lively discussion about the genre of biography and the role of the biographer in the prefaces and introductions to Puran Singh's *SSR* and Sharga's *LSRT*. Puran Singh and Narayan Swami, who themselves played prominent roles in the Swami's life, were keen to explain their approach to writing as participant observers. As they reflected on what should be the proper method for writing biography, they reflected typical concerns of their era such as the quest for absolute accuracy and objectivity. At first glance, one might suspect that each author sought to write some sort of critical historical biography of Swami Rama Tirtha (and indeed they presented their efforts as such). Yet all three authors made clear that their goals were different than those of a critical historical biographer; at heart, their enterprise was more spiritual than historical in nature. The real questions were not about critical biography (Swami Rama Tirtha as a man), but more properly hagiography (Swami Rama Tirtha as a saint), even though none of the authors used the term "hagiography" in characterizing their efforts.

In his preface, Puran Singh openly wondered whether it was even possible to write a biography of a man such as Swami Rama Tirtha.

> What can be the materials for the biography of a man who was silent on the secret of his joyous life like a lotus that springs up from its humble hidden birth-place, and bursts forth into the glory of its own blossom? And what can be his biography but that whoever happened to see him, a flower amongst men, stood for a while, looking at him, and having looked at him, went past him, deeply suspecting the existence of golden lands beyond this physical life, whose mystic glimpses shone on his smiling face. This full blown lotus refused to give any further details of the story of his life, though much to the agitation

> of many a soul, he kept on flaunting the perfume of his soul in air. . . . A rough pencil-sketch of this inspired personality with whom I first came in contact at Tokyo is given in the following pages in the form of impressions, as it is evidently impossible to trace an authentic history of the development of his mind and his secret love-making with Krishna, God. (*SSR*: v-vi)

For Puran Singh, then, it was virtually impossible to write an "authentic history" of the Swami, for his spiritual power was so great as to preclude the normal means of explanation and analysis. Singh acknowledged the Swami's own misgivings about revealing the details of his life, but also asserted that the true "biography" of the Swami lay not so much in those details as in the experiences of those who saw him and breathed in the "perfume of his soul." For Singh, what was most important was that when people saw Swami Rama Tirtha they experienced something profound. Those experiences could not be captured by the mere details of the Swami's words or actions, for the experiences were brought about by whatever mysterious power the Swami exuded from his soul. The heart of the Swami's true biography, Puran Singh believed, was in those experiences. His "rough pencil sketch" depended heavily on "impressions"—Puran Singh's own reading of events—and not just the voluminous factual material that he and the other early hagiographers had at their disposal. Since Singh placed so much emphasis on the experience of seeing and being with Swami Rama Tirtha, he was very much aware of his own role in the text as he attempted to convey what it was like for him to see the Swami. Narayan Swami, however, took an opposing tack, suggesting in his preface to Sharga's work (which significantly also serves as an explicit critique of Puran Singh) that only the "facts"—not Puran Singh's "impressions"—could reveal the true power of the Swami.

> The work of a biographer is that of a scientist who must make use of bare and solid facts rather than dwell in regions of poetic imagination. He should be neither biased nor prejudiced and should give more importance to facts than to preferences. His work must be free from all 'isms. (*LSRT*: i)

Narayan Swami, adopting a positivist model of biography, envisioned a text which would be purely objective, "scientific" in its approach, free from all prejudices. Naively showing the positivist faith in the possibility of objectivity, he believed that readers would themselves be able to draw the unavoidably correct conclusions. "Poetic imagination" is an unsubtle reference to the work of Puran Singh the poet. While emphasizing the importance of "bare and solid facts" over Puran Singh's impressions, Narayan Swami betrayed no awareness of the role that the author (whether himself or Sharga) played in selecting and arranging those "pure" facts. Nor did he anywhere acknowledge that in his own hagiography his own impressions might be central to his narrative strategy. Though Narayan Swami did not admit it, impressions in and of themselves were not so much the problem as were impressions Narayan Swami deemed incorrect. Puran Singh, he believed, most definitely had the wrong impression of Swami Rama Tirtha.

Of the three, Sharga seemed to be the most aware of the biographer's role in selecting and evaluating information.

> A biographer's task is not completed by the mere narration of the life-story of his hero; he is expected to review his work also. A biographer is not a mere story-teller, but also a judge, a literary critic and a guide. (*LSRT*: 13)

Sharga recognized himself as a guide to the Swami's life, not just narrating facts, but placing them in the appropriate context. As a biographer, he believed, it was his responsibility to select the most important information, and further give a critical appraisal of the Swami's work. Nonetheless, his conception of himself as a "guide" to Swami Rama Tirtha was primarily related to his critique of Swami Rama Tirtha's writing, and not so much his own role in guiding readers through the Swami's life. Still, he did his best to distance himself from the creation of the text, and in his own preface placed responsibility for any of its strengths or weaknesses on the shoulders of his guru Narayan Swami (*LSRT*: 16).

Each of the three hagiographers, then, had a different approach to writing about Swami Rama Tirtha's life. For Puran Singh, it was to record "impressions," for Narayan Swami, "bare facts," and for Sharga, it was to assume the responsibility of properly choosing and presenting those facts. Of the three, Puran Singh was the most forthcoming about his sense of his own limitations and his own role in shaping the text. He believed that he could not even begin to understand the greatness of the Swami, and that there could be no "details" which could possibly express it. Thus he could only hope to convey something of his power through describing the effect that the Swami had on those around him. As he recognized, his text was as much about his and others' impressions of the Swami as it was about the Swami himself. Narayan Swami and Sharga, however, attempted to detach themselves from their own narratives, suggesting that the "facts" would tell the true story. What they did not acknowledge was that their selection and organization of those facts would help shape a particular picture of the Swami. Despite their different methods, however, each of the hagiographers hoped that his text would serve the same purpose for readers.

Hagiography as Spiritual Inspiration

The authors' comments about what they hoped readers would take away from their books indicate that they intended their works not just as historical records, but more importantly as sources of spiritual inspiration. Puran Singh wished to show readers that Swami Rama reminded "the people of India to rise from empty idle dreams and take to incessant work to win the freedom which is the fruit not of conquest over others but over one's self" (*SSR*: 11). He wrote about the Swami's life because he believed it could serve as an example of self-realization for others to follow. Similarly, Narayan Swami hoped that readers would pattern their own lives on Swami Rama's; thus students could follow his example as a dedicated student, swamis could follow his example as a renunciant, and even those in poor health could learn from Swami Rama Tirtha's diet (*KeR* 2:350). Sharga presented his work as his humble offering before the respected Narayan Swami, and hoped that his readers, even if they found the experience of reading "bitter," would be inspired to seek further knowledge and happiness (*LSRT*: 16). Through conveying something of Swami Rama Tirtha's extraordinary spiritual character, each author hoped to present the inspirational example of Swami Rama Tirtha's spiritual attainment to the reader.

And therein lies the primary source of contention. None of the hagiographers doubted that Swami Rama Tirtha was a man of extraordinary spiritual accomplishment. It was indeed the power of this accomplishment that attracted them to him, a power that all three authors experienced firsthand. But how could they convey it? For Puran Singh, the task seemed virtually impossible. He insisted that he was qualified only to sketch his own impressions, and hoped that the reader would thereby be left with some sense of Swami Rama. For Narayan Swami, however, the only option was to write as a "scientist" and present the "bare facts" which would in and of themselves convey Swami Rama's spiritual power. In his foreword to Sharga's *LSRT*, he expressed his hope that Sharga's text would present as many facts as possible to make available a complete account to readers that would counter Singh's misrepresentations of Swami Rama Tirtha.

> Mr. Puran lived with Rama and his *Story of Rama* is a record of his impressions rather than anything else. It is a common mistake of biographers to thrust their own feelings [into their work], and they so colour the facts that it is difficult to separate the two. This defeats the aim of biography and gives a distorted vision, which, to my mind, is a mis-representation. (*LSRT*: ii-iii)

To Narayan Swami, Singh's choice to convey his impressions of the Swami was a fatal flaw of subjectivism, for it influenced the way he conveyed the "facts." He proposed Sharga's account of the Swami as an antidote to Puran Singh's faulty "impressions": "This book and the *Story of Rama* by Mr. Puran Singh are in no way convertible. . . . Mr. Puran's *Story of Rama* cannot be said to be a biography, for it mostly embodies the author's personal impressions, which, like a chameleon, change their colour from time to time according to his environments and surroundings" (*LSRT*: iii-iv). In contrast, in Narayan Swami's estimation, Sharga's book was "a simple life-story, made of stern facts, an exact exposition, supplying us with detailed data without any conclusion. This policy of non-interference, with facts coupled with the true spirit of research, is a vital necessity in a true biographer" (*LSRT*: iv). Narayan Swami revealed his positivist bent in bestowing his approval on Sharga, whom he imagined as an objective researcher working with "stern facts" as his data, coming to no impressionistic conclusions.

Narayan Swami's foreword to Sharga's work confirms that he considered it the definitive version of Swami Rama Tirtha's life:

> Mr. Sharga wrote this life-story after a very careful study of the various manuscripts, auto-biographical notes and other available documents. He has studied them like a research student intelligently but coolly. In the calm of night we together discussed many a point which required deep thinking and careful analysis. . . . I went through the manuscript and gave my best thought to it. So I can say unreservedly that the book is reliable in almost every respect. (*LSRT*: ii-iii)

Narayan Swami rejected his own text because he could not separate his experience from the facts. As a "scientist," he did not think that he could be properly objective about his own role, but he did believe that he could be objective when presented with the views of others such as Sharga and Singh. He therefore reserved for himself the right to be a judge of other texts, in part because of his firsthand experience of the Swami, which again suggests that what is at issue is not so much "impressions" based on experience as incorrect impressions. While Narayan Swami conceded that there was some disadvantage in the fact that Sharga was not a close disciple of Swami Rama Tirtha, he believed that this disadvantage was outweighed by Sharga's resultant ability to look at "historical facts" without resorting to sentimentality (*LSRT*: ii). Sharga, cool and levelheaded, with less direct experience of the Swami, could present the "facts" properly, and Narayan Swami therefore deemed his book reliable. The implied assessment of Puran Singh was that he was not levelheaded and scientific, but emotional, wrapped up in his own experience; he was subjective (the antithesis of positivist "science") and therefore not to be trusted.

Narayan Swami's stress on the importance of facts through his use of the rhetoric of scientific method masks a very different concern. Puran Singh, Narayan Swami, and Sharga actually had no serious disagreements about the basic facts of Swami Rama Tirtha's life, the information used to construct their narratives of his life, or larger questions about selection, organization, and objectivity. Neither Narayan Swami nor Sharga, for example, mentioned any quarrel with Puran Singh over the details of the events—the "facts"—he described, nor did they suggest that Puran Singh left out anything significant. Sharga, in fact, quoted copiously from Puran Singh without challenging or modifying any of his statements. What was really at stake, though not directly addressed, were concerns that are more properly in the realm of hagiography, the writing of the life of a saint, and not the "science" of historical biography, as Narayan Swami argued. Narayan Swami believed that Puran Singh's impressions were inextricably knotted into the facts he presented, thereby making it impossible for the facts to reveal their truth. What Narayan Swami clearly believed but did not openly concede was that the facts could be deemed reliable only if they revealed Swami Rama Tirtha as a great saint who had no doubts about his mission. In theory, according to Narayan Swami's own "scientific method," Puran Singh's faulty impressions should have been immaterial, for anyone could take his facts (the same facts Narayan Swami and Sharga had) and draw the proper conclusions. Yet Narayan Swami himself did not believe this; he wanted Sharga's text to supercede Puran Singh's. The final irony was that Puran Singh's text would become the most successful.

Puran Singh, Narayan Swami, and Sharga all hoped that their texts would demonstrate that Swami Rama Tirtha was an extraordinary man whose life itself could serve as an example for their readers. The Swami could serve as an example not just as a student or world traveler, but most importantly as a man of exceptional spiritual attainment. To learn about his life could help others move toward similar spiritual attainments. In the concluding passage of his own text, Narayan Swami suggested that reading about the Swami's life could itself be a means of experiencing the Swami's presence. He wrote, "even though Rama is lost to the sight of his admirers, Emperor Rama [*Rāma Bādshāh*] is nonetheless himself present and visible everywhere. Just look!" (*KeR* 2: 356), a statement which was clearly not so much an objective, scientific point of argument as an assertion of his faith both in Swami Rama Tirtha's status as a spiritual "emperor" and his eternal presence for his followers. Yet Narayan Swami firmly believed that only reporting the "facts" about Swami Rama

Tirtha's life could lead people to accept his claim that the Swami was indeed visible and present everywhere.

Although all three authors considered Swami Rama Tirtha a great saint and wanted to convince others of this, it seems to have been Puran Singh who chose the most effective rhetorical strategy for conveying Swami Rama Tirtha's status. Puran Singh's "impressions" (i.e. his chronical of others' and his own experiences with the Swami), though they suggested that the Swami had doubts, were infinitely more effective in conveying Swami Rama Tirtha's power than the "bare facts" approach of Narayan Swami and Sharga. Swami Rama Tirtha was considered a saint because other people perceived him as such—his sainthood was established through his relationships with other people. Puran Singh, who thought that relationship (his "impressions" of it) was the most important aspect of Swami Rama Tirtha he could write about, thus produced a text which presented far more compelling evidence for the Swami's sainthood than Narayan Swami's and Sharga's compilations of "bare facts." Indeed his "impressions" may have been the most important "facts" of all in communicating Swami Rama Tirtha's status as a great saint.

This debate about impressions and facts among the early hagiographers is especially well-illustrated in each text's account of the final two years of Swami Rama Tirtha's life, from his return to India from the United States in 1904 until his drowning in 1906. After his return from the United States, Swami Rama Tirtha made important decisions about the public role that he would play. Why he made the decisions he did, and what really happened when he drowned, were questions that the Swami's followers could not easily answer. Ultimately, the debate between Puran Singh and Narayan Swami centered not upon the proper means of presenting facts scientifically, but rather the correct way to interpret those facts (i.e. relating one's impressions) to support a particular image of sainthood.

Impressions and Facts: Swami Rama Tirtha, 1904-1906

For the earliest hagiographers, there were three key issues in the last two years of Swami Rama Tirtha's life: his position on India's growing nationalist movement, his willingness to become a public figure and reformer, and finally his reasons for deciding to leave public life and retire to the Himalayas. It was only a short while after making that decision that he drowned while bathing in the Ganges river, prematurely ending his career as a religious leader. When the Swami had first returned to India from the United States, that career seemed especially promising. His stay in the United States received a fair amount of press coverage in India, and when he returned, people in north India and the Punjab in particular were curious to see and hear this Swami who had traveled abroad. Would he, like Swami Vivekananda before him, create an organization to propagate his ideas and promote social reform? Would he become a leader in the growing Indian nationalist movement? When Swami Rama Tirtha landed at Bombay in 1904, Swami Shivagunacharya (whom Puran Singh termed an "old Pharisee"[5]) was apparently anxious to capitalize on Swami Rama Tirtha's fame and develop plans for some sort of organization. Whatever Swami Shivagunacharya's intentions may have been, Swami Rama Tirtha did spend some time at his *āśram* in Mathura pondering his options and giving occasional public addresses.

Swami Rama Tirtha's speeches and letters from this time (*IWGR* 4) show that he was concerned about India's growing movement for independence from British rule, and debating whether he should be involved in any social and religious reform organizations. After tentatively exploring a public role for himself as a social, political, and religious leader, he abandoned the idea of forming any sort of organization, and stopped talking about India's need to be politically independent. But there is no consensus on how to interpret Swami Rama's actions on these issues among the three authors. Puran Singh, who was with Swami Rama during much of this period, painted a picture of a man who became disillusioned with the requirements of a life of renunciation, who had grown uncertain as to his purpose, and as a result was unconvincing as a nationalist leader. Singh reported that when he and Swami Rama Tirtha were travelling in the Himalayas, the Swami complained to him that the ochre robes of renunciation had become symbols of slavery to formality and convention, and announced that he intended to tear his robes to shreds in front of an audience the next time he visited the plains. Puran Singh believed that the Swami's disenchantment with the renunciant's life largely stemmed from his confusion after his wife and younger son came to visit him upon his return to India (*SSR*: 246). According to Puran Singh, Swami Rama Tirtha first refused to see them, but then relented after Puran expressed his shock that the Swami could ignore his own wife and child. Later, he told Puran Singh that he had enjoyed seeing his former family, but felt constrained by the requirements of the renunciant's life (*SSR*: 243-246).[6] Puran Singh's assessment showed a man riven with doubts, uncomfortable with the demands and strictures of a life of renunciation, a man who was not sure that he could fulfill the leadership role that was being thrust upon him. Yet for a while he had explored the possibility of adapting his religious ideas to the political arena.

In some of the speeches he gave to audiences in north India when he first returned from the United States, Swami Rama told audiences that they could incorporate nationalist ideals into Vedantic practice by imagining themselves to be at one with the nation (e.g. through imagining their bodies to be the Indian subcontinent). Although later hagiographers would make much of Swami Rama's comments on Indian nationalism, Puran Singh thought such talk rang hollow, noting with some distaste, "all the lectures that Swami Rama delivered at this period have a strong odour of patriotic fervour" (*SSR*: 152). As he saw it, Swami Rama Tirtha had been too impressed by the success of the independent United States and so toyed with the idea of being a nationalist leader, but eventually abandoned this and went back to being "himself" (*SSR*: 152). That Swami Rama Tirtha quickly severed his ties with Swami Shivagunacharya, moved to the Himalayas, and eschewed public contact became direct evidence for Puran Singh that the Swami was not overly enamored with the notion of becoming involved in India's quest for independence from the British or working for socio-religious reform. To Singh, Swami Rama Tirtha's religious life was incompatible with patriotism and political action and the Swami spoke of India's quest for political freedom only because he thought it was expected of him. Finally, Singh believed, Swami Rama Tirtha could take such pressures no more, and retired to the Himalayas, longing for solitude and freedom from the expectations of others.

It was this frank reading that particularly roiled Narayan Swami. In his own account of Swami Rama Tirtha's life, he argued that the Swami was actually an ardent nationalist, a position which was a perfectly natural consequence of his overall love for humanity (*KeR* 2:278-280). In his preface to a later edition of Puran Singh's hagiography, he directly challenged Singh's interpretations: "to give a few examples of his weak vision: whereas Swami Rama advocated married life as alphabets of expansion of self, Mr. Puran thinks that Swami Rama thought of it as a life of bliss; whereas Swami Rama was submerged towards the end of his life in speechless joy, the source of the river of peace, Mr. Puran takes it as an emblem of sadness; and lastly whereas Swami Rama was rising above all the rituals, Mr. Puran thinks he was tired of the ochre garb" (*SSR*: xvi). Narayan Swami would not brook the possibility that Swami Rama had any doubts about his life as a renunciant; to him, the problem lay with Puran Singh's faulty impressions. Narayan Swami believed that Swami Rama Tirtha had no confused feelings about his former family, and saw them out of a spirit of compassion but also detachment. To Puran Singh's untrained eye, the Swami's profound spiritual joy appeared as sadness. For Narayan Swami, Swami Rama Tirtha's rejection of the traditional regulations for renunciants marked his advanced state of spiritual understanding, but Puran Singh could see it only as misgivings about having left his family. Whereas Puran Singh chose to view the Swami as a man with doubts and misgivings, Narayan Swami insisted that he was beyond all doubts, thus according himself the authority to declare as "bare facts" what actually seem to be his own impressions. There is no disagreement here between Narayan Swami and Puran Singh about the basic facts; rather, the disagreement is over interpretation.

In contrast, Sharga (who, other than hearing the Swami speak in Lucknow, did not have direct contact with him during this period) glossed over these conflicting interpretations, relying most heavily on Swami Rama Tirtha's speeches and letters and extensive quotations from Puran Singh, with little or no comment on either (*LSRT*: 306-377). He drew particular attention to Swami Rama Tirtha's ongoing struggles with physical illness (*LSRT*: 364-365), but did not speculate about his mental state, leaving the reader to contend with his quotations of both Puran Singh and Narayan Swami's interpretations. Nonetheless, a careful reader of the text would have been forewarned by Narayan Swami's foreword that Puran Singh's interpretations were suspect.

Narayan Swami and Puran Singh often accompanied Swami Rama in the last two years of his life. Both agreed that Swami Rama wished to retire from public life for some time but their views on his frame of mind were diametrically opposed. What Puran Singh reported as sadness and doubt, Narayan Swami reported as speechless joy. Their different positions on the Swami's mental state subsequently conditioned their interpretations of Swami Rama Tirtha's drowning in the Ganges river in October, 1906. In 1905, Swami Rama Tirtha had begun to minimize his contact with the public and had moved from the plains of north India to the foothills of the Himalayan mountains, sometimes living alone, and sometimes summoning Narayan Swami and other followers to be with him. Swami Rama Tirtha was studying Sanskrit and had announced his intention to write a book called *Dynamics of Mind*, which was to be a complete exposition of his philosophy of Practical Vedānta. Sometime in 1906, he established residence outside the town of Tehri in an area known as Vasishtha Ashram. That summer, Puran Singh and some other admirers of Swami Rama Tirtha came to visit (*KeR* 2:288-290). In September of that year, Puran Singh returned to his job, and shortly thereafter, the remaining members of the group moved to a new location closer to the town of Tehri. Finally only Narayan Swami remained, and Swami Rama Tirtha instructed him to visit only once weekly to collect what he had written for publication. As noted earlier, before he could make his first scheduled weekly visit, Narayan Swami received word that Swami Rama Tirtha had drowned. He quickly rushed to Swami Rama Tirtha's hut, and Puran Singh also hurried to Tehri after hearing the news.

In his original account of the final months of Swami Rama's life, Narayan Swami made little comment on the Swami's mental state in the months leading to his untimely death. He reported their moves to different locations in the

Himalayas, proffered rather pointed opinions about the visitors who came, and described how he had received word of the Swami's death. But clearly he disagreed with Puran Singh's reading of those same events. In *SSR*, Puran Singh reported that he was puzzled by Swami Rama's sudden interest in "stale and musty" Sanskrit grammar and found him increasingly "sober, serene, and quiet" rather than what Puran considered to be his usual cheerful self (*SSR*: 156,158). According to Singh, Narayan Swami had attributed this change in mood not to sadness or depression, but dyspepsia, and out of his "wild love" tried to get Swami Rama to agree that diet was his only problem (*SSR*: 162). Singh reported that Narayan Swami had many "bitter discussions" with Swami Rama, and that Narayan Swami also frequently indulged his tendency to "mercilessly dissect" other people. Puran Singh maintained that because Narayan Swami was so contentious, Swami Rama finally asked him to live at least a mile away from him (*SSR*: 163). Narayan Swami made no mention of Puran Singh's uncomplimentary assessment of his character in his own version of the events of this period, but Singh's criticism of him may well have something to do with his overall distaste for Singh's account. When Puran Singh's *SSR* was published in 1924, Narayan Swami was heading the Swami Rama Tirtha Publication League and other publicly visible organizations, and it may have been troubling to him to find himself so negatively portrayed in a book by a well-known poet.

Sharga chose to gloss over the tension between Puran Singh and Narayan Swami in his version of this period of the Swami's life, just as he had in their debate over the Swami's patriotism. Sharga used Puran Singh's text as a primary source of information, but remained silent on the disagreements between Singh and Narayan Swami. His narrative of events erased virtually all conflict among the Swami's followers and produced no hint of doubts or uncertainties on the Swami's part. Sharga did not try to explain to his readers why Swami Rama Tirtha did what he did at this time; instead, he quoted Puran Singh's text and the Swami's own writings (*LSRT*: 336-382). Puran Singh's faulty "impressions" were left to stand on their own (albeit with Narayan Swami's prefatory cautions about Singh's unreliability), perhaps because he left the only firsthand account of some of the events of the Swami's last two years.

The mysterious farewells that Swami Rama Tirtha had bade some of his followers at the end of the summer of 1906 figured heavily in attempts to understand Swami Rama Tirtha's death. As he prepared to return home in September, 1906, Puraṅ Singh had a conversation with the Swami which he later concluded was the Swami's forecasting of his own death. That day, Swami Rama Tirtha asked Puran Singh to help him bathe, and told him that he would soon become silent (*SSR*: 164-165). When Swami Rama Tirtha shortly thereafter made arrangements with Narayan Swami to visit weekly, he bade a similar farewell, telling Narayan Swami that his body was weakening and that he soon would become silent. He asked Narayan Swami to be his representative since he would no longer leave the mountains (*LSRT*: 380). Sharga, whose text was approved by Narayan Swami, confirmed this account. According to Puran Singh, "both these farewells were the farewells of his approaching death" (*SSR*: 165). The unstated implication is that Swami Rama Tirtha somehow knew that he was soon to die, and was perhaps even planning it. Narayan Swami, however, argued that what had really happened was that Swami Rama Tirtha realized that Puran Singh's devotion had reached its limit, that he would forsake Vedānta for the Sikhism of his family, and therefore was bidding goodbye to Puran Singh as a close disciple (*KeR* 2:293). As for the Swami's apparent farewell to him, he had no comment, though he never denied that the conversation took place.

Interpreting the Facts: Swami Rama Tirtha's Death

For Singh, Narayan Swami, and Sharga, those farewell conversations were crucial for understanding what happened next. Puran Singh was back at home with his family, Narayan Swami was living a mile away, and Swami Rama Tirtha was alone with no one to visit him but his cook. Narayan Swami interviewed the cook shortly after the Swami drowned, and all three hagiographers used his transcription of their conversation. According to the cook, this is what happened on October 17, 1906: some days earlier, Swami Rama Tirtha, weakened from chronic digestive difficulties, had injured his knee while exercising and had given up his customary daily bath in a tributary of the Ganges. On October 17, which was Diwālī, however, the cook told him that it was an astrologically auspicious day, so the Swami decided to leave his hut for a bath in the river. The cook bathed first, and then sat on the riverbank watching Swami Rama dunk himself underwater. After a rock shifted under his feet, the Swami got caught in a whirlpool and began to struggle. He made several vain attempts to swim against the whirlpool and the swift current, but then stopped struggling, intoned "*oṃ*" several times, and was washed downstream.[7] The area was virtually deserted, and the cook could see no way to help the Swami himself.

Swami Rama Tirtha's life thus ended at the young age of thirty-three, and the sudden, tragic nature of his death posed an interpretive challenge to his hagiographers. In his speeches, letters, essays, and poetry, Swami Rama Tirtha had often proclaimed his power over death, yet he died struggling against the current of a river. Statements made by Singh and Narayan Swami hint that there were those who maintained that the Swami, in a depressed state, had committed suicide, and Sharga mentioned the possibility of suicide explicitly. All three authors vehemently argued against this interpretation of Swami Rama's death (evidence, perhaps, of its popularity), but Puran Singh and Narayan Swami's conflicting interpretations of the Swami's emotional state prior to his drowning led them to different conclusions about why he had died.

Narayan Swami was deeply saddened and troubled after hearing how Swami Rama died, and felt guilty that he had not been there to try to save him. The Swami had always said that death could not take him without his permission. Yet the cook's account suggested that Swami Rama Tirtha had fought valiantly to save himself, and gave himself up to the river current only when he realized there was no hope. In the days after Swami Rama's death, Narayan Swami wandered aimlessly in the area near Rama's hut, afraid to enter it for fear of what he might find. As he described it, he found himself questioning everything—the validity of Swami Rama Tirtha's Vedānta, Swami Rama Tirtha, sometimes himself (*KeR* 2:304). Why would Swami Rama Tirtha permit himself to die just as he was embarking on a major project?

Then one day he ran into Puran Singh, who had also come to Tehri, experiencing many of the same doubts. How could a man who had always proclaimed his power over death have drowned while taking a bath? Puran Singh suggested that the two visit Swami Rama's hut to organize his books and papers and perhaps find clues to the Swami's state of mind; Narayan Swami had thus far avoiding doing this. The next morning, they found in Swami Rama's hut a few books and a rough draft of an essay in Urdu.[8] Amidst the unnumbered pages of the essay they found a brief, scrawled paragraph in Urdu, apparently the last that the Swami had written, which read:

> Indra. Rudra. Marut [Mārut]. Brahma [Brahmā]. Vishnu [Viṣṇu]. Shiva [Śiva]. Ganga [Gaṅgā]. etc. Bharat! O death! Please blow up this body. I have no shortage of other bodies. Wearing only the beams of the moon will I have any peace, living with the stars. Clothed in the rivers and streams of the mountains, I shall wander singing. Clad by the stormy ocean, I shall undulate. I alone am the graceful wind, I am the blowing of the maddened breeze. My wanderer's face is never still. I descended from the mountains in that form; I brought wilted seedlings back to life. I made the flowers laugh. I made the nightingale cry, I knocked on all the doors. I awakened the sleeping, and wiped away someone's tears. I lifted someone's veil. Tease him, tease him. Tease you. He has left, he has left. He took nothing with him, no one was with him. (*KER* 2:305)[9]

All the hagiographers quoted this final paragraph in full assuming that it was somehow linked to the Swami's death. Did this paragraph show that the Swami was planning his own demise, or was it simply yet another example of his poetic style of expressing his Vedantic sense of identity with everything around him? Both Narayan Swami and Puran Singh acknowledged the anguish they suffered and the doubts that were brought about by their Swami's death by drowning. Puran Singh ventured a possible connection between what he took to be Swami Rama Tirtha's sadness and his death, but could not be certain whether the Swami indeed had planned to die. Narayan Swami could not settle on any one explanation, but believed that there was some spiritual reason for what happened. Neither would ever offer a conclusive explanation, but both tried to quell any suspicions that the drowning was intentional.

Indeed Puran Singh wavered in his interpretation of Swami Rama's death. In the first edition of *SSR*, he declared that the Swami's last paragraph was an explicit forecasting of imminent death, but in later editions he revised his argument, speculating that it was simply another example of Swami Rama's characteristic style in which death received frequent mention, more as a metaphor for forsaking egoism than a reference to bodily death (*SSR*: 166).[10] According to Narayan Swami, Puran Singh came to him some years after his *Story of Swami Rama* was published and said that there were many things he would revise if he had the chance (*SSR*: xiv-xv). In spite of the wavering, he always believed that the Swami had been depressed and unhappy before he died. Yet the closest that Narayan Swami would come to suggesting that Swami Rama Tirtha was depressed was to concede that he was in a strange state [*'ajīb hālat*] prior to his untimely demise. The Swami's cook told him that the morning of his death, Swami Rama sat in his hut, tears streaming down his face, seemingly in some kind of trance as he wrote. He was so absorbed that for some time he did not notice the presence of his cook, who had come to tell him that their meal was ready, and to ask whether Swami Rama wished to bathe in the Ganges.

To Puran Singh, these were tears of sadness; to Narayan Swami they could only be tears of joy welling from his advanced spiritual state. To strengthen his claim for his own interpretation of the Swami's tears, Narayan Swami considered several possible explanations for the Swami's death: first, that he realized that his frail, weakened body was to be of no further use, and therefore summoned death; second, his spiritual bliss was so great that he could no longer tolerate worldly life, and therefore summoned death to claim his body; or third, Swami Rama Tirtha intentionally offered his body to the Ganges. On the basis of Swami Rama's struggle against the current, Narayan Swami ruled out the third possibility and leaned strongly towards the first, that his death was somehow connected to his weakened physical condition and had nothing to do with his mental state (*KeR* 2:334-335). He presented this as the conclusion of a logical argument, but did not explain the full progression of his logic. While Narayan Swami contested Puran Singh's portrayal of the Swami's mental state in the months before his death, he joined Singh in concluding that there was no adequate means of explaining exactly how and why the Swami died just as he was beginning a major project. Finally, neither Singh and Narayan Swami, who were close to the Swami in the months before he died, could themselves produce a conclusive explanation of what happened, nor could they reconcile the Swami's death at thirty-three with his frequent statements about his power over death. Both ended their texts with unresolved questions.

It was Sharga who offered what Narayan Swami eventually deemed the definitive explanation of the Swami's death. Sharga, who was not with the Swami in those final months, avoided analyzing his mental state as a possible explanation for his death, and rejected Puran Singh's and Narayan Swami's speculations that the Swami's death was perhaps accidental (*LSRT*: 388-389). He argued that if indeed the drowning were accidental, it would negate the Swami's many proclamations of his power over death. Rather than focusing on the Swami as a unique individual whose actions must be explained within the context of his state of mind or personality, Sharga assumed that the explanation for the Swami's death lay in his status as a *jñānī*, one who possesses the highest spiritual knowledge.

> There is, therefore, a deeper cause of Rama's body getting a watery grave. For a *jnani* all actions cease, not in the sense that his physical body is idle, but in the sense that while the organs of senses and actions are moving among their respective objects, his will is not behind them—if he seems to do or suffer, it is so by force of his *prarabhda karma*, which is exhausted, not by *jnan* [knowledge], but by actual operation. . . . Now a *jnani* becomes one with the universal Self, without Whose order not a leaf quivers, not a blade of grass grows, not a drop of water falls from the clouds. Rama's claim of subduing death was therefore a true claim, but he had to undergo the *prarabdha karma*. (*LSRT*: 390-391)

According to Sharga's analysis, Swami Rama Tirtha had merged into the "universal Self" even before he died; his state prior to his death, whether seen as deep sadness or profound joy, was merely the result of the workings of *prārabdha karma*, or that *karma* which was to be worked out within his lifetime.[11] When the effects of all his actions from the present lifetime were finally exhausted, there was no reason for Swami Rama Tirtha to continue to lead a mundane bodily existence. That he struggled against the current was simply a reflection of the physical body's tendency to avoid death, but finally the physical will to live succumbed to his spirit's desire to move on. His death, then, had nothing to do with doubts, or poor health, much less a depression so severe that it led to suicide. Instead, the explanation lay in the Swami's status as a *jñānī*. His *ātman* no longer had any reason to function within the confines of an ordinary human body, and although the Swami appeared to act, his will was not involved in those actions. As a result, when he died, there was no remaining *karma* that would cause him to be reborn. In Sharga's account, the Swami's death was thus revealed as a triumph over worldly life, and not the tragedy it seemed to Puran Singh and Narayan Swami.

Sharga's explanation obviated any need for speculation on Swami Rama Tirtha's mental or physical state at the time of his death; his death had a perfectly defensible explanation supplied by the Hindu tradition itself, the advanced state of the *jñānī* who is "at one with the universal Self." Puran Singh and Narayan Swami made no such overtly religious claims about Swami Rama's spiritual status when he died, but Narayan Swami endorsed Sharga's interpretation. That he did so is noteworthy, for Sharga's analysis goes far beyond the "bare facts," the approach that Narayan Swami originally found most credible. Sharga's interpretive strategy is significant, for it signals the beginning of a shift that would characterize the developing hagiographical tradition—explaining Swami Rama Tirtha not as a mere human defined by aspects of his character or historical circumstances, but as a saint who transcended such mundane concerns. Significantly, Puran Singh's interpretation could retrospectively be made to fit within such a model as well, for Singh ultimately concluded that the Swami's death was beyond his comprehension; since the Swami was of such advanced spiritual status, an ordinary man such as Puran Singh could not understand him.

Although Narayan Swami sought only the facts, and directed Sharga to do the same, both reached a point at which those facts were no longer sufficient, and some sort of overt interpretation was acknowledged. Both Puran Singh's interpretation (that he could not understand why the Swami had died) and Sharga's interpretation endorsed by Narayan Swami (that as a *jñānī* the Swami's actions could not be interpreted by normal means) presupposed the "fact" that the Swami was no ordinary man, and that ordinary means of explanation could not be applied.[12]

Experience as Fact: The Stage is Set

When they discussed their aims and methods, all three of these western-educated authors demonstrated some familiarity with standards of critical historical biography, and presented themselves as working within this genre.

Using the terminology of a positivist approach to historical biography, Narayan Swami expressed his disagreement with Puran Singh over the issue of "impressions." He believed it was possible to write a biography consisting only of "bare facts" unencumbered by intrusive personal impressions. For readers, those facts would be like the different ingredients used in an experiment, with the implication that when done properly the same results would always appear. Yet Puran Singh used those same ingredients to reach what Narayan Swami thought was a wrong reading, and Narayan Swami's critique of Singh's approach suggests that his true purpose was not as firmly grounded in "scientific objectivity" as he believed. Narayan Swami wanted to present the facts not "bare," but clothed in such a way that readers' experiments would reproduce Narayan Swami's results—the conviction that Swami Rama Tirtha was a great saint, a man without doubts.

It is especially revealing that Narayan Swami's anxieties revolved around the role that personal experiences of the Swami played in texts about his life. Puran Singh clearly saw the Swami first and foremost as a man with a distinct personality, a man with doubts and weaknesses, but whom he nonetheless admired greatly. Yet among the Swami's followers, who share Narayan Swami's appraisal of him as a great saint, Puran Singh's text has remained the most popular. The reason for his enduring popularity lies in a fact that Narayan Swami failed to understand—that Puran Singh's impressions, however flawed they might have been, played a critical role in creating an enduring image of Swami Rama Tirtha as a great saint, because it was the personal element of Singh's experience of the Swami and not just an enumeration of facts which made Swami Rama Tirtha real to people.

Both Puran Singh and Narayan Swami traveled with Swami Rama Tirtha, corresponded with him, and heard him speak publicly and privately. They witnessed his ongoing struggle with poor health, and they saw him in many guises: as a student, a husband and father, a renunciant, a successful public lecturer accepting the adoration of the public, and as a quiet, contemplative man who craved solitude in the mountains. Both men found themselves inexplicably drawn to Swami Rama Tirtha, and in writing of his life, they sought to convey something of the power that drew them to this man, the devotion that compelled both of them to renounce their families and careers (albeit temporarily in Puran's case) to follow him. In writing about him, they had to decide how to present the information that was available to them in order to convey that power. Both obviously considered Swami Rama Tirtha to have been important enough that some account of his life should endure; each independently made the decision to write about his life. They both sought to preserve Swami Rama Tirtha's memory by creating books that would allow readers who had not had the experience of meeting Swami Rama Tirtha to experience something of his power. As noted above, Narayan Swami concluded his account of the Swami's life by exhorting readers to look around them to find the Swami. Though Swami Rama Tirtha was no longer alive, his biography (or, more accurately, his hagiography) could provide a way for devotees to re-establish his presence, to experience him for themselves.

Puran Singh and Narayan Swami understood their project as the writing of biography, and thus framed their discussions in terms of what they thought constituted good biographical writing. Narayan Swami's attitude towards "facts" and "true biography" was very much akin to that of many of the early western critics of Christian hagiography who were dismayed to find that the typical Christian hagiography did not provide much in the way of reliable historical data about the lives of saints. Narayan Swami wanted an "objective" biography to reveal what was essentially the subjective perception that Swami Rama Tirtha was a great saint; in a sense he thus conflated the genres of biography and hagiography (exemplifying what Reynolds and Capps [1976: 5] termed "confessional biography," texts which combine modern biography with traditional hagiographic elements). Puran Singh too was aware of the positivist approach to biography, but believed there really was no way to write a true biography of a man such as Swami Rama Tirtha, for there was no way to explain or interpret his actions. Thus he abandoned all hope of an objective, "scientific" approach.

> He enchants the very air around himself with his bird-like speech that was all poetry, all music. His body was a lake which trembled seeing the sun enter its depths. He confounds logic by his divine madness. He contradicts himself in a thousand ways in his self-intoxication which alone is both his creed and religion. (*SSR*: vii)

How could Puran Singh possibly explain the actions of a man intoxicated by a divine madness that confounded all logic? Puran Singh's operating premise was that ultimately, Swami Rama Tirtha could not be explained. Those who found themselves in his presence while he was alive could only marvel at his enchantment; those who read about him may perhaps rekindle some sense of that divine madness.

Narayan Swami, on the other hand, began with the unstated premise that Swami Rama Tirtha was a great saint, whose greatness, although it precluded explanation by the average devotee, could be exposed through a "scientific" approach—a cool, clear exposition of the facts. Using the idiom of positivism, he hoped to enlist the ideals of science in order to create a scientific model of the ideal of sainthood. Indeed his approach presupposed such a model. He apparently assumed that if certain characteristics identify an animal or plant as belonging to a particular species, that there must be certain characteristics ("bare facts") which similarly identify a person as belonging to the class or "species" of saints. The characteristics of the species as a whole, then, could be used to explain the behavior of a single member of the species. Narayan Swami, initially skeptical about Swami Rama Tirtha and all that he stood for, put him to the test and found him a genuine saint. Thus according to Narayan Swami's "scientific" model of sainthood, the proper biography presents the components of an experiment, the "bare and solid facts." Narayan Swami believed that if readers analyzed these components with the proper method, they would replicate the results of Narayan Swami's experiments, reaching the same conclusion—that Swami Rama Tirtha was a great saint. Narayan Swami's mistake, perhaps, was in assuming that Swami Rama Tirtha's sainthood was an objective classification. Puran Singh's reliance upon his own experience—and the subsequent success of *SSR*—suggests that such subjective "impressions" are in fact a critical part of what characterizes a saint.

Given the positions of Puran Singh and Narayan Swami, we might expect that Puran Singh would have written an adulatory text, presenting the Swami's every action as a wonder to behold, impossible to understand, and in contrast we would expect Narayan Swami, defender of facts and objectivity, to have written a straightforward narrative, with logical conclusions supported by strong historical evidence. But this is not what happened. Despite his protestations to the contrary, Puran Singh did venture to speculate about why the Swami did what he did, and even dared suggest that the man had doubts. Although he emphasized the Swami's "divine madness," it was his all-too-human frailties which Puran Singh used to explain the Swami's actions in the final years of his life. Narayan Swami, the cool scientist, we might assume, would have presented readers with a reasoned account of the Swami in which the facts would speak for themselves. If the facts led readers to conclude that perhaps the Swami was uncertain about his role, troubled, or unhappy (a reading which is virtually inescapable if one reads the Swami's complete works), then so be it—the "true biographer" would have to allow such conclusions. In his prefaces to both Sharga's and Singh's books, Narayan Swami asked readers to use their own judgement in assessing Swami Rama Tirtha: "it is hoped that the reader will go through the book impartially and meet Rama directly rather than through any medium" (*SSR*: xvii). Yet Narayan Swami did not follow the model he so heartily endorsed. His presentation of the "facts" was intended to guide the reader away from the Swami's more "human" side, steering them instead towards viewing him as an ideal, an infallible saint. Puran Singh took the same facts and confessed his inability to arrange them in any way that would truly reveal the Swami. These early hagiographies thus complicate the distinctions between two major divisions within sacred biography (or hagiography) which Reynolds and Capps (1976: 3) noted: texts which "'humanize' the biographical subject by including episodes which reflect his common humanity" and those which "'spiritualize' the subject by expunging references to his human weaknesses, mental lapses, signs of occasional cruelty and so on." Whereas Puran Singh in one sense adopted a "humanizing" approach, his emphasis on his own experiences in the Swami's presence served to "spiritualize" the Swami; Narayan Swami ostensibly aimed for the more "humanizing" approach, but his critique of Puran Singh revealed that "spiritualization" was his true goal.

Deciding how to convey to their readers something of the spiritual power of their subject is the central challenge that hagiographers face. These early hagiographies suggest that "humanizing" or "spiritualizing" is not simply a matter of the way that the hagiographer presents the events in the subject's life, but is just as much a function of the way the hagiographer portrays the subject's relationships with his followers. People such as Narayan Swami recognized Swami Rama Tirtha as a saint because of their understanding that he had experienced something of divinity, of the true nature of reality itself. It was the power of this experience that drew followers to the Swami; as a saint, he could point the way towards that same experience of divinity. He lived in this world among ordinary humans, but seemed to draw power from something beyond this world, a reality beyond expression in ordinary language. For his followers, he stood as a mediator between the mundane and ultimate reality. For Puran Singh, this was what made Swami Rama Tirtha "contradictory"—his experience of divinity which came across as madness in the world of ordinary humans. Swami Rama Tirtha himself lamented that he could not adequately convey his experience of realization in language. Puran Singh found it even more difficult as a man of lesser realization, and therefore he tried to write about what he thought himself capable of understanding—Swami Rama Tirtha the man—his education, his family, his travels, his experiences, his doubts. He produced an account which, however poetic, was most firmly rooted in historical, mundane details—the "facts" that Narayan Swami ostensibly sought.

Narayan Swami, however, set before himself the virtually impossible task of expressing the Swami's realization through a quasi-scientific method of presentation. How could the facts be presented in such a way as to lead readers to the proper conclusions without Narayan Swami's or Sharga's own impressions somehow coming into play? To convey something of the power attributed to a great saint goes far beyond the realm of Narayan Swami's scientific method, and what Narayan Swami did not acknowledge, and perhaps could not, is that the role of the hagiographer is central. The hagiographer's experience of the saint itself becomes a crucial element in creating an image of sainthood. Swami Rama Tirtha became a saint on the basis of other people's recognition of him as such, and there was no escaping that fact. Whether he can be objectively described as a saint, as the positivist position would require, yields completely to the reality that he was made a saint by the many people who accepted him as such not on the basis of "facts," but what Puran Singh called "impressions."

Narayan Swami instinctively understood something of this when he declared Puran Singh unworthy of the task of conveying Swami Rama's spiritual power: "Mr. Puran had a dumb devotion towards Rama, and it continued till he was in physical contact with Rama's divine personality; but when Rama's physical garb dropped off, Puran was, as if clipped of his wings" (*SSR*: xv-xvi). It was not Puran Singh's presentation of facts which Narayan Swami found wanting, but the quality of his devotion. Hence his distaste for Puran Singh's *Story of Swami Rama.* In his eyes, Puran Singh's fault as a biographer was that his devotion was "dumb." He had somehow been able to experience something of the Swami's power (something which none of his critics challenged), but he hadn't the spiritual capability, the "smarts," to know what he was dealing with, nor could he sustain his devotion after the Swami died. Therefore, in Narayan Swami's estimation, Singh's account of the Swami's life was flawed, because his experience of him was incomplete. Thus Narayan Singh's real challenge was to the nature of Puran Singh's experience of Swami Rama Tirtha, not the facts about his life that he presented, because Puran Singh presumed to be able to explain the Swami's actions.

Narayan Swami, however, considered himself smart enough to judge the true Swami Rama Tirtha, the one whose life should be recorded for others to read and experience. Indeed he acted as the self-appointed arbiter of the earliest hagiographers. Yet he could not express what he felt in the Swami's presence, and did not try to do so (it was, as he put it, "beyond the powers of the pen"). Rather than attempting, as Puran Singh did, to convey something about Swami Rama despite the difficulties involved, Narayan Swami did his best to provide what he considered a strictly fact and detail-oriented account, hoping that a true picture of the Swami as a great saint would emerge as a result.

Sharga hinted that he too struggled with the role of his own experience of Swami Rama Tirtha in writing his text. When Narayan Swami first asked him to write about Swami Rama, he was reluctant. When he finally agreed, and Narayan Swami provided him with information about the Swami, he was overwhelmed. "I waded through it all, but I discovered that I was interested more in reading than in writing on Rama" (*LSRT*: x). He was doubly constrained—he thought first of all that he was not up to the task of presenting the life of a saint such as Swami Rama Tirtha, and he had been commissioned to write a text that would correct the "errors" of Puran Singh's account by avoiding the danger of personal impressions. As he began the project, he found that he reveled in his own experience of Swami Rama Tirtha through reading about him, but was not sure if he could adequately express that experience. Narayan Swami wanted "stern facts," an "exact exposition," and no "direct interference." While Sharga was most intrigued by his own encounter with Swami Rama Tirtha through his letters and the other information that Narayan Swami gave him, he was under orders not to write about that experience. It is no wonder that he relied so heavily upon lengthy quotations for which he provided virtually no comment or interpretation, and that he described the experience of writing as "almost involuntarily blackening sheet after sheet of paper."

Thus Narayan Swami and Sharga both tried to divorce themselves from their tellings of Swami Rama Tirtha's life. This approach presumed that the reader would be able to recognize Swami Rama Tirtha's saintliness solely by virtue of the presentation of facts in a suitable framework. Both authors attempted to convey the saintliness of a man using what they understood to be the methods of historical biography, leaving their own experiences of him out of their texts as much as possible. At the same time, however, their underlying organizational strategies suggested that they were clearly trying to steer readers towards believing that the Swami was a great saint. What they ended up producing was something that unsuccessfully melded two genres; it was really neither quite critical historical biography nor hagiography. The facts were meant not to support a particular reading of the Swami's life revealing how he was shaped by specific historical circumstances, or how he made certain contributions to his own era, but to support the reading of his life as that of a man of profound spiritual realization—something which the methods of critical historical biography were ill-suited to confirm. Nor did their texts convey much of what it was like to be a devotee of the Swami, a critical strategy in much hagiographical writing. For Swami Rama Tirtha did not proclaim himself a saint—his followers did. Their experience of him as such is perhaps the central "fact" in the construction of his sainthood.

This may help explain why Puran Singh's *The Story of Swami Rama* has remained the most popular of the three texts both in the original English and in Hindi translation, and may also account for its extensive quotation in subsequent hagiographies. Despite what Narayan Swami saw as flawed interpretations of Swami Rama Tirtha's actions, Puran Singh's text is not simply a compendium of detail, but an attempt to describe what it was like to be a devotee of Swami Rama Tirtha, what it felt like to hear him speak, or simply chant the syllable "*oṃ*." Puran Singh's failure at this attempt was ironically his greatest success in readers' eyes, for the Swami's very inexplicability stood as testimony to his greatness. Indeed if we understand hagiography as chronicling an *experience*, then it is clear why Puran Singh's text has been the most successful hagiography of the three. In 1974, when the SRTP released a new edition of *SSR* fifty years after it was first published, Ayodhia Nath, then the Honorary Secretary of the SRTP, wrote:

> Sardar Puran Singh has done great service to the humanity, by writing this book, "Story of Rama," in beautiful English and he deserves all praise for this unique work which is the outcome of the pourings of his heart from the depth of his devotion for him. . . . Sardar Puran Singh's nerves tingled, his heart thrilled and, like an overjoyed child, oblivious of the environment, he would start jumping and dancing with tears of ecstasy at remembering his blissful association with his beloved Master, Swami Rama. (*SSR*: xxv-xxvi)

Ayodhia Nath, who headed the organization which Narayan Swami had founded, chose to highlight the intensity of Puran Singh's experience of Swami Rama Tirtha, and praised him for expressing it so eloquently. What Narayan Swami characterized as "dumb" devotion Ayodhia Nath championed as a great service to humanity at large. Significantly, there were no such reissues of either Narayan Swami's text or Sharga's *LSRT* on the fiftieth anniversaries of their publication.

Narayan Swami thought of Swami Rama Tirtha as a quintessentially "modern" figure who presented eternal truths in a fashion suited to the modern era. In his own writings, Swami Rama Tirtha often asserted that his Practical Vedānta could reconcile religion and science in a way that no other religion or philosophy could. Perhaps Narayan Swami hoped that his and Sharga's accounts of the Swami's life could accomplish something similar as scientific, objective texts which nonetheless revealed Swami Rama Tirtha's religious power. Ironically, Swami Rama Tirtha's later followers would seize upon this image of him as a saint with a message specifically tailored to the "modern" twentieth century, but they would construct this image not through the "scientific" approach advocated by Narayan Swami, but by building upon the subjective, "impressionistic" approach of Puran Singh.

And so at this stage in the nascent Swami Rama Tirtha hagiographical tradition, Narayan Swami, Puran Singh, and Brijnath Sharga have established the basic "facts" about the Swami's life; their books mark the end of any substantive research into the details of the Swami's life. While Narayan Swami's brief Urdu hagiography will receive little subsequent attention, the works of

Puran Singh—and occasionally Brijnath Sharga—will be paraphrased and quoted extensively (often without attribution) by later hagiographers. Memory of the conflict between Puran Singh and Narayan Swami will fade away, and only the memory of their devotion to the Swami will remain. The outline of Swami Rama Tirtha's life that these three authors agreed upon will become the foundation for future hagiographies. The role of experience will remain central both in the writing of hagiography itself, and in the stated goals of hagiography—helping others to experience the power of the Swami. Indeed the focus on the authors' and the readers' experience of Swami Rama Tirtha will eventually eclipse what might seem to be a significant element in remembering the Swami—his extensive descriptions of his own self-experience.

4

Fragments for an Autohagiography?

Swami Rama Tirtha Tells the Story of His Life

What might Swami Rama Tirtha have thought about the controversies that emerged as followers wrote about his life? As it turns out, he had a great deal to say about how he hoped he would be remembered.

> The ignorant biographers watch only the outside bearings and attribute the achievements, now to the style of writing and then to the number of followers, etc., ignoring the real soul of success, as if my work depended on what birds are perching on the tree under which I sit and write. (*IWGR* 1:240)

So wrote Swami Rama Tirtha in a letter to Narayan Swami. Long before Narayan Swami and Puran Singh took pens in hand to write about the life of Swami Rama Tirtha, the Swami was already pondering what the "ignorant biographers" might write about him, and his words read almost as an explicit warning against the "bare facts" approach that Narayan Swami himself would later adopt. Would a conventional biography, detailing the numbers of his followers and assessing his writing style (one of Sharga's concerns), create a record that would reflect his true work, the "real soul" of his success? The fact that Swami Rama Tirtha addressed this question indicates that he wondered if it would be possible to guide his future biographers towards his "true work" so that they might write about him in the way he wished. A careful reading of the autobiographical anecdotes in his lectures, essays, and letters, along with his teachings on Practical Vedānta, suggests that the Swami very clearly attempted to guide his future biographers to read and write about his life a particular way in spite of his admonitions to pay him no mind. He left a detailed record of how his life might serve as an example to others, and his hagiographers too expressed the wish that their readers could pattern their lives on his. Would his hagiographers follow his example and adopt the model of his life he so pointedly left for them? Because the corpus of Swami Rama Tirtha's writings is clearly defined, his writings in an autobiographical vein provide an ideal opportunity to compare a saint's self-presentation with his hagiographers' presentation of him. In the hagiographical traditions surrounding many earlier figures such as the poets of the north Indian *bhakti* movement, hagiographers often used biographical statements from the writings attributed to those poets to legitimate their own portrayals. This is a problematic approach, however, because in many instances the poems attributed to these figures are later compositions in the poet's name, and therefore not the most reliable source of biographical information. In Swami Rama Tirtha's case, however, we may clearly contrast his own autobiographical statements with his hagiographers' readings of them.

As part of his exposition of Practical Vedānta, Swami Rama Tirtha carefully described his own spiritual experiences. Indeed one of the fundamental premises of his Practical Vedānta is that personal experience must be the ultimate authority in spiritual development, not another person or a text. He urged his followers not to accept his words because of their faith in him, but to test them for themselves. He wrote in one of his notebooks:

> Spare not, respect not, believe not anything I have written. Rest not till you have ground it to smallest meal between your teeth. And looking me in the face, accept not anything that I do or say . . . for it does not call for acceptance. (*IWGR* 7:50)

Swami Rama Tirtha recognized that his followers were intrigued by what he did and said. He knew that some were willing simply to accept whatever he told them on the basis of his authority as a man of advanced spiritual realization, and with this apparently in mind, he admonished them not to accept unquestioningly his every word. They were to consider each statement thoroughly, test it, and accept it for themselves only if they found it true. Thus if he were to function as an exemplar for his followers, it was only so that they might test for themselves his words and actions. In spite of this emphasis on self-validation, however, Swami Rama Tirtha still tried to exert a guiding hand. So that his followers could do as he bade them, he frequently wrote and spoke in an autobiographical vein in his letters, essays, and lectures, leaving a wealth of material about himself to "grind to the smallest meal."

As he grew older, Swami Rama Tirtha became increasingly more explicit about the example he was providing for others to put to the test themselves. The evidence is scattered, but if we piece together the Swami's chronicle of his own experience, what clearly emerges is that he began to see a pattern to his own spiritual development. He charted a series of phases in his spiritual life and explicitly related each phase to his theory of Practical Vedānta. He thereby created a model of his life that would lend itself to a controlled image for his future "biographers." According to his model, the initial phase of his spiritual development was his struggle with the demands of a worldly life, followed by his move towards renunciation and gradual attainment of spiritual knowledge, and finally his increasing sense of his importance not as a spiritual leader seeking the adulation of devotees, but as a guide showing the way for others to reach his level of attainment. Though he never explicitly described it as such, the pattern that he saw in his life in some ways echoes the traditional Hindu model of *varṇāśramadharma* according to which a Brāhmaṇ male should first live as a celibate student [*brahmacaryāśrama*], then as a householder [*gṛhasthāśrama*], then retire to the forest [*vānaprasthāśrama*], and finally live as a renunciant [*sannyāsāśrama*].

If we understand hagiography in part as the chronicle of the writer's experience of his subject, then Swami Rama Tirtha sought to chronicle reflexively his own experience of himself as a spiritually advanced person. In other words, he intended his autobiographical statements to function as a kind of self-directed hagiography, or autohagiography. He wished to leave a record of his own experience to guide his biographers, so that their biographies might guide others. What is intriguing, however, is that there is a wide chasm between what Swami Rama Tirtha wanted others to remember about him, and what his hagiographers would choose to record. His estimate of their ability to convey what he considered most important about himself proved prescient. Ultimately, his goal in recording his own experience, and the goals of hagiographers in recording theirs of him, could not be reconciled. Because there is historically accurate documentation of Swami Rama Tirtha's own perspective, the gulf between the Swami's view of himself and that of his hagiographers illuminates a fundamental issue in the construction of sainthood—the role of the saint as exemplar—and shows that it is a saint's devotees, and not the saint himself, who determine what is exemplary. For Swami Rama Tirtha, what was most important about his life was the lesson he meant it to teach about Vedantic self-realization. For his hagiographers, what was most important about his life was the lesson in devotion [*bhakti*] it taught.

The first source of information about Swami Rama Tirtha's self-presentation, though not explicitly autobiographical, is the over eleven hundred letters originally written in Urdu (and occasionally Hindi) which he sent to his guru Dhanna Ram. The letters chronicle his diet and health, study habits, family matters and financial woes, as well as increasingly elaborate descriptions of his spiritual experiences. Tirath Ram began composing essays about his own spiritual development and growing understanding of the concept of spiritual evolution for his journal *Alif.* These essays constitute an important second source of autobiographical information because many of the unsystematic statements from his earlier letters then began to take a coherent form. From the year 1900, when Tirath Ram took vows of renunciation and the name Swami

Rama Tirtha, until his death in 1906, he publicly charted his experiences in letters to his followers and critics, as well as privately in entries in his notebooks.[1] He not only attempted to describe himself, but often reflected upon what he had learned and done. Parallel to these explicit statements, in his lectures he would often tell stories of his own spiritual practice, connecting patterns and phases in his personal spiritual development to a larger theory of Practical Vedānta. Placing these pieces of the Swami's autobiographical material in chronological order against the outline of his life reveals that he was successful in articulating a pattern of development for his own life.

The Plains and the Mountains/The Body and the Soul

In May, 1886, Tirath Ram wrote the first of his eleven hundred letters to his guru and father-figure Dhanna Ram. Tirath Ram apprised his teacher of everything he thought significant, and his earliest letters present a rather tedious chronicle of matter-of-fact statements about what he ate, how much money he spent, and how long he spent studying, always punctuated by his fervent admiration for Dhanna Ram. He was particularly preoccupied with his body. In 1888, he wrote Dhanna Ram, "this body is your slave," (*RP*: 2-3) and in a manner consistent with that belief, kept him well-informed of virtually every detail imaginable about his body as he completed his bachelor's and master's degrees in mathematics. Over the next few years he bemoaned his chronically poor health, compiling a litany of ills: constipation, persistent coughing with phlegm, fever, stomach pain, leg pain, diarrhea and vomiting, chills, trembling, even an enlarged spleen (*RP*: 12, 28, 39-40, 62-63, 65). In 1891, he regaled Dhanna Ram with graphic descriptions of toothaches, bursting pus-filled boils, and nosebleeds (*RP*: 70, 78). Tirath Ram tirelessly experimented with remedies for his ailments, and after many less-than-successful treatments, he settled upon diet as the key to his well-being, following the popular Ayurvedic strategy of giving up "heating" [*garam*] foods such as onions and chutney (*RP*: 70). Also essential, he believed, was solitude, and so rather than take advantage of the relative comfort of the college hostel while studying in Lahore, he rented a series of small, dingy, poorly lit rooms where he was repeatedly troubled by thieves, snakes, and the activities of prostitutes living nearby (e.g. *RP*: 82).

Over the next several years a second important theme began to take its place alongside the health and dietary reports in Tirath Ram's letters—his increasing devotion to the god Krishna. His daily routine included not only studying, but long walks along the Ravi river in Lahore, during which he longed for a vision of Krishna. In the months of the monsoon, he would cry to the dark rain clouds and ask them to carry his message of love to Krishna. Eventually he began to connect his diet and health to his devotion to Krishna, informing Dhanna Ram that having a healthy stomach was a sure means of becoming closer to God (*RP*: 124-125). By early 1895, he proclaimed that the best diet for a devotee was milk alone as a means to health, and thereby Krishna (*RP*: 161). At about the same time, he ventured that something was "not quite right with his head (*RP*: 188)," and began to express his growing conviction that his true identity was separate from his body (*RP*: 193). In spite of these changes in perspective, he managed to earn his M.A. in mathematics that year, and also became a member of the Lahore Sanatana Dharma Sabha Education Committee (*RP*: 170). From September, 1895, until April, 1896, he taught mathematics at a high school in Sialkot, and began giving speeches throughout the Punjab on Krishna-devotion for the Sanatana Dharma Sabha. His dietary experiments continued, and he reported to Dhanna Ram that he often went for six or seven days consuming nothing but milk (e.g. *RP*: 182).

As he juggled his teaching job with lectures in towns throughout the Punjab, Tirath Ram began to see the world in terms of a profound disjunction—a contrast between life in a noisy, crowded city amongst people, and peaceful solitude at the ocean's shore or in the mountains on the banks of a river. This contrast would occupy him for the rest of his life. Tirath Ram's quest for physical well-being was not limited to an attempt to control what went into his body, but also the control of the environment surrounding his body. He sought greater solitude than that afforded by his own room, and longed to leave the crowds of the city. When he traveled to the coastal city of Karachi on a whim to see the ocean, he expressed this sense clearly. In a short essay, he related his wonder at seeing the vastness of the ocean for the first time.

> It is all water, nothing but water which washes away from the mind the very idea of dry land. The big cities, the bazars, the busy markets, the crowded roads, and the din and deafening noise of the citizens' quarrels appear like dreams. This dry world appears to be nothing, when compared with the endless ocean. (*IWGR* 6:139)[2]

On the ocean's shore, Tirath Ram had discovered a place in the world that suddenly made everything about his daily life appear insignificant. Back in the Punjab, he had many responsibilities—not only his studies, but constant financial struggles which were worsened by the demands of his extended family who depended upon his salary (*RP*: 193). Curiously, Tirath Ram focused on his body more and more as the source of all his woes, sensing that it was his body that tied him to job and family.

In April, 1896, Tirath Ram left Sialkot to accept a position teaching mathematics at his former college in Lahore. He continued to give lectures on

Krishna-devotion for the Sanatana Dharma Sabha, and through his affiliation with that organization met many visiting religious leaders (*RP*: 193-197). As his letters make clear, he searched for reasons not to return to his village and family during his vacations. In the summer of 1896, rather than visit his family, he performed a pilgrimage to Mathura and Brindavan, the land of his beloved Krishna (*RP*: 197-199). But when he returned, family pressures continued to trouble him. Now that he was able to afford better accommodations in Lahore than during his student days, relatives began to arrive from his village for indefinite stays, and Tirath Ram had to take out loans to feed them (*RP*: 201).

In 1897, Tirath Ram wrote Dhanna Ram about the English translations of Vedānta texts he was reading in his spare time. Though his family woes continued and his health was still poor, reading about Vedānta brought him comfort (*RP*: 205), and his letters throughout 1897 reflect his increasing acceptance of Vedānta philosophy and a corresponding detachment from family woes. During the festival of Diwālī that year, Tirath Ram sent a letter to his father announcing that he had sold his body and was absolving himself of all responsibilities.

> . . . the body of your son Tirath Ram has been sold, sold before God [*Rām*]. Nothing of his remains. Today, on Diwālī, he has defeated his body and won over the lord. Thank you. Whatever you need now, request from my master. . . . It isn't right for us to give up the true, priceless wealth of our selves for the false wealth of the world.[3] (*RP*: 218-219)

Tirath Ram's body somehow linked him to his family responsibilities; requiring constant care, troubling him with its countless ills, it seemed to be the tie which bound him to his family and job and the greatest obstacle to his spiritual progress, and so he "sold" it.

In his letters, Tirath Ram then began to express openly his sense of worldly disgust [*vairāgya*], but this was met with resistance by not only his family, but even his teacher Dhanna Ram, who had previously supported him in his spiritual pursuits (*RP*: 223). While Tirath Ram still referred to himself as Dhanna Ram's slave and devoted disciple, he now tried to explain the ideas that captured him, and began sending to his teacher Urdu translations of Vedānta texts (*RP*: 226). In February, 1898, he started his Vedānta study group (whose members included Narayan Swami), the Advaitamrita Varshini Sabha. But his health still troubled him, and he continued to experiment with his diet. That summer, he decided to escape Lahore; rather than returning to his village, he again took a journey that reflected the emerging primacy of his spiritual interest. But it was no longer the land of Krishna which captivated him. Instead, he traveled to Hardwar and Rishikesh, towns on the banks of the Ganges in the Himalayan foothills, home to countless renunciants.

Tirath Ram spent the 1898 summer vacation wandering in the Himalayas, meditating, meeting with other spiritual seekers, and trying to put his ideas about Vedānta into practice. Still, family ties kept him from breaking entirely the bonds to his physical body and his life in the Punjab. His family worried that he was seriously considering taking vows of renunciation. When his father wrote to insist that he return home immediately, Tirath Ram sent a reply to his father, but addressed it to god.

> O lord! I am fulfilling your command, going to my true home, meeting with your true form. I have renounced my body, this misperception made up of the five rivers of the Punjab (blood, semen, urine, sweat and saliva) and found my real home, Hardwar ["the door to the lord"]. (*RP*: 234)

Thus began the struggle that would continue for the rest of Tirath Ram's life. It was not simply a struggle with his family, nor just an allegorical struggle, but one with himself as a member of his family with ties to the real land of the Punjab, land of five rivers. When he wrote of forsaking all allegiance to his body of five rivers, he was effectively rejecting his family as well. The body which lived in the Punjab was to be left behind as the true Tirath Ram made his way to Hardwar in the Himalayan foothills, the "door to the lord." Hinting at his more formal renunciation of home and family to come, Tirath Ram wrote further of sacrificing his body to the Ganges.

> We all end up as dried-up flowers in the Ganges, so why should I not submerge the green flower of my new body into the Ganges of knowledge? Or else I should make wood out of my bones, ghee out of my marrow, recite "*svāhā*" as I offer my life's breath into the fire of knowledge, and thus obtain the merit of human sacrifice. (*RP*: 235)

Alluding to the Punjabi Hindu practice of submerging the ashes of the dead in the Ganges river at Hardwar, Tirath Ram made an even more explicit reference to his withdrawal from his life in the Punjab. His use of the imagery of the ritual of cremation suggests his desire to be dead in the eyes of his family (indeed formal rites of renunciation typically include the renunciant's performance of his own funeral). His young, "new" body was a more fitting sacrificial offering than his aged body of the future would be, and it was an offering not just to the physical Ganges river, but to the knowledge it represented. His mountain journeys became outward expressions of his inner detachment from his physical body and everything to which it was connected. The body that tied him to his family coursed with impure fluids that the rivers of the Punjab could not purify, for those rivers flowed through plains polluted with family and responsibilities. When Tirath Ram left the Punjab—literally, his responsibilities in its city of Lahore, and metaphorically, his attachment to the five rivers of his body—both were washed away by the cool waters of the Ganges as it flowed from the mountains. The earlier wanderings along the Ravi river in Lahore had been but preparation for his later encounters with the Ganges river. After this break, he expressed his willingness to sell or even sacrifice his body, whatever was necessary to gain the knowledge he sought.

Swami Rama Tirtha would later identify these years as the initial phase of his spiritual development. Preoccupied with the notion that the body is ill and impure by nature and therefore an impediment to spiritual progress, he concluded that the body must be controlled and eventually sacrificed or sold to God. But to be a suitable offering, the body had to be purified. Initially, Tirath Ram sought to make his body literally worthy of sacrifice through changing his diet, first by modifying his food intake, and then by taking the more drastic step of subsisting on milk alone. As he began to make regular trips away from Lahore, Tirath Ram's practice moved beyond dietary modification. Rather than purifying his body, which required ongoing attention, he would simply renounce all attachment to it, and allow the water of the Ganges (metaphorically equated with spiritual knowledge) to replace the waters of the Punjab (equated with impure body fluids).

Late in that summer of 1898, Tirath Ram began to sense a profound change in his relationship with his body. Living on the banks of the Ganges, imbibing the river's knowledge, he joyfully proclaimed that the river had begun to flow within him. His letters to Dhanna Ram, previously full of complaints, now heralded his happiness. "The lake Mansarovar of the mind fills with nectar, and a river of joy flows from my heart" (*RP*: 239). No longer a sacrifice for the Ganges, he understood himself as the Ganges itself: "Where is the Ganges? I am it. What is the meeting? I am it. Even the word 'alone' has fled from me" (*RP*: 238). When Dhanna Ram relayed the serious nature of these sentiments to Tirath Ram's family, they grew ever more fearful that he would abandon them. But in September, to his family's great relief, Tirath Ram returned to Lahore and began another year of teaching, but back in the plains of the Punjab, his sense of *vairāgya* continued to intensify. He wrote to Dhanna Rama but occasionally, signing his letters with Dhanna Ram's name rather than his own, suggesting his detachment from his identity (and responsibilities) as Tirath Ram, as well as his sense of complete identity with his teacher. He continued to fill these increasingly infrequent letters with graphic descriptions of physical ailments, but the descriptions assumed a very different style. In November he wrote to Dhanna Ram: "It's been a long time since the courtesan of health has sung her song and danced in the palace of my body. Instead, fever, abdominal pain and breathing difficulties are dancing there" (*RP*: 234). His separation from his physical body seemed complete to him. Whereas before he saw illness as an impediment to spiritual progress, and good health as a sign of successful spirituality, both were now immaterial. Even health itself was a beguiling courtesan, distracting him from his true identity.

As his writings attest, Tirath Ram by then believed that his body had become a possession to be renounced rather than simply purified; it was no longer even suitable as an offering. Having symbolically replaced bodily fluids with the purifying fluid of the Ganges, Tirath Ram had returned to the plains, able to live with a new understanding of his body—it went places, but Tirath Ram's essential location was no longer physical (*RP*: 247). As he articulated it, he himself was the Ganges, and therefore could no longer conceive of surrendering to it. Tirath Ram's body, a palace in which courtesans or vile illnesses might dance to no effect, was no longer a distinct entity that was in any way constitutive of his identity.

Though Tirath Ram's letters to Dhanna Ram continued to taper off, he would later describe the powers he developed in this phase of his life.[4] In a 1905 lecture, after he had returned from his successful tour of the United States, Swami Rama Tirtha described to his audience his state in the months before his vows of renunciation. Using his characteristic form of reference to himself in the third person, he said:

> At that time Rama's condition was so changed that if he ordered air to blow, it would start blowing. All the elements of nature obeyed him. If he needed a book, someone would come from somewhere and give that book to him. Such a condition of Rama lasted for about six months. This was not peculiar only to Rama; this stage can be achieved by anyone else. (*IWGR* 4:300)

As Swami Rama Tirtha later understood it, once he experienced a sense of oneness with the natural world (which he most commonly expressed through his union with the Ganges river) and lost his individual body-consciousness, he could control the natural world. Especially telling is his assertion that anyone could do this—it was not a unique power that Tirath Ram acquired. He did not describe it to convince others of his greatness, but to demonstrate that others were just as capable as he of acquiring such power. He claimed that his miraculous powers were not a manifestation of something unique, but were available to all who would follow his example. It was for this reason alone, he then maintained, that he agreed to discuss his life before he became a renunciant (illustrating his belief that information about his life was useful only insofar as it served as a teaching for others).

Experiences such as the ability to control the air apparently made it increasingly difficult for Tirath Ram to continue with his career, and early in 1899, he resigned his position at Mission College and took a less demanding job as a reader for Oriental College (*RP*: 247-248). In February, when Dhanna Ram wrote that Tirath Ram's wife had given birth to the couple's second son, Tirath Ram expressed indifference. "If a river flows into the ocean, the ocean becomes no bigger. If a river doesn't reach the ocean, the ocean is not diminished" (*RP*: 249). The child (in part a product, after all, of the bodily fluids he had already renounced) had no connection to him in his spiritual world.[5] Instead, Tirath Ram tried to develop new relationships with people based on his developing theory of Vedānta, meeting regularly with his Vedānta study group.

Renunciation, Rebirth, and Death

As we earlier learned from Narayan Swami's chronicle of this period, late in 1899 Tirath Ram enlisted Narayan Swami and other members of the Vedānta study group to start a magazine called *Alif* in which he could publish his spiritual essays (*RP*: 254). After three issues had appeared, Tirath Ram decided that he could no longer lead the life of a householder in Lahore. His break with family life was gradual; when he first left Lahore, he took his wife, children, and several friends and admirers with him on what was to be an extended stay in the Himalayas (which he may have understood as something akin to the classical conception of *vānaprasthya*, or retirement to the forest as a prelude to renunciation). His wife was apparently unhappy with the conditions under which they lived and soon returned to Lahore with their children. There is little record of what happened in the following months, but sometime early in 1901, Tirath Ram became Swami Rama Tirtha. A few years later, he wrote several essays about the first months of his life as a *sannyāsī* wandering in the Himalayas, occasionally climbing its peaks.

His essays demonstrate that as always, the status of his physical body was crucial. Earlier, he had "sold" the body of Tirath Ram, renouncing responsibility for it to god, and thereby distancing his sense of identity from his physical form and consequently his family. As a renunciant, he fully severed his bodily ties—ties of blood which bound him to life in the Punjab (likened to the five bodily fluids). Yet however much he spoke of his disconnection from his physical form, he was still very much an embodied human being. Now, he spoke of his physical form as an instrument which he could use to climb mountains, his external bodily actions metaphorically representing his inner spiritual journey. The higher he climbed, the further he was from his former life in the plains of the Punjab below, and the closer he moved to the spiritual realization he sought. Earlier, he had written of his complete identity with the waters of the Ganges river; now he climbed to its very source, reasoning that if a river such as the Ganges is purifying, then it must be at its purest at its source, before it has been polluted by the increasingly densely populated world below. Since he saw himself as the Ganges, his journey to its source symbolized his quest for the realization of his own true identity.

Sometime during these months, the Swami climbed Mt. Sumeru, a journey he later recounted in a letter. To climb the mountain was to "move along in the jaws of death." Guided by local shepherds, the Swami climbed higher and higher. One by one his companions had to turn back, unable to withstand the thinning air, until finally, Swami Rama Tirtha stood alone at the top of the mountain in a blinding snowstorm. In his letter, he recalled asking, "is it not an ocean of radiant milk, splendid, sublime, wonderful and wonderful?" (*IWGR* 3:289). Literally and metaphorically, climbing represented his increasing self-realization—he went ever higher, leaving others behind. Here too are the recurring images of oceans and rivers, the snowstorm on the mountain creating an "ocean of milk" that washed over him in a way his constant cups of milk in Lahore never could. Having reached the summit of Sumeru, the Swami surveyed his surroundings.

> At last on a snowy mound, the red blanket was spread. Rama sits on it, all alone, above the noise and the turmoil of the world, beyond the fumes and furies of the multitude. Perfect silence reigns here. What perfect peace prevails! . . . The veil of clouds became a little less thick. The rays of the sun sifted through the thin clouds, fell on the scene and immediately turned the silver snows into burning gold. (*IWGR* 3:290)

Here the Swami extended his metaphor of self-realization: the clouds that cleared for Swami Rama Tirtha were the "clouds of ignorance" that had hung over him before, and still hung over the rest of India. After taking vows of renunciation, the climb became a journey of initiation into a fully spiritual life. It began with a confrontation with the jaws of death, symbolized by the treacherous mountain. Leaving everything in the plains behind him, Swami Rama Tirtha alone withstood the confrontation, as the shepherds who lived their lives on the mountain were unable to keep up with the Swami. He finished the journey alone, bathed in a chilling ocean of milk. Dead to his family, his physical body, the Punjab, he was finally reborn, the birth lit by the rays of the sun. Whereas earlier Tirath Ram spoke of forsaking or "selling" his body, as Swami Rama Tirtha he understood himself to have thoroughly transformed his experience of his body.[6]

Yet however much he progressed in his spiritual practice, Swami Rama Tirtha could not fully sever contact with other people—he could not forever remain atop Mt. Sumeru. He accepted food from people in the mountains, and met Narayan Swami and other close acquaintances regularly. As he wandered, people began to seek him out, hoping for spiritual instruction or even the blessing of a renunciant. It was thus that Swami Rama Tirtha met and spoke with the Maharaja of Tehri. The Maharaja had heard that there was to be a Parliament of Religions in Tokyo, similar to the one held in Chicago in 1893, and he thought that Swami Rama Tirtha could replicate Swami Vivekananda's success in representing India and Vedānta. Swami Rama Tirtha was now prepared to come out of the mountains and share what he had learned with others; he agreed to sail for Japan as a representative of Vedānta. He and Narayan Swami spent several weeks in Japan, where they first met Puran Singh, who arranged for Swami Rama Tirtha to give a series of lectures.

Swami Rama Tirtha then sailed alone to the United States, where he spent almost two years (1902-1904). American followers carefully transcribed Swami Rama Tirtha's lectures, which he brought back to India with him; these lectures constitute the most thorough surviving record of the Swami's teaching. Some letters he wrote to Indian friends from the United States have survived as well, and he later spoke of his stay in the United States in lectures to Indian audiences. Just as in India, Swami Rama Tirtha was drawn to rivers and mountains. When he was not travelling and giving public lectures, he spent most of his time in the United States in northern California on the banks of the Shasta river; he also climbed Mt. Shasta. Swami Rama Tirtha returned to India in 1904 with a certain amount of fame because of reports on his successful lecturing in the United States, and faced pressure from other swamis to participate in the nationalist movement, or to found an organization dedicated to the promotion of his ideas. As we saw in the previous chapter, the interpretation of this period of the Swami's life was a major source of contention between Narayan Swami and Puran Singh. Ultimately, the Swami decided that he could not remain in the plains, and returned to the Himalayas once more, away from the public gaze.

His admirers hoped that he would follow in the footsteps of Swami Vivekananda, who enjoyed great success abroad, and founded the Ramakrishna Mission in his guru's memory. Indeed all the pieces were in place for Swami Rama Tirtha to become, perhaps, a nationally prominent leader. He had received favorable press coverage, had the support of other swamis, and drew large crowds when he spoke publicly. But his essays and letters highlight his indecision about his plans, and his reluctance to meet the expectations of those around him. Once he had abandoned the idea of becoming a leader, he tried to explain his decision to his disappointed followers. While others saw him on a clear path towards nationwide renown, Swami Rama Tirtha was uneasy with the idea that he was on a path towards any kind of worldly achievement; his life as he saw it could have no identifiable worldly destination, as he wrote in English in a letter:

> . . . Honour-winners, knowledge-gainers, social reformers, political workers, religious messengers, dear labourers! . . . Rama is on a different ticket. He cannot break journey and sojourn long at any between station. Good bye! Darlings! The terminus! The interminable terminus. (*IWGR* 3:303)

And so Swami Rama Tirtha sought to shrug off the roles being thrust upon him, uncertain of where it might all end. He found it difficult even to have people visit him. "Rama feels offended when people come and worship the body of Rama" (*IWGR* 1:279). It was as if people saw his power in the very part of himself he had worked hardest to deny—his physical body. Yet every day, people came to touch his feet and take his *darśan*. He saw no benefit that people could gain from merely basking in his presence, and asked that people instead "digest" him—digest, that is, that which he now understood himself to be—not an ordinary body, but an edible embodiment of Vedānta:

> Not to produce millions of followers like Buddha, Mohammad, Christ and other prophets or incarnations, but to produce, evoke or express Rama himself in every man, woman and child is *Rama's mission*. Trample over this body, eat up this personality, grind, digest and assimilate this *Vedānta*, then alone you do justice to Rama. (*IWGR* 3: iii)

As a young student, Tirath Ram struggled to overcome the illnesses that weakened his body, and finally declared himself free of it. As a foreign-returned Swami, he was surrounded by people clamoring to touch that very same body. To followers, he was an embodied being whose presence and gaze were powerful; Swami Rama Tirtha wished instead that they could perceive the transformation that had taken place in his own conception of his body, and digest his real body—the body of Vedānta. He saw no need for people to approach his physical body, because he believed that in essence, he was everywhere, as he expressed through equating his body with India in its entirety.

> The land of India is my own body. The Malabar and Coromandal are my two legs, Cape Comorin is my feet, the deserts of Rajputana my breast, the Vindhyacals are my loins, and I spread my arms to the west and to the east. The Himalayas are my tressed head, and in my curls winds the pure silver Ganges. I am India. I am Shiva. (*IWGR* 2: xxiv)

By announcing his identity with all of India, Swami Rama Tirtha may in part have been attempting to express his sympathy with the nationalist movement, but he was distancing himself from it at the same time. He maintained that he sought no attention at all, even as a focus of worship and admiration; people could know him from anywhere in India without having to be in his presence. But he created a paradoxical position for himself: he wanted to be left alone, but he was making what some might find rather grandiose, attention-grabbing claims. His style of expression is in part a reflection of the Advaita Vedānta concept of the individual self's [*ātman*] true identity with the fundamental reality of the universe [*brahman*], and not the result of a massive ego. Yet to proclaim that he was India in its entirety, that he was Shiva, and in the same breath demand to be left alone, was perhaps an unreasonable expectation. People were naturally curious about a man who understood himself this way. Still, Swami Rama Tirtha continued to try to draw people's attention to his identity, not his physical body. Early in 1905, he wrote of himself in an English letter to be published in a Lahore newspaper:

> Beating in thy breast, seeing in thy eyes, throbbing in thy pulse, smiling in the flowers, laughing in the lightning, roaring in the rivers and silent in the mountains is Rama. Fling aside Brahmanhood, burn up swamiship, throw overboard the alienating titles and honors. Rama is one with you, darling. (*IWGR* 3:350)

Earlier, the Ganges flowed through him and he was at one with the Ganges and then all of India; now, he understood himself to permeate every corner of the universe. As such, he proclaimed himself to be inescapable, beating in everyone's hearts. He wished desperately that people would focus not on his fame as a Swami, his birth as a Brāhmaṇ, or the honors he had received, but nonetheless keep him in their thoughts at every moment, and see him everywhere, even within themselves. He longed to escape from those who wanted to see him in the flesh, and not instead look within themselves to find him. His advanced state of realization made it hard for him to live among ordinary people, but that very state drew people to him rather than pushing them away.

To escape the difficult situation he had created for himself, Swami Rama Tirtha withdrew even further from contact with people in what would be the final months of his life. As he had as a young man, he fled to the mountains for solace, vowing to remain there indefinitely. In lectures, he had often drawn the contrast between the Punjab and the mountains, the life of the body and the life of the spirit, emphasizing the need to sustain the kind of peace he found in the mountains while working in the plains. It was a struggle he never won; before retiring to the Himalayas, again and again he spoke of his need to be away from rest of the world. In March, 1905, he wrote in English to one of his favorite American devotees, Mrs. Wellman:

> People are coming in crowds to see Rama, and this must be closed. God and I! All this day we will go together, the night ever insatiate of love we will sleep together and rise early and go forward in the morning wherever the steps shall lead, in solitary places or among the crowd, it shall be well. We shall not desire to come to the end of the journey nor consider what the end may be. Is not the end of all things with us already. Om! Om! Om! Soon will Rama be beyond the reach of letters—in forests, on hills, in God, in you. Don't know when next you may hear from Rama. (*IWGR* 3:329)

The letter suggests that he wished simply to detach himself from all the activity around him and make no definite plans; while he hoped that all would "be well" whether he was alone or in a crowd, the demands of people wanting to see him were too much. He had renounced one family only to acquire a much larger and more demanding family of followers. He wrote (in English) in one of his notebooks:

> Believe not your admirers, worshippers and flatterers. They ruin. Keep no disciples. Keep no connection with any person; be free from all relations. . . . The greatest hindrance[s] in the way of realization are accursed newspapers, critics, reviewers, admirers, friends, flatterers, disciples. They hynotize you into misery by their indirect suggestions. Historians, novelists, poets and ordinary writers and periodicals are the worst enemies of realization. Let all ties snap. Why should ties keep you bound? (*IWGR* 7:12)

Around the same time, Puran Singh recalls that the Swami told him:

> Puranji! The world is concerned only with my blossoms, and they taste me when I appear before them in my flowers. But they do not know how much I have to labour underground, in the dark recesses, in my roots that gather the food for the flowers and fruits. I am now in my roots. Silence is greater work than the fireworks of preaching and giving off our thoughts to the world. (*SSR*: 159)

This image illustrates the recurring theme in the Swami's self-presentation of the contrast between what he saw as real, and what he saw as false or unimportant. To be devoted to God,[7] he had to abandon his sense of the importance of his physical body. To experience himself at one with god, he had to transform his sense of his body once more to realize that it could be the vehicle not just for illness, but for divinity. Having done that, he attracted the attention of spiritual seekers and the curious. While he could express himself only through silence, they wanted him to speak. He had transcended his sense of bodily identity and the sense that as a human being with a physical body he could somehow be important or even worthy of worship, but his admirers were not so advanced. As a man who had experienced realization of the unity of his spirit with the entire universe, and proclaimed it publicly, he represented something far beyond the experience of most ordinary people. He wanted others to replicate that experience for themselves, not worship him because he had had it. Yet most people seem to have been interested not in learning how to follow his example, but in being near him, as if something of his spiritual power was contagious. It seemed to him that his admirers could only gaze upward at his "branches," or his outward appearance, not realizing that to him his true identity lay in his "roots," which he could not show anyone.

So Swami Rama Tirtha retreated to the Himalayas once more, far from the crowds of north Indian cities, seeing only a few of his closest followers. When even the presence of his closest disciple Narayan Swami troubled him, and he told him to stay at least one mile away, visiting only at scheduled times, he wrote in his notebook: "The presence of N[arayan] and other Swamis near you is like the presence of fats in stomach. The ghee, etc. demand more bile from liver; but their very presence diminishes the secretion of bile" (*IWGR* 7:389). It was not just the crowds of ordinary people who troubled him; even the adoration of other Swamis was too draining. It reminded him of his earlier struggles with diet, when food loomed as an obstacle to his spiritual life. In the mountains, the Swami felt free from his own body-consciousness as well as others' consciousness of the power of his physical presence. But when his devotees were with him in the mountains, they seemed to carry the body-consciousness of the plains with them. He wanted them to ingest him (just as he had earlier lived on milk alone, he was now himself an "ocean of milk," sufficient sustenance for others), to understand him as constituting their very essence, yet he could not stomach their actual presence. Nonetheless he wanted people to know what he was doing, and wrote many letters to his followers, explaining why they had to leave him alone.

Late in July, 1906, Swami Rama decided to visit Sahasru-tal, a lake high in the Himalayas. He reveled in the silence and the fresh mountain air, and wrote of his journey in an English letter (whose recipient is not named):

> O! The joy of leaving behind the prosaic plains of parching body-consciousness! . . . *God is, and nothing else exists but God*! Glory! Glory! Perish this body and mind, if for a single second the idea of defence lodges therein. My bodies are millions, my Self is God and needs no protection. (*IWGR* 3:302)

The journey upwards echoed the climbs he made in the first months of his life as a renunciant; once more, he felt tainted by life in the plains. He no longer wished to speak of his individual self, much less his physical body. His body now stretched far beyond India, and rather than being confined to one, he found himself inhabiting millions of bodies. Having escaped the crowds who came to see him, he renounced even his earlier wish to defend himself from them.

Finally, living alone in a hut on the banks of the Ganges, seeing only the cook who brought him food, he one day thumbed through the magazine *Sat Updesh* (published in Lahore) and came across a letter addressed to him. He began an essay in response to some of the questions about sainthood that the letter posed,[8] and it was this Urdu essay, entitled "Stamped Deed of Progress [*tamassuk-e-'urūj*]," that Swami Rama Tirtha was working on the morning he died.[9] The letter-writer wondered if saints had to wear ochre robes to be genuine. The Swami's response was that saintliness could be found in many guises, and that the true saint or God-intoxicated person was at peace anywhere in the world: "he peacefully enjoys the solitude of the forest in the midst of hectic activity" (*IWGR* 5:381). Further along in his freewheeling response, he considered the responsibilities of a true saint in modern India.

> Rama cannot advise true saints to devotes themselves to work for the industrialization of the country rather than enjoying the nectar of God intoxication. Rama has never done so, nor can he ever do so in the future. Yes, when saints neglect their real kingdom of Godhood and come down from their spiritual throne, it is no wonder that the dogs of the world chase after them and bite. They are themselves responsible for their humiliation and downfall. They themselves, in a way, invite their misfortune. (*IWGR* 5:384)

There is a hint of regret here; Swami Rama Tirtha conceded that he had brought his problems upon himself. After making a tentative foray into social and nationalist issues (such as the need for greater industrialization), he found himself chased by dogs. The Swami went on to tell the story of the god Indra who once dreamed that he was an itchy, hungry pig. Who was responsible for those problems, asked the Swami? Indra himself. "So too is the case with saints who forget their real self and become involved in worldly temptations" (*IWGR* 5:385). Swami Rama Tirtha's words clearly echo his own struggles; he had earlier traveled through the towns of northern India speaking on topics more far-ranging than God-intoxication, making recommendations about India's need for industrialization, only to find himself chased by "dogs" and "pigs." He apparently thought the fault was his own, concluding that any efforts in this regard could not be his "true work" and that he must give up everything in his quest for self-knowledge. Of the true saint, he wrote,

> When you see your own light in the sun and the moon, when you are fully convinced that in the past, present and future you alone are manifested in all beings, when you are above body, mind and intellect, and when you have fully identified yourself with the universal self, then alone may you be called a God-intoxicated saint. (*IWGR* 5:387)

Was Swami Rama Tirtha making such a claim about himself? It is worth reconsidering here the hastily scrawled paragraph that Narayan Swami and Puran Singh found among the pages of this essay after Swami Rama Tirtha drowned in October, 1906.

> Indra. Rudra. Marut. Brahma. Vishnu. Shiva. Ganges. etc. Bharat! O death! Please blow up this body. I have no shortage of other bodies. Wearing only the beams of the moon will I have any peace, living with the stars. Clothed in the rivers and streams of the mountains, I shall wander singing. Clad by the stormy ocean, I shall undulate. I alone am the graceful wind, I am the blowing of the maddened breeze. My wanderer's face is never still. I descended from the mountains in that form; I brought wilted seedlings back to life. I made the flowers laugh. I made the nightingale cry, I knocked on all the doors. I awakened the sleeping, and wiped away someone's tears. I lifted someone's veil. Tease her, tease her. Tease you. He has left, he has left. He took nothing with him, no one was with him. (*KeR* 2:305)

Clad in moonbeams and the ocean, Swami Rama Tirtha identified himself as a part of everything in the world, the "universal self," precisely the definition he gave of a God-intoxicated saint. Taken with his earlier musings about his body, the paragraph is revealed as a continuation of a long-standing theme—the Swami's analysis of his physical body and its relation to his spiritual experience. When he wrote this paragraph, tears streaming down his face, he believed that his identity had no connection with his physical body, and that he needed it no more. What puzzled Puran Singh and Narayan Swami was whether Swami Rama Tirtha meant this literally or not, and neither ever found a fully satisfactory answer.

Swami Rama Tirtha's Writings as Autohagiography

Although he craved solitude, the Swami consistently drew attention to himself as he described his ongoing spiritual quest. He hoped that his audience would attempt to replicate his experiences by putting his recommendations into action, testing them for their accuracy and effectiveness. Yet there is an intriguing disjunction between his exhortations to followers to do as he did, and actual explanations about how to do so. For example, when he told an audience that anyone could attain the same miraculous powers to control the wind as he had in his early days as a renunciant, while he emphatically asserted that anyone could do this, he gave no specific instructions on how to go about it. Throughout his career as a Swami, he steadfastly avoided giving direct instructions.

> Moral pauperism is produced by the giving of precepts.
> Spiritual pauperism is produced by religious instructions. Each man must make his own religion. He must form his own ideals. (*IWGR* 7:167)

Giving specific instructions, he believed, would be ineffective, and instead people should adopt a "do-it-yourself" approach, finding their own ways to replicate his experience. Although the Swami was averse to precepts and instructions, he constantly wrote and spoke about his experiences in his lectures and essays. These anecdotes were the closest things to specific instructions he provided to his followers.

Swami Rama Tirtha clearly hoped that others would learn from what he described about himself. Indeed his autobiographical musings were to serve as the only instructions for replicating his experience. Hagiographers often open their texts by expressing the wish that others may learn and be inspired from the example of their subject; Swami Rama Tirtha wished to construct an account of what he considered the salient features of his life to serve as an inspirational example for others, and for that reason we may understand his autobiographical writings as "autohagiography." In other words, the Swami recorded his experience of himself so that others might have that same experience. That this was the Swami's intention becomes even more clear when we consider his ongoing discussion of body-consciousness in his letters and essays through the lens of his teachings on Practical Vedānta.

The Practical Vedānta Life

Swami Rama Tirtha's perceptions of his body and its relation to his spiritual experience were a recurring theme in his descriptions of his experiences, from his early experiments with diet to his later proclamations of himself as all India. At every step of the way, the Swami shared his perceptions of his bodily and spiritual identity with others. When he spoke of himself as being all of India, the god Shiva, the heart beating in everyone's chest, he brought adulation upon himself. His grandiose statements drew followers who saw spiritual benefit to be gained from the physical presence of a man who understood himself to be so much more than the ordinary person. Paradoxically, after finally managing to distance his sense of identity from his physical body, he found that suddenly others wanted to be near that very body, making him aware of it once more. He yearned to find the forest of solitude even in the midst of hectic activity, but was unable to do so; as he put it, he had to retreat from his "blossoms" (his public persona) to his "roots." Ultimately he could not bear to have others in the presence of his physical body, and in the last few hours of his life, he pleaded with death to "blow up" his body, concluding that this was the duty of the genuine God-intoxicated saint. His request to death, it is worth remembering, was part of an essay he planned to publish in a Lahore journal. Whatever he meant by his desire for death, he certainly did not want to be forgotten.

How are we to understand the Swami's preoccupation with publicly reporting his every thought, though he pushed people away? A cornerstone of Swami Rama Tirtha's Practical Vedānta was the necessity of individual spiritual experimentation rather than following the directions of others. Everything that he taught, he said, he taught because he had confirmed it for himself, accepting no outside authority. Rather than accepting his teachings on faith, Swami Rama Tirtha asked his followers to begin the same journey of spiritual exploration that he had. He could offer no specific instructions other than the example of his own life. Those who followed his example, he believed, would surely evolve towards an understanding of Practical Vedānta.

Swami Rama Tirtha argued in his essays and lectures that all individuals and all religions are involved in a process of spiritual evolution whether they realize it or not.[10] This evolution proceeds through a series of phases leading inexorably to Practical Vedānta. In his doctrine of spiritual evolution, Swami Rama Tirtha adopted much of the same imagery he used in representing his personal spiritual experiences and his own experiences were the primary examples he used in presenting his theory. Religions in their entirety could be classified according to the evolutionary phase in which they operated, and individuals could move through the phases themselves. The first phase he termed "I am his (*tasyaivāham*)." In this phase (exemplified by Christianity and Hindu *bhakti*), people conceived of ultimate reality as a personal God, and perceived themselves to be distinct from this God. In the second phase, "I am yours (*tavaivāham*)," the distinction began to blur. Finally, in the third phase (exemplified by Vedānta), "You are I (*tvamevāham*)," there was no sense of distinction between the individual and ultimate reality (*IWGR* 4:296-7). According to Swami Rama Tirtha, this was the path that he followed in his own spiritual journey, and he applied these phases to the developments that he described in his early letters and essays.

As a young man, devoted to Krishna, he exemplified the "I am his" phase. As he moved away from Krishna-devotion to Advaita Vedānta, he entered the second phase of "I am yours." He went from declaring himself a slave (first to Dhanna Ram, then to Krishna) to offering himself as a sacrifice to the Ganges river. Finally, he entered the third phase, "you are I," understanding no difference between himself and the Ganges. As time passed, he saw no difference between himself and the rest of the world, proclaiming all bodies as his own. He asked his followers to realize that they could find him anywhere, for his very body was India itself. Near the end of his life, he realized that what had seemed to be a journey (or series of phases) with a particular destination (self-realization, the "interminable terminus") was not in fact a journey at all, for he finally perceived no distinction between himself and that which he sought.

By applying his theory of spiritual evolution to his own life (and vice versa), the Swami effectively set out a path for his devotees to follow. He insisted over and over again that anyone could learn from and replicate what he did, and that anyone who set out to gain realization would have the very same experiences as he. Using a quasi-scientific idiom, he argued that he had conducted an experiment whose results could be replicated by anyone who conducted the same practices under the same conditions. This made reporting and explaining his experiences to his followers absolutely critical. He repeatedly advised his followers to ignore him as a swami or spiritual leader, and instead concentrate on trying to duplicate his experience—he wanted them not to worship his body, but to "digest" it, make it their own. If he were to offer instructions about how to make spiritual progress, it would defeat his purpose, for he believed that people would accept the instructions because of their respect for him, and not because they had tested the instructions themselves and found them useful.

The fact that Swami Rama Tirtha did not want to leave any specific instructions made the prospect of a biography especially important to him. After his death, his biographies would become the means whereby people might learn of his life, which was in effect his teaching. Confident that he would attract the attention of biographers, the Swami nonetheless anticipated their "ignorance" (suggesting, perhaps, that he believed that the process of evolution towards Practical Vedānta was so slow that he would likely not find a qualified biographer). He was careful, therefore, to leave not just the raw material for his biography, but a framework for presenting it. The "ignorant biographers" would find the three-stage doctrine of spiritual evolution, a ready-made model for understanding and presenting his life. Thus Swami Rama Tirtha wished to show others that his life could be understood and explained, and even replicated. His biographers' task would be to present the Swami's life experiences as the Swami himself had described them, thereby preserving his life as an example for others to guide their own lives. But what would the "ignorant biographers" make of all this?

The Fate of Autohagiography

The Swami's hagiographers, from the earliest to the most recent, freely employed his autohagiographical writings. The way the hagiographers used this material, however, shows that the Swami's attempt to shape the memory of his life was a failure. The hagiographers ignored the Swami's own model of gradual spiritual evolution in favor of their own models. Rather than following the example Swami Rama Tirtha left, they would choose to construct their own exemplary images of him. As we saw in the previous chapter, what made Puran Singh's *SSR* so successful was his consistent emphasis on his own experience of Swami Rama Tirtha. Later hagiographers would adopt a similar tack. Because the reporting of experience is so central to hagiography, it was the hagiographers' own experiences of Swami Rama Tirtha—not his reports of his experiences—that would become the basis for his exemplary role.

During his life, Swami Rama Tirtha recognized and was troubled by the gap between his own idea of how followers should regard him and what his followers actually tended to do. Instead of focusing on replicating his experience, his followers focused on him personally. Swami Rama Tirtha argued that while what he accomplished was noteworthy, it was not unique, and could be easily explained. Yet even during his life, that message was difficult to convey. When he proclaimed that he was India and had millions of bodies, he did so with the hope that others would see not only him, but themselves in the same way. The grandiosity of such claims, however, far eclipsed the idea that followers could be the same themselves. Ordinary devotees could not hope to understand or explain such a man, much less achieve the same level of spiritual realization as they imagined he experienced. That the Swami could so confidently make such statements became more evidence for his status as a saint. The Swami's hagiographers themselves were first and foremost devotees, and they wrote as devotees of the Swami, not as his equals. Their own spiritual practices had not taken them to his level of spiritual realization, and for that reason it would have been difficult for them to see themselves as qualified to present the Swami's life in the way he had; their own experiences had apparently not confirmed what he taught. What their experiences had confirmed, however, was that being in the Swami's presence was incredibly powerful, so powerful that it made the Swami worth remembering, and in that their experiences converged.

When Swami Rama Tirtha said that others could understand him, and do as he did, his hagiographers took it more as a reflection of his humility than a genuine exhortation. What remained most important about their own experiences of him was that he was so extraordinary, and that to be in his presence was unforgettable (and often indescribable). Their purpose in writing hagiographies about the Swami, then, could not help but be different from Swami Rama Tirtha's guidelines, because the Swami's experience of his spiritual power was so far removed from their own. Swami Rama Tirtha's followers experienced the effect of his own experiences, rather than duplicating those experiences themselves. Thus the hagiographers used the Swami's descriptions of his spiritual life to serve their own purpose of recording their experience of a saint. Part of what made that experience so profound was that in his spiritual attainment, the Swami appeared so different from the ordinary person. To adopt the framework that he had provided for understanding his life would suggest that anyone could be like him. In effect, the hagiographers concluded—on the basis of their own experience—that Swami Rama Tirtha's own experience, however carefully he had documented it, was so vastly beyond that of the ordinary devotee that even his explicit command that others imitate him was unrealistic.

This was true even for his closest disciple and confidant, Narayan Swami. Narayan Swami indeed chose a different path in his own life than the one Swami Rama Tirtha set before him; after Swami Rama Tirtha's death, he devoted the rest of his life to social and political work in Lucknow. He carried out this work in the Swami's memory, but never spoke of himself as India or Shiva as the Swami had. When he sat down to write about Swami Rama Tirtha's life, he thought the only way to report it accurately was to present what he thought were the "bare facts" that were in his view devoid of interpretation, even if it were the Swami's own interpretive framework for his life. And although Narayan Swami quoted copiously from Swami Rama Tirtha's own writings in his account of the Swami's life, he did not include quotations from those lectures in which Swami Rama Tirtha set out his theory of spiritual development. As we saw earlier, Narayan Swami found Puran Singh's attempt to interpret the Swami's life misguided; it was then left to Brijnath Sharga to produce a compendium of "bare facts." In choosing not to adopt the Swami's own interpretive model for his life, ironically all three seemed to be following the Swami's command that they accept nothing until they themselves had experienced it to be true. What was true, and what they could accept, was their devotion to the Swami. But they could not explain the Swami himself as he had hoped they might.

Instead, what the hagiographers could hope to explain was their own experience of Swami Rama Tirtha—not their attempts at replicating his spiritual experiences, but their own or others' experiences of being with him. It was something about Swami Rama Tirtha himself which attracted them to him and made them want to be in his presence. None of them wrote about wanting to be *like* him—they wrote about wanting to be *with* him. They made no claims to having attained anywhere near the same level of realization as he. Thus when the hagiographers incorporated the Swami's statements into their own texts (Puran Singh in particular), they did so as a means of conveying what it was like to be with him and listen to him. To listen to what he said was a part of being in his presence (recall Narayan Swami's exhortation that "Rama is everywhere!"). Yet this was not something that one must necessarily understand, and therefore the hagiographers made little attempt to explain what Swami Rama Tirtha was saying about his own spiritual experience. Puran Singh, for example, craved being in the Swami's presence, but could not make much of what the Swami actually said to him:

> I heard nothing, for I was agitated with the joy of a young woman that falls for the first time in love with the man of her dreams. I was much too vibratory to have any patience for listening to him. I would go out of his room aimlessly and come back aimlessly. I neither could stay with him for long, nor could stay away from him by any means at my command. I loved him, I liked him, and if I were a girl, I would have given anything to win him. But one thing is certain that I heard not a syllable of what he said, yet every word that fell from him was treasured by my mind, and whatever I am producing now is true in its every syllable. (*SSR*: 113-14)[11]

Puran Singh's experience was like that of a young girl who wants only to be with the object of her passionate love. He believed that his experience of being in the presence of and hearing Swami Rama Tirtha was more important than the content of whatever the Swami said (which reflects the elementary *bhakti* or devotional phase much more than that of the Swami's own Practical Vedānta). Nonetheless through no effort of his own, everything that Swami Rama Tirtha said was somehow all accurately preserved in his mind. The power of that experience itself was the guarantee that whatever he remembered would be true (and not his own testing of what the Swami said, as the Swami himself would likely have advocated). It is the hagiographer, not the Swami himself, who is left to tell the "truth" about Swami Rama Tirtha.

These hagiographies are in part records of their authors' experiences of the Swami (despite Narayan Swami's and Sharga's protestations to the contrary) and as a result, it is the author's understanding of the subject (and not the subject's own) which dictates the organizational framework of the hagiography. Puran Singh, who by his own hyperbole "heard not a syllable" of what Swami Rama Tirtha said, perhaps did not register the importance that the Swami placed on his followers trying to replicate his experience of self-realization. He expressed his admiration for Swami Rama Tirtha not through trying to replicate his experience, but through a frenzied, inexplicable devotion that was as intense as first love. While Swami Rama Tirtha, using his conception of Vedantic self-identity, pleaded with his followers to recognize that he was accessible everywhere, even if not physically present, his hagiographers instead used imagery based upon the traditional *bhakti* model wherein the devotee is willing to forsake all simply to be in the presence of the beloved God. By disregarding Swami Rama Tirtha's own explanation of his spiritual life, the hagiographers highlight what Robert Cohn has identified as a tension at the very core of the saint's identity as a mediator: the "tension between imitability and inimitability, between likeness to us and otherness to us" (1987: 1). The saint on the one hand is human like everyone else, but by virtue of his spiritual attainment, reaches far beyond ordinary human life. Through his attempt to set an example for his followers, the Swami emphasized his likeness to his followers, yet it was a likeness that apparently only he could see. His otherness—the uniqueness of his spiritual realization—drew followers to him. That otherness, as the central experience of the Swami's devotees, became the central focus of the hagiographers. When the Swami was alive, his followers longed to be in his presence. After his death, his autohagiographical writings became a tool not for imitating him, but for recalling his unique presence. The hagiographers chose to focus on that presence without necessarily trying to explain the example the Swami meant it to provide.

It was Swami Rama Tirtha's extraordinary "otherness" to his followers, after all, that made him a worthy subject for hagiographies. For Puran Singh, Narayan Swami, and Sharga, the Swami's sainthood provided the motivation as well as the fundamental framework for understanding and organizing the events of his life. The experiences that Swami Rama Tirtha hoped would serve as exemplary they chose to present as evidence of his otherness as a saint. Yet despite neglecting Swami Rama Tirtha's vision of himself as an exemplar, the earliest hagiographers all expressed their desire that readers should pattern their lives on the Swami's. What they meant, however, was that readers could imitate not the Swami's spiritual example (for that was assumed to be out of reach), but the more mundane aspects of his life. For example, all three hagiographers presented young Tirath Ram's dogged devotion to his studies as an example for young Indians, and his love for India as an example for nationalists to follow.

His sainthood (his "otherness") may not be imitable, but his activities in this world (his "likeness") are. His studiousness and his love for his country were thus heralded as examples for all Indians. The Swami's example—those areas in which others could be like him—was all the more compelling because of the authority he carried by virtue of his otherness.

Through his autohagiographical writings, the Swami sought to establish a relationship with his followers wherein the content of what he said and wrote was more important than the fact that he said or wrote it. He asked that rather than worship him, they "digest" the essence of his teachings. His followers, however, focused on him as a saint rather than his teachings. In a study using Jesus and the Buddha as examples, Joachim Wach distinguished between the teacher/student relationship (Swami Rama Tirtha's conception of his relationship to his followers) and the master/disciple relationship (the way his followers understood it), and his distinction is useful in understanding the disjunction between the exemplary roles that the Swami and his followers each created.

> The disciple does not understand the master, though the master means everything to him; he loses himself in the greatness of the master and seeks to comprehend him existentially. His highest goal is to be most intimately related to his master. (Wach 1962: 3)

Puran Singh said that he could not understand a word the Swami said (and whether he really meant it or not, it shaped his approach to the Swami's life), yet longed for him like a young girl in love; Narayan Swami wrote of the futility of capturing in words the "deep wound" the Swami left on his heart; Brijnath Sharga despaired of ever being able to write about Swami Rama Tirtha, so engrossed was he in reading about him. The master, in Wach's analysis (1962: 2), must "renounce all hope of being fully understood, because to understand him fully would mean to become the master, to know the great mystery of renunciation. . ." Swami Rama Tirtha himself, who had taught high school and college mathematics before he became a renunciant, could never renounce the hope that he might remain a teacher, his followers students not of math, but self-realization. His hagiographers, however, saw him as their master, and they were content to remain as disciples, unable to understand him fully, but entirely capable of being enriched by his presence.

In the end, it was not Swami Rama Tirtha but his followers who dictated the nature of their relationship. After the Swami's death, his hagiographers assumed the responsibility for chronicling that relationship. It was their experience of him as devotees that compelled them to write, and that experience defined the way they approached the Swami's life. They chose to focus on his "otherness" rather than his "likeness" to them, on his inimitability as a saint rather than his imitability, because that was what their own experience had confirmed. Their powerful experiences of the Swami became the authority on which they created hagiographies that others could read to experience that power themselves. The hagiographers had the ultimate authority in creating and maintaining the memory of Swami Rama Tirtha. Their image of him as a master beyond explanation—and thus inimitable—would come to dominate the subsequent hagiographical tradition. Future hagiographers, however, would not have the experience of being in the Swami's presence. As a result, the nature of the experience of Swami Rama Tirtha would change, and with it, so would the nature of the hagiographical tradition.

The cover of *Rām Jīvan Citrāvalī*. Courtesy of the Swami Rama Tirtha Pratishthan

5

From "Bare Facts" to Myth

Swami Rama Tirtha as Avatār

Swami Rama Tirtha hoped that he could shape the way people would remember him through his autohagiographical writings, but the earliest hagiographers disregarded the Swami's recommendations and argued amongst themselves about how best to shape and preserve the Swami's memory. Ultimately neither they nor the Swami would be able to control the ways the Swami would be remembered, but they did succeed in laying the foundation for a record of the Swami that could keep his memory alive. In the late 1980s, more than eighty years after the Swami's death and over sixty years after the first hagiographies were published, the Swami's community of followers was still active across north India and beyond. Their image of the Swami shows that they had gone even further than the earliest hagiographers in constructing an image based on their own experience of the Swami, and not necessarily what he said. To follow the example of a man who considered reform societies unnatural and ultimately futile, the Swami Rama Tirtha Mission, a society registered with the government of India, has branches throughout north India which sponsor weekly devotional programs, operate schools and clinics, and work for social reform. To preserve the words of a man who was deeply suspicious of formal organizations, the Swami Rama Tirtha Pratishthan (in Lucknow, Uttar Pradesh) continues to publish the Swami's works, as well as hagiographies and other works by the Swami's followers.

To understand how the memory and experience of Swami Rama Tirtha have changed, we must consider how his followers now tell the story of his life. The best example of typical trends in the third and most recent phase of the hagiographical tradition is a Hindi text published in 1989 by the Swami Rama Tirtha Pratishthan entitled *Rām Jīvan Citrāvalī* ["Illustrated Life of Ram", hereafter *RJC*]. Interspersed with many illustrations, the text is aimed at the young people of India. The anonymous author of the *RJC* wrote to introduce the Swami to yet another generation so that his community of devotees could add new members. Like most of the texts from the third phase of the tradition, the *RJC* is in Hindi, India's national language, and the choice of Hindi (rather than English, the dominant language of the earlier hagiographical tradition) reflects the tendency to link Swami Rama Tirtha directly to Indian nationalism. As the *RJC* demonstrates, by the third phase of the hagiographical tradition, memory of the tensions between Puran Singh and Narayan Swami had long since faded, as had the debate over "true" vs. "ignorant" biography; these concerns had been replaced by new interests in Swami Rama Tirtha's historical legacy and his relevance to independent India. The *RJC* illustrates a significant shift in the way that Swami Rama Tirtha's memory is being perpetuated.

Puran Singh, Narayan Swami, and Brijnath Sharga were in many instances eyewitnesses to the events they reported, and suspecting that their texts would become one of the most important sources of information about the Swami, they endeavored to preserve every possible "fact" they could. They were in agreement on the basic outline of the Swami's life, but argued about the interpretive frameworks they used to explain it. After their initial collecting and recording of the facts, investigation into the Swami's life effectively came to a close. Though many hagiographies were written after the first three, none of them presents any substantial new research. The *RJC* works with the same basic set of facts established by the first hagiographies, but also significantly adds much new material to the life of Swami Rama Tirtha, and in so doing provides a new interpretive framework for the Swami's life.

The change in the portrayal of Swami Rama Tirtha is of course in part due to the passage of time. The first hagiographers had the advantage of having firsthand information to record, but also the disadvantage of being unable to step back from that firsthand experience to place the Swami in a larger context. They could not know what the ultimate legacy of his life and work would be; they could only do their best to preserve as much information as possible so that the Swami's legacy would have a chance to unfold. Sixty years later, the *RJC*'s author was in a better position to assess the Swami's legacy and his relevance to independent India. His interpretation of the Swami could take into account not just his immediate memory, but the significance of that memory in the years after the Swami's death.

The *RJC*'s author had an advantage over the earlier hagiographers in that he could decide what about the Swami's life and teachings had remained important, and what was no longer relevant for a contemporary audience. But the advantage of historical perspective was tempered by the disadvantage of distance. The *RJC*'s author did not know the Swami, and did not live in the same era as he; instead, he met the Swami primarily through the medium of earlier hagiographies, stories told by the Swami's followers, and the writings of the Swami himself. His experience was thus partially filtered through the experiences of other devotees, and could not carry quite the same authority as the firsthand accounts of the earliest writers. To make his text credible, the author of the *RJC* had somehow to establish his authority to write about his experience of a man he never knew, a task more challenging than that of the earlier writers. The credibility of his enterprise was crucial, because without it, how could he convince young readers that Swami Rama Tirtha's life might be relevant to them? The strategy which the author adopted to establish his credibility was based upon the power of experience, a strategy not unlike Puran Singh's, but what is different is that the experiences were not his own, but those of others, reported with an intriguing blend of mythical imagery and historical reflection. Placed against the backdrop of Swami Rama Tirtha's own writings and the earlier hagiographies, the *RJC* affords a wonderful opportunity to trace the ongoing interaction between the historical fact of an individual life and the placement of that life into a larger mythical framework, a process which Reynolds and Capps (1976: 28) identified as basic to what they termed the "biographical process."[1]

Ayodhia Nath's Introduction to the 'Rām Jīvan Citrāvalī'

The first clue to the nature of this text's portrayal of Swami Rama Tirtha is the cover, on which Swami Rama's figure with outstretched arms is superimposed on a map of the Indian subcontinent, a flag with the word "*oṃ*" flying behind him. "*Mãĩ bhārat hũ. Viśva ke āliṅgan ke liye mere hāth phaile hãĩ. Mãĩ prem hī prem hũ* " ["I am India. My arms reach out to embrace the world. I am love, love alone"] reads the caption below. The Swami's outstretched arms beckon the entire world to listen to his message, which will have a new resonance in independent, secular India. The brief introduction (*Do Śabda*) by Ayodhia Nath, who served for many years as the secretary of the Swami Rama Tirtha Pratisthan, further hints at themes which the text of the *RJC* will elaborate.[2]

> Swami Rama Tirtha Maharaj was one of those epochal men who sometimes descend upon [*avatarit hote hue*] this world's stage like a flash of lightning in the sky, giving just a little hint of the development of spirituality to the confused souls of this world, and then merging once more into the limitless universe. (*RJC*: vi)

While the earliest hagiographers situated Swami Rama Tirtha in the context of their own region and time, colonial north India and Punjab of the late nineteenth and early twentieth centuries, in the *RJC*, the Swami's scope has been expanded, making him an "epochal man" who appeared briefly not on the stage of the Punjab, but the stage of the world, only to merge back into the "limitless universe." Nath assigned Swami Rama Tirtha a place among the great saints and leaders of Indian and world history. His words hint at the concept of the descent of god [*avatār*] who comes to earth in times of trouble, an idea which would emerge more clearly in the text of the *RJC* itself. For Nath, the Swami's status as an epochal man made his life of great educational value (*RJC:* vi). What the *RJC*'s version of the Swami's life teaches, then, will illustrate the ongoing construction of Swami Rama Tirtha as an exemplar.

Significantly, Nath not only emphasized Swami Rama Tirtha's place within the larger constellation of Indian saints throughout history, but also the Swami's role within the context of independent India. "Swami Rama was not just a propagator of *dharma*, he was a fearless social reformer, a politically knowledgeable religious patriot, and a supporter of independence" (*RJC:* ix). In Nath's hands, the man who publicly announced that he found social reform work futile had been transformed—the Swami was not simply a religious teacher, but a man whose life is relevant to important issues in modern-day, independent India. For Nath, he understood and could successfully meld religion and politics, and supported the cause of independence from the British. His importance in all these areas brought him to the attention not just of Indians, but people the world over.

While earlier hagiographies named and discussed particular followers, and made passing reference to the largely anonymous audiences who heard Swami Rama Tirtha speak, Nath declared the Swami's impact to have been more far-reaching.

> In America, the Christians called him the "living messiah." In Egypt, the Muslims experienced in him the simplicity of Hazrat Muhammad and his firm faith in God. And Buddhists saw in him the Lord Buddha's supreme renunciation and spiritual splendor. (*RJC*: ix)

Using a common hagiographical image, Nath accentuated the universal appeal of Swami Rama Tirtha, who traveled the world to speak before not just other Hindus, but Christians, Muslims, and Buddhists as well. For Nath, so compelling was the Swami's power that those who heard him speak could not help but equate him with the highest leaders of their own religion. As one man, Swami Rama Tirtha embodied the finest qualities of the founders of some of the major world religions. It is significant that Nath has focused on the idea that people *experienced* Swami Rama Tirtha as equal to Jesus, Muhammad, and the Buddha. Whether or not Swami Rama Tirtha ever declared himself their equals is not the issue; assertions about other people's experiences of Swami Rama Tirtha will remain a significant strategy in the *RJC*. Indeed Nath's introduction closes with a prayer that the experience of reading the text be beneficial to its readers.

> We request of God [*paramātmā*] that the readers of this *Citrāvalī* will taste the experience of *brahma*, and finding truth, love, and knowledge, make their lives meaningful and successful, become filled with Rama in a practical way, and find release from the endless cycle of life and death. (*RJC*: x)

Thus the text aims to generate both the experience of the imperishable reality of *brahman*, and practical, worldly success through the medium of Swami Rama Tirtha's life. The author's challenge will be to introduce the Swami's life to a new generation of young Indians, making his life relevant to their own so that they too will want to "become filled with Rama."

Tirath Ram, Emperor of Knowledge

The *RJC*'s opening passage sets the stage for the Swami's birth, a stage which is not simply a small village in the Punjab, but the entire world. The author explained that in the late nineteenth century, India was under the rule of the British, and her citizens were so demoralized by the British critique of their civilization that some considered abandoning Indian religions for Christianity. Hinduism in particular was under siege. What connection could this have had to the birth of a baby in a small Punjab village?

> In such a depressing era of religious [*dharmik*] ignorance and political hopelessness, in accordance with the words of Lord Krishna in the *Gītā*, Swami Rama Tirtha descended to earth [*avatarit*] on 22 Oct. 1873, as an emperor of knowledge, to enlighten India, caught in the darkness of ignorance, with knowledge. (*RJC*: 1)

What Nath hinted at in his introduction, the *RJC*'s author has now made explicit. Swami Rama Tirtha came to earth not as an ordinary human being, but as an *avatār*, a fulfillment of the famous passage from the fourth chapter of the *Bhagavad Gītā* in which Krishna promises that when *dharma* is in decline, he will descend to earth to restore it.[3] Thus at the very beginning of the text, two linked trends emerge. Swami Rama Tirtha is placed both within the specific historical context of colonial India, and within the mythological context of the *avatār*. It has become a truism to state the tendency of many hagiographical traditions to become more "mythological" and less historical over time, and the *RJC* on one hand would seem to be no exception. Yet the author has provided the basis for "mythologizing" the Swami through his placement of him in a specific historical context. Only from the vantage point of the late twentieth century could the author and readers conclude that Swami Rama Tirtha lived on the cusp of dramatic historical developments, and only now is it clear to them that it was he who ushered in a new era. In retrospect, the colonial period reveals itself to his followers as a perfect example of *adharma* on the rise, when Hindus and non-Hindus alike called into question many of the beliefs and practices of Hinduism and some Hindus even converted to other religions. Thus the historical perspective afforded by the passage of time has provided the author the opportunity to place the Swami in a more traditional mythological context; the prestige that the Swami gains through association with figures such as Krishna highlights the value of the knowledge he brought to enlighten an India caught in darkness.[4]

The *RJC*'s opening claim for Swami Rama Tirtha's status as an *avatār* foreshadows the way his life will unfold. The author assumed he addressed readers familiar with the Hindu tradition who would understand that as an *avatār*, Tirath Ram's ultimate goal would be to help restore the true Hindu *dharma*. An *avatār* is an *avatār* even before he is born, and everything that happens from the moment of his birth is a manifestation of his *avatār* status. The *RJC* thus has a built-in interpretive model for selecting and presenting information. The significant events will be those which contribute to the text's image of the Swami as *avatār*, while the *avatār* model absolves the author from any need to suggest a specific developmental pattern in the Swami's life. By relying on this traditional framework, the questions that troubled the earliest hagiographers are pushed aside. In the life of the *avatār*, doubts or uncertainty are only apparent, for *avatār*s are not ordinary human beings, they are divine descents. We should note that the *RJC*'s use of the term *avatār* is not part of a larger theological explication of the nature of *avatār*s (e.g. as compared with the complex theology regarding Caitanya as *avatār* in the Gauḍīya Vaiṣṇava tradition[5]); rather, its usage reflects the tendency in nineteenth and twentieth century Hinduism to name saints as *avatār*s in a very general sense implying that the saint is not fully human, but also godlike in some way.[6] In that sense, *avatār* in much contemporary Hindu usage, including the *RJC*, has come to mean something like its frequent (but misleading) translation into English as "incarnation," which suggests the idea of a god made flesh.[7] (In classical Sanskrit, the term *avatār* was applied to the descent or appearance of a deity upon earth; in current Hindi/English dictionaries, it is often translated as "incarnation," not "descent."[8])

While defining the Swami as an *avatār* has given the author a ready-made organizational scheme, it also places upon him the burden of defending his claim. Readers presumably bring to the text expectations about what *avatār*s are like based on their knowledge of other *avatār*s and will of course expect the Swami to live up to those expectations. The author must therefore establish the

Swami's qualifications. Lacking direct experience of Swami Rama Tirtha himself, he places particular emphasis on the way that people around Tirath Ram reacted to him. Other people's experiences of the Swami (and not simply the Swami's character or actions themselves) become the primary evidence for his *avatār* status, making the basis of the hagiography itself the very proof and foundation of the author's argument. The first significant experience the text reports is that of Tirath Ram's grandfather, who was, readers are informed, a famous astrologer who could foretell the future of a young child. According to the *RJC*, he cried when he cast his grandson's horoscope, for it foretold that either Tirath Ram or his mother would soon die, and that if it were the boy who lived, he would become one of the great men of his era (*RJC:* 2). A skeptical reader might conclude that the *RJC* has already moved wholly into the realm of fiction, and dismiss it, yet Swami Rama Tirtha's horoscope has not been invented out of thin air. A copy of it did survive and was noted in some of the earliest hagiographies, although only one of the earliest texts made any mention of any such predictions by the Swami's grandfather.[9] Tirath Ram's mother did die shortly after his birth, and Tirath Ram did in fact become a religious leader. The *RJC*'s story is not simply fanciful fiction; while the details may reflect some elaboration, the horoscope has become a means of reorganizing specific historical facts about the Swami to make them fit the mythical ideal of the *avatār*, whose future is clear from birth. Writing over a century after the Swami's birth, knowing what happened to him, the *RJC*'s author concludes that the horoscope must have made these facts clear. The *RJC* has begun to blend myth and history by very consciously grounding mythological claims in specific historical facts, a common move in hagiographical traditions around the world.

The subsequent events in Tirath Ram's childhood which the *RJC* reports add to the growing body of evidence that he is no ordinary child, and are *topoi* familiar to readers of hagiography: readers learn that Tirath Ram demonstrated an unusual spiritual precocity, preferring religious stories at the temple to candy or toys, and was an unusually gifted student who mastered virtually effortlessly whatever he was taught. The earlier hagiographers reported similar stories, and used them to show that Tirath Ram had the potential to become a religious leader even as a young child. Such stories in the *RJC*, however, take on a special significance because they are preceded by the assertion that Tirath Ram was an *avatār*. The author does not present young Tirath Ram's precocity as a means of suggesting a path of development that he might take (as did earlier texts); rather, it is simply confirmation of what he was from the moment of his birth.

The author of the *RJC* has asserted the Swami's power through linking him to the familiar class of the *avatār*s (whose power is already well-established) rather than relying on an account of his own direct experience of Swami Rama

Tirtha to establish his power as a saint (recall, for example, that Puran Singh began *SSR* by first describing Swami Rama Tirtha as a monk and not his birth and early childhood, because "we all met him first as a monk," thereby emphasizing the centrality of direct experience). The skeptic might conclude that the *RJC* is making young Tirath Ram into more of a "type" than an individual simply to prove that he was an *avatār*, for what readers have learned of him thus far is very similar to the hagiographical accounts of the early lives of countless other saints. At first glance, this does not seem like a winning strategy for an author who seeks to show the relevance of the Swami's life to young Indians of the late twentieth century. If Swami Rama Tirtha was just like so many other saints, then one might wonder why readers should take the time to learn about him in particular. The answer comes from stories that relate Tirath Ram's life to the specific concerns not just of his own lifetime, but of independent, secular India. The new mythical claims about Tirath Ram as *avatār* establish him as a figure who has appeared to address the specific problems of the historical period in which he lived. Indeed this is a particular advantage of adopting the *avatār* model. It is up to the *RJC*'s author, who is constructing the mythical image of Swami Rama Tirtha as *avatār*, to determine what those problems were, and it is not surprising that they are the problems of the author's own era. Having established Tirath Ram's power by linking him to other *avatārs*, the author links him to the *RJC*'s audience by choosing to highlight issues relevant to them from among the many the Swami addressed.[10]

To do this, the author expands upon some of the Swami's anecdotes about his life. For example, in one of his American lectures, Swami Rama Tirtha briefly related this incident from his childhood:

> When Rama was a boy, one day he was walking along the roadside, reading a book. A gentleman came along and cracked a joke with Rama. He said, "What are you doing here? This is not a school, young sir, throw away your book." Rama replied, "The whole world is my school." (*IWGR* 1:344)

This skeleton-like tale is fully fleshed out in the *RJC*. When Tirath Ram was studying at a school outside his village, the *RJC* recounts, he would make the seven-mile journey to his village by foot every weekend, studying along the way. One week he met a Muslim landlord who told him that he might get hurt by not paying attention as he walked, but Tirath Ram assured him that the whole world was his school (*RJC*: 6). The *RJC*'s author has added significant details to the Swami's simple anecdote because those details contribute to his portrayal of Swami Rama Tirtha as an exemplar for young Indians of the late twentieth century. Tirath Ram was not just walking along a road, he was walking home from school, and the message, however trite on the surface, is actually polyvalent. He was willing to walk miles for his education and was so committed to knowledge that he viewed the whole world as his school. The man whom young Tirath Ram met was not just any man, but a Muslim landlord. The message: the encounter between Tirath Ram and the Muslim man was a friendly one of mutual concern, for the young man destined to save India from "religious ignorance" had cordial, not hostile dealings with Muslims. His life, then, may serve as an example for young Indians coming of age in an era in which Hindu/Muslim conflicts are all too common.

By making the Swami's life relevant to his audience, even with such apparently superficial stories, the author has established his technique for demonstrating both Swami Rama Tirtha's authority as a spiritual leader and his own authority as an author. He interweaves incidents in which Swami Rama Tirtha can best be understood as representing an ideal type of saint (the *avatār* whose spiritual destiny is clear from his horoscope and childhood tendencies) with incidents in which he makes a point aimed at a contemporary audience, such as the story of Tirath Ram meeting the Muslim landlord. This strategy allows the author to establish both the Swami's authority (through the myth of the *avatār*) and relevance (through incidents whose lessons are applicable to young Indians). Assigning mythical status to the Swami does not create a timeless, ahistorical image of him (as hagiographical images have frequently been characterized); rather, it serves to link the Swami's era to the *RJC*'s late twentieth-century audience.

In the *RJC*, myth and history are thus in a mutually dependent relationship. Historical perspective has given the Swami mythological status. The author of the *RJC* has created the role of *avatār* for the Swami (who himself made no such claim), but it would have been difficult if not impossible without finding the evidence for it in what he knew of the Swami's life. Swami Rama Tirtha's specific actions, however, take on new meanings because of his status as an *avatār*, and different actions are emphasized. Yet the hagiographer must present those specific actions to validate his claim for the Swami's *avatār* status, and the assumption of that mythological status, in turn, discounts much of the specific historical information about his life as no longer important or at least of diminished value. The fact and details that so consumed Narayan Swami have served their purpose by becoming the foundation upon which later followers built an image of the Swami as an *avatār*; for a later audience, however, that image requires a rebuilding or renovation which preserves and reorders only those facts which make the Swami relevant to them.

The *RJC*'s initial assertion that Tirath Ram is an *avatār* effectively allows the text to condense much of the information about his early life. The horoscope and few childhood incidents are a quick sketch that confirm the direction Tirath Ram's life will take. If readers know that Tirath Ram will become a great religious leader, then there is little need for information that does not pertain directly to his destiny. The *RJC*'s author was therefore able to reduce the voluminous information about Tirath Ram's high school and college days into a few key points. Unlike earlier hagiographies, there is very little direct quotation from Tirath Ram's letters to Dhanna Ram. Instead, the letters, like the Swami's story about meeting a man on the road, serve as threads out of which the author weaves a newly textured cloth.

According to his letters to Dhanna Ram, as we saw earlier, Tirath Ram lived in a series of small, decrepit rooms while studying in Lahore, unable to afford anything better. Several times he came home to find snakes in his rooms, and quickly recruited neighbors to kill them for him. His letters chronicled in excruciating detail his experiments with his diet, and his fondness for extended milk-only fasts. In the *RJC*, Tirath Ram's poverty, fear of snakes, and chronic digestive problems are transformed into a kind of proto-asceticism. The same snakes make an appearance in the *RJC*, but as Tirath Ram's dear friends, whom he fed milk and spoke to lovingly.[11] Dangerous animals recognized him as an ally, a theme found in hagiographies the world over (and serpents in India are particularly associated with divinity). He lived frugally not simply because he was poor but because he knew that worldly wealth was of no use to him (*RJC:* 8-9). His fasting was preparation for a life of renunciation, an indication that he knew as if instinctively what he was to do, although he had not yet fully discovered his own divinity. All the details of his student life that the *RJC* reports presage events to come. The *avatār* is moving ever closer to his destiny as a religious leader, and the *RJC* is constructed to propel the reader to that conclusion.

Whereas earlier hagiographies dutifully rehearsed in great detail the events that Tirath Ram described in his letters (the titles of books he had read, what he ate for dinner, where he bought his new shoes and how much he paid for them, etc.) the *RJC*'s account of Tirath Ram's student days in Lahore focuses primarily on his devotion to Krishna. Given that the *RJC* began with the assertion that Tirath Ram was born as a fulfillment of Krishna's promise to descend to earth himself, the *RJC*'s continued emphasis on Tirath Ram's relation to Krishna helps strengthen the case for his role as an *avatār*. The author continues to build an interplay between such "mythologizing" constrasted with specific incidents that convey something about the contemporary historical context of colonial India and Swami Rama Tirtha's role in it.

One of the few direct quotes from Tirath Ram's letters in the *RJC* comes in the section on his school days, and deals with his refusal to consider entering the Indian or Punjab Civil service: "Whatever knowledge I have gained through my hard work I will not sell for slavery. I have gained my knowledge to spread it as a teacher or lecturer, for the good of the people" (*RJC:* 10-11). In the *RJC*'s portrayal, young Tirath Ram realized in the earliest days of the Indian nationalist movement that to work for the British was a form of slavery. Once again the author of *RJC* emphasizes Tirath Ram's innate understanding of the historical situation, as befits an *avatār* sent to remedy the wrongs of his age, for he already knew that his mission was to become an emperor of knowledge, not a "slave" for the British. The author's vantage point from the late twentieth century affords a kind of proof of the Swami's prescience and success; India has indeed become independent from British rule.

Hand in hand with his understanding of the historical situation came Tirath Ram's growing understanding of his own spiritual status. Using images commonly associated with devotees of Krishna [*bhaktas*], the *RJC* explains that it was during his years as a teacher in Sialkot and Lahore that Tirath Ram's destiny further unfolded. His interest in worldly affairs diminishing, he drenched his pillow with tears each night as he desperately longed to meet Krishna. The mere sound of Krishna's name or the sound of a flute would send him into unconsciousness. Once while walking outside Lahore, the *RJC* reports, he chased a black snake, crying out that it was black, just like Krishna and his own heart. He was so maddened in his quest for Krishna that he tried to clutch the snake to his breast, only to have it quickly slither away (*RJC:* 11-13). Although the details differ, these tales about Tirath Ram's Krishna-devotion convey essentially the same story as those in earlier hagiographies. The *RJC*'s portrayal of Tirath Ram's transition from *bhakti* to Vedānta, however, is significantly different from earlier accounts. In his lectures and essays, the Swami himself explained that he had moved beyond the lesser stage of Krishna-devotion to what he considered the more advanced approach of Vedānta, but in the *RJC*, the author reframes the same basic events in order to attribute the initial transition to Vedānta to Krishna himself. One night, readers learn, Tirath Ram dreamed that Krishna had hidden from him, and Tirath Ram grew frustrated looking for him. When Krishna finally appeared Tirath Ram angrily slapped him, only to awaken from his dream and realize that he had slapped his own cheek (*RJC:* 13). The *RJC* opened with an allusion to Krishna's promise to incarnate himself in times of trouble, and now it is Krishna himself who literally and figuratively awakens the *avatār* Tirath Ram to his true identity as a manifestation of Krishna. Krishna's appearance in Tirath Ram's dream serves as further confirmation that Tirath Ram is indeed an *avatār*, and Tirath Ram's new awareness of himself as a manifestation of Krishna provides a smooth transition to his adoption of the Vedantic idea that everyone has God or ultimate reality within. The mythical image of Krishna revealing himself to Tirath Ram has been woven in with the historically verifiable image of Tirath Ram gradually adopting Vedānta, erasing the less dramatic transition that Tirath Ram described in his letters as he began to read Vedānta texts in English translation; as such, the *RJC*'s *avatār* model dramatically alters the Swami's own concept of religious development and evolution.

The *RJC* further recounts the years before Tirath Ram would leave Lahore to become a renunciant by illustrating his noble poverty, his selfless service, and a naïveté that masked profound spiritual wisdom. The *RJC* tells the story of a hot summer day when Tirath Ram happened upon two Muslim women who were seeking alms. One of the women was pregnant, and told Tirath Ram that they had come from their village to seek medical treatment but had been reduced to begging on the street because they had no money and no one in their family could help them. Tirath Ram had no money himself, but moved by the women's plight, he approached strangers on the street to get money for the women. When a friend passed by and told Tirath Ram that these women were famous for regularly using this story in different parts of the city, Tirath Ram became very grave. He gave the money he had collected to the women anyway, telling them that they should work rather than beg, and that they should rely upon Allah, who would provide for them if they would but ask. Ashamed, the women began to pray as they walked away (*RJC:* 15-16).[12]

In his surviving writings, Swami Rama Tirtha did not mention such an encounter, nor does the story appear in earlier hagiographies. The story is nonetheless plausible; as with many of the stories in the *RJC*, its significance lies less in its veracity than in its purpose. First, it shows that Tirath Ram could bring about a spiritual transformation even in Muslims. Second, it shows that he advocated charity, reliance upon God, and honest work over begging. This didactic message aimed at an audience in secular, independent India illustrates that Hindu leaders can reach out to Muslims, that all able-bodied people should work, and that all Indians, regardless of their religious affiliation, should be sincere practitioners of their own faith. Nearly a century ago, Tirath Ram demonstrated values which the *RJC*'s author asserts must still be maintained. As he put it, "What is this but a sense of unity with everyone? To whatever extent possible, we too should perform such selfless service and aid—this is Rama's Practical Vedānta." And so even before he becomes a renunciant, Tirath Ram has been cast in the role of exemplar, not just on the basis of his spiritual practice, but on the basis of his interactions with non-Hindus. He has already mananged to impress a Muslim landlord with his dedication to study, and two Muslim women with his honesty.

The Professor's Miracles

This theme is further highlighted by the *RJC*'s report that Tirath Ram not only began to study Vedānta texts, but also Persian Sufi texts. The *RJC*'s mention of Sufi texts is especially interesting, and marks a departure from earlier hagiographies. Tirath Ram's letters, lectures and notebooks make it abundantly clear that he had a lifelong passion for Sufi literature, but this is rarely mentioned in the early hagiographies. In the late nineteenth and early twentieth centuries, when religious communities in India sought to define themselves and distinguish themselves from one another, many Indian thinkers were sharply critical of those whose religious practices seemed to transgress the new boundaries that reformers established. In the hagiographies of that era, Swami Rama Tirtha's fondness for Sufi poetry received only passing mention. But in independent India, a nation which struggles to find some common ground amidst the vast diversity of its people, such a bridging of traditional boundaries between Hinduism and Islam becomes an example worth following, and is thus highlighted in the *RJC*.

As further evidence of his effort to focus on those aspects of the Swami's life which are relevant to a contemporary audience, the *RJC*'s author expands the role of figures who have become important for India in the years since Swami Rama Tirtha's death. According to both Narayan Swami and Tirath Ram's letters to Dhanna Ram, Tirath Ram studied Vedānta and discussed his plans to become a renunciant with Swami Madhva Tirtha (then head of the Dwarka Math) who spent some time in Lahore when Tirath Ram was a student there. According to Narayan Swami, it was Swami Madhva Tirtha who encouraged Tirath Ram to become a renunciant, and Tirath Ram even chose the name Swami Rama Tirtha as a sign of respect for Swami Madhva Tirtha. The earliest evidence thus suggests that Swami Madhva Tirtha played an important part in Tirath Ram's spiritual life. As a member of the Sanatana Dharma Sabha, Tirath Ram not only met Swami Madhva Tirtha, he also helped make the arrangments for Swami Vivekananda's visit to Lahore in 1898, although this visit receives little mention in the earliest hagiographies. In contrast, the *RJC*'s author virtually ignores Swami Madhva Tirtha, and instead describes the immediate bond between Tirath Ram and Swami Vivekananda when they met. The bond was so strong, the *RJC* recounts, that as Swami Vivekananda was preparing to leave Lahore, Tirath Ram presented his prized pocketwatch as a sign of his respect. Swami Vivekananda returned the watch on the grounds that it would nonetheless remain with him because he and Tirath Ram were one and the same body. Gazing intently at the watch, Swami Vivekananda told Tirath Ram,

> "Look, it's one o'clock now. The time means that you should spread oneness, meaning *Advaita* [*Vedānta*]. I have the distinct feeling that you will be the one to spread *Vedānta* after I am gone. I have found the worthy young man I have been seeking, and he is you. You will definitely spread India's leadership, culture, and eternal religion [*śāśvat dharma*]. This is God's plan." (*RJC*: 17)

According to his letters, Tirath Ram did help arrange Swami Vivekananda's visit to Lahore, but his letters included no mention of this momentous exchange reported in the *RJC*.[13] The reason for Swami Vivekananda's prominence in the *RJC* lies in his current renown. As founder of the Ramakrishna Mission, promoter of Hinduism as a world religion with wisdom for the west, Swami Vivekananda has become a symbol for modern Hinduism. While Swami Rama Tirtha has not achieved quite the same fame, there are many similarities between the two men. Like Swami Vivekananda, Swami Rama Tirtha taught a form of Practical Vedānta, and he spread his message of Vedānta beyond India (he reached the United States in 1902, the year that Swami Vivekananda died). Swami Vivekananda, however, is a much better-known religious leader whose ideas have been appropriated for a number of different causes in independent India. His name presumably carries far greater authority for the average contemporary reader than that of Swami Madhva Tirtha, who arguably had a closer relationship and more profound influence on Tirath Ram. And so through a subtle interplay between historical fact and probable fiction, the *RJC* asserts that it was Swami Vivekananda who designated Tirath Ram as his successor in spreading Vedānta, India's eternal religion. Here again a specific historical incident forms the basis for further "mythologizing" of Tirath Ram, but within a context relevant to the late twentieth century reader. Young Tirath Ram's status has been recognized not only by Krishna, but by a renowned human leader as well. The *RJC* continues to build its case for Swami Rama Tirtha's incontrovertible status as a great religious leader, and also explains why the Swami adopted Vedānta in favor of devotion [*bhakti*] to Krishna.

Along with meetings with well-known figures such as Swami Vivekananada, the *RJC* also describes Tirath Ram's encounters with ordinary people. In both kinds of stories, it is people's experience of Tirath Ram—their spontaneous response to his power— that confirms his status as an extraordinary man. Whereas the stories of meetings with well-known figures such as Swami Vivekananda tend to expand greatly on minor incidents mentioned only briefly in earlier texts, the stories of Tirath Ram's encounters with ordinary people in contrast appear to have little or no basis in the earlier tradition. As with the tale of the begging Muslim women, the stories are plausible enough, but often not confirmed either by the Swami's own writings or earlier hagiographies. Given that the *RJC* is based upon the earlier hagiographies and not new historical research, it seems likely that these stories are the oral traditions of later followers or the invention of the author himself. When there is already such a wealth of information about the Swami in his own writings and those of people who knew him, the fact that the author or the Swami's followers embellish old stories or even "make up" new tales suggests that they must serve an important purpose; in the *RJC*, the stories of Tirath Ram's meetings with ordinary people reveal his simplicity and innocence in worldly matters, an innocence which nonetheless masks a profound wisdom. Their presence also reveals something about the hagiographer's enterprise.

In the *RJC*'s story of the tailor and the cloth merchant, for example, readers learn that even after he secured a well-paying teaching position, Tirath Ram lived very frugally with little regard for basic household necessities. At one point, an acquaintance convinced Tirath Ram that he should have a warm quilt made. Tirath Ram finally agreed, and went to a tailor, who got the cloth for the quilt from a cloth merchant. When the quilt was ready, Tirath Ram paid the price the tailor asked. When he told his friends what the quilt had cost, they were shocked, and insisted that Tirath Ram had been cheated. Unperturbed, Tirath Ram calmly explained that the tailor and the cloth merchant could not possibly cheat anyone because they were forms of God like everyone else. At that very moment, the two businessmen arrived to return Tirath Ram's money and beg his forgiveness for overcharging him (*RJC*: 23-24).

The inspiration for this story likely lies in a brief anecdote from one of Tirath Ram's *Alif* essays, in which he described buying two silk quilts. The context of Tirath Ram's account, however, is significantly different. It comes as part of a dialogue between Tirath Ram and an acquaintance; the acquaintance challenged Tirath Ram to explain why he (Tirath Ram) was wearing expensive silk clothes and buying expensive silk quilts when he had ostensibly adopted a philosophy of renunciation. Tirath Ram's response was that his fashionable silks were like the "perfect makeup" of a woman preparing to become a *satī* (i.e. immolate herself on her husband's funeral pyre). When asked whether the price for the silk quilts was too high, Tirath Ram replied that it did not matter. The tailor and cloth merchant did reappear, and in Tirath Ram's words, it was not he, but God who "filled their hearts with repentance" so that they admitted their guilt (*IWGR* 5:249-250). The *RJC*'s version of this story subtly alters Tirath Ram's own account so that it is Tirath Ram, not God, who sways the tailor and cloth merchant, and the message is clear: Tirath Ram had the power to affect other people positively. Effortlessly he moved them in such a way that they could not help but be honest. He affected the merchants not through reasoning with them, or threatening them, but simply through the power of his presence, and his actions became a living example (whereas in Tirath Ram's own version, he was actually defending himself against the accusation that he was living rather grandly for a man who espoused the values of renunciation).

While Puran Singh could wax rhapsodic about his passionate love for Swami Rama Tirtha, and Narayan Swami could declare the wound on his heart beyond even the powers of the pen to describe, the *RJC*'s author had recourse to no such compelling personal experience. As a substitute, the author recreates the kinds of experiences that he assumes ordinary people must have had; in his version of the story of the tailor and the cloth merchant, the focus is shifted from Tirath Ram's defensiveness to the experience of the tailor and the cloth merchant themselves. Through the experiences of others rather than his own, the author demonstrates that Tirath Ram's presence in and of itself was powerful. While the tale is a largely fictitious dramatic embellishment of Tirath Ram's anecdote, it functions as a kind of "mythological fact" which helps to build the image of the Swami as *avatār*. The contrast between men caught up in the pursuit of wealth and the innocent saint who nonetheless manages to convince them of the futility of their worldly concerns is a common theme in Indian hagiography. The quilt story's similarity to stories told about other saints helps to establish Swami Rama Tirtha among their number. Tirath Ram managed to affect the people around him profoundly, even though they had not yet realized that an *avatār* was in their midst. What was not immediately apparent in Tirath Ram's own lifetime is abundantly clear to the *RJC*'s author in hindsight, and part of its power is the fact that it was not immediately recognized. The *RJC*'s author can thus steadily build a case for Swami Rama Tirtha's greatness to come as a religious leader. Even before Tirath Ram took vows of renunciation, his power and authority had been recognized by those close to him (his grandfather), a god (Krishna), dangerous animals (the snakes in his room), a famous religious leader (Swami Vivekananda), and countless ordinary people (e.g. the Muslim women, the tailor and cloth merchant). The *RJC*'s author again and again returns to the theme of what it was like to experience the presence of Tirath Ram. What he lacks in direct personal experience himself, he makes up for with the authority of others' experiences enhanced by mythical imagery.

The *RJC*'s author's use of mythical imagery becomes even more important in his demonstration of another form of Tirath Ram's power—the power to perform miracles. It is quite common for miracle stories to play increasingly prominent roles in developing hagiographical traditions, but that this should happen in the Swami Rama Tirtha tradition is somewhat surprising. Swami Rama Tirtha argued that apparent miracles were simply a reflection of an incomplete understanding of the laws of nature, and in fact not miraculous at all but completely explainable. The first miracle story in the *RJC* does not appear in any of the earlier hagiographies, although it does circulate orally among members of the Swami Rama Tirtha Mission.[14] According to the *RJC*, on the morning of July 14, 1900 (one of the only specific dates in the text, and central to the author's defense of the miracle), Tirath Ram was so absorbed in meditation that he neglected to give his mathematics lecture. Later that day, when he realized he had missed his lecture, he rushed to the college office only to find that according to the clerk he had already signed in that morning. Tirath Ram was at first puzzled, especially when some of his students told him that his lecture that morning had been the best they had ever heard. Soon Tirath Ram realized that Krishna himself had been watching over him as he meditated, stepping in to teach his class when he saw the intensity of his meditation. Tirath Ram then concluded that if Krishna had to fulfill his teaching responsibilities, it was time for him to give up his job. He immediately resigned his position and quietly left the college (*RJC:* 25).

There are many interesting components to this miraculous tale. The earliest hagiographies report that Tirath Ram was asked to leave his teaching position because the Christian officials at his college disapproved of his incorporating devotional material into his math lectures. Tirath Ram is then reported to have supported himself by working as a grader for Oriental College before giving up teaching completely. None of that is mentioned in the *RJC*; instead, Krishna has again himself guided Tirath Ram to his destiny, making him realize that he could no longer live a householder's life. Tirath Ram's decision to leave his job, and soon thereafter his home, is presented as a firm, immediate decision. In contrast, according to earlier accounts it was a difficult decision for Tirath Ram which led him to vacillate for several years before finally leaving Lahore, and even then wait several months before taking formal vows of renunciation. But in the *RJC*'s presentation of Tirath Ram the *avatār*, Tirath Ram's decision to become a renunciant was immediate and firm. There were no doubts, no pressures from Tirath Ram's family, and Krishna himself once again made it clear to Tirath Ram what he must do. In this respect, the story of Krishna's miraculous intervention fits in comfortably with the *RJC*'s strategy of recourse to mythological images to demonstrate Tirath Ram's power.

However, this miracle story conflicts with the *RJC*'s wish to make Swami Rama Tirtha's life relevant to a late twentieth-century audience. Judging from the way he presented the story, the author evidently believed that his audience would likely not be willing to accept this story without some discussion of the nature of miracles. The story of the miracle is immediately followed by a lengthy analysis of whether such a story can be true. The *RJC*'s author defends the miracle as not only plausible, but true by arguing that many things in the world make no sense even though they occur regularly. He cites as proof the work of astrologers, palm readers, and clairvoyants, as well as those who can remember past lives. After all, the author asks, could we have imagined that a man would walk on the moon, and that we would be able to see and hear him in our own living rooms? Scientific progress produces events that earlier would have seemed miraculous. Saints, astrologers, and people with similar talents are themselves practicing a kind of science, but most people do not have the knowledge to understand it fully (*RJC:* 24-27). The author presumes that readers will accept the notion of scientific progress (everything will eventually be explainable) as verification of a miracle.[15] This defense of miracles is remarkably similar to Swami Rama Tirtha's own argument about them, even though *RJC* makes no reference to it. Without the reference we can only speculate about the connection, but the effect is to make the miracle episode palatable to those who might question such miraculous happenings. A member of the Swami Rama Tirtha Mission proffered a similar argument when telling me this story, and offered ostensible proof that it had happened. The proof, he said, was that the registers of the college were still available in Lahore, and anyone who doubted the story could go to Lahore and see that Tirath Ram had indeed signed in on July 14, 1900. While this of course would not prove that it was really Krishna who signed Tirath Ram's name (the proof hinging on the unassailable "fact" of the date), it does show that there is concern among the Swami's followers to make miracle stories plausible and even provide some form of corroborating evidence if possible.

Given the challenge of justifying a miracle to a modern audience, at first glance it might seem strange that the *RJC*'s author would include miracle stories in a tradition where they were not found before. The *RJC*, after all, is aimed at a late-20th century audience, especially young students who presumably have some training in the sciences. If readers are unlikely to take such stories seriously without extensive explanation, then the *RJC*'s author is perhaps running the risk of losing his audience. What makes such a risk worthwhile? The miracle is yet another piece of evidence that establishes Swami Rama Tirtha as an *avatār* whose work was watched over by Krishna himself, who promised to send such *avatār*s in times of trouble. Unlike earlier texts, including the Swami's own writings, which show that the Swami met with resistance to his growing interest in his spiritual life, the *RJC* has Krishna himself pave the way for Tirath Ram to prepare himself for his work as *avatār*. The miracle story was perhaps a calculated risk, but an ingenious strategy, for it served both to legitimate the Swami as an *avatār* (with direct connections to Krishna) and to legitimate the author's authority as well. As a man of science, his own experience of Swami Rama Tirtha helped him to believe in miracles. And so, he presumably hoped, would his readership.

Tirath Ram's Renunciation Revisited

In the *RJC* narrative, Krishna's miraculous manifestation as substitute math lecturer was a pivotal event, for Tirath Ram decided to leave Lahore the very next day. The *RJC* thus conveniently collapses a period of several months into several days. Its treatment of Tirath Ram's family is also markedly different from earlier hagiographies in which Tirath Ram's wife and children received only passing mention, while the exact circumstances under which she and her sons accompanied him to the Himalayas were not made clear. In the *RJC*, however, Tirath Ram's wife assumes a greater role. She insisted on accompanying Tirath Ram to the mountains because as a dutiful wife she wished to follow the example of Sita [Sītā], who accompanied her husband Ram (note the reference to another Vaiṣṇava *avatār*, Tirath Ram's namesake) to the forest when he was exiled from his kingdom. Tirath Ram finally allowed her to join him, but insisted that she leave their children behind. Ultimately, out of deference to her husband she agreed to deny her maternal instincts, but just as their train was about to leave a mysterious stranger (who, the author speculates, may have been God himself) delivered the children to them. This is the only appearance of Tirath Ram's wife and children in the *RJC* (*RJC:* 28-30).

The new version of Tirath Ram's wife's role in his leaving Lahore suggests that the author sensed the need to justify Tirath Ram's decision to become a renuciant even though he was the primary earning member of a family that included not just his wife and children, but many other relatives as well.[16] Thus Tirath Ram's wife assumes the role of Sita, the princess who gave up a life of luxury to live in the forest with her husband, thereby becoming the classic model of wifely devotion and sacrifice. Tirath Ram's wish to abandon his children becomes a test of his wife's devotion, and her steadfast dedication to her husband is rewarded by the return of the children. God himself looked after Tirath Ram's wife and children, so readers are assured that there was no reason to worry about them. The author has deftly accomplished two tasks here—readers' potential concerns about a young family with virtually no means of support are assuaged, and Tirath Ram is explicitly compared to and identified with another well-known mythological figure, the *avatār* Ram.

The earlier hagiographies devoted more space to reporting the interval between the time Tirath Ram left Lahore and when he took vows of renunciation, although what happened after Tirath Ram's family returned to Lahore has never been entirely clear. That Swami Rama Tirtha would become a renunciant the *RJC* had already presented as a foregone conclusion,[17] so in the *RJC*'s version of events, the narrative sequence is clear: Tirath Ram left behind his life as a householder, spent time meditating in a cave to make his final preparations for his mission to bring the light of knowledge to a darkened India, and then emerged, reborn from the womb-like cave, ready to spread his message to the world rechristened as Swami Rama Tirtha.[18] The pieces continue to fall neatly into place as Swami Rama Tirtha's mission unfolds. Now, others began to recognize his growing power. Soon after taking vows of renunciation, the Swami earned the support of a political leader. Kirti Shah, the Maharaja of the mountain kingdom of Tehri, met Swami Rama Tirtha while he was wandering in the Himalayan foothills. The Swami convinced Kirti Shah to abandon atheism for Vedānta, and once converted, the Maharaja would play a key role in helping the Swami to spread his message, for his patronage conferred status (*RJC:* 35-36). The meeting with the Maharaja is yet another instance in which Swami Rama Tirtha's authority is affirmed by the recognition he receives from others. Gods, animals, religious leaders, political leaders, and ordinary people—all are moved by the Swami's presence. Not only did the Maharaja of Tehri sense that he had met a great man, so too did the humble farmer who brought food to Swami Rama Tirtha when he lived in the mountains. As the author of the *RJC* explains it, this simple man may not have understood much of what the Swami said (much like Puran Singh's earlier "dumb devotion"), but he became more pious and kind after spending time with him. The author writes,

> The truth is this. Even wet wood dries out when it lies next to a fire. And just from sitting in the presence of a *mahātma*, an atheist can become a believer. This is the greatness of *satsaṅg*. (*RJC*: 40)

The point is clear, and becomes a refrain throughout the *RJC*: being in Swami Rama Tirtha's presence [*satsaṅg*] transforms people. This refrain consistently reinforces the Swami's authority, and is meant to lead readers to the inevitable conclusion that Swami Rama Tirtha could have such an effect on them as well. Again and again, the author returns to others' experience of Swami Rama Tirtha's power. At this juncture, the author has openly declared that reading the hagiography itself can thus become a form of *satsaṅg* with Swami Rama Tirtha; the Swami's absence does not mean that the experience must remain vicarious.

For the reader who might still have doubts, the *RJC* steadily builds more and more evidence of the power inherent in other people's experiences of Swami Rama Tirtha. Mixing myth and history yet again, the author details the response to a lecture the Swami gave in Faizabad. In the audience were a member of the Arya Samaj and his friend, a Muslim scholar. According to the *RJC*, both were vehemently opposed to the Swami's views, the scholar so much so that he announced after the lecture that if Faizabad were under Islamic rule, Swami Rama Tirtha would be executed for maintaining that he and indeed everyone was in fact god. The next day the scholar returned to see Swami Rama Tirtha, bearing a dagger. But hearing him sing a Farsi song about sincere prayer to God, the chastened scholar immediately dropped his dagger and fell at the Swami's feet, begging forgiveness. It was not long before he too had become one of the Swami's most ardent devotees (*RJC:* 42-43).

This is yet another story which substantially elaborates upon earlier accounts of the Swami's life, and its inspiration may come from an anecdote in Sharga's *LSRT* not found in other early hagiographies (*LSRT*: 226). According to Sharga's account, Narayan Swami spoke before a meeting of representatives of different religions, and a Muslim scholar raised some objections. Swami Rama Tirtha, who had been listening, asked the scholar to return the following day. The next day, the Muslim scholar returned to apologize to Swami Rama Tirtha, and from then on was an "ardent lover of God." In Sharga's account, he neither carried a dagger nor became a devotee of Swami Rama Tirtha. The *RJC* version of the story, however, glosses over the *LSRT* report that it was Narayan Swami who actually gave the offending speech, and also adds the figure of the Arya Samaj member. Whereas the *LSRT* version suggested that it was Swami Rama Tirtha's explication of Vedānta which convinced the Muslim scholar that his objections were unfounded, the *RJC* emphasizes the power of Swami Rama Tirtha as an individual, as opposed to the power of Vedānta itself. The Swami swayed the scholar not through a reasoned lecture, but through the immediate power of a simple Farsi song, Farsi being a language closer to the Muslim scholar's heart. Once again, the *RJC*'s author shows that it is possible for Hindus and Muslims to find common ground, even in the case of a Muslim so devoted to his faith that he was prepared to kill a man whom he considered to have expressed heretical ideas. As in the *RJC*'s earlier tales of Swami Rama Tirtha's encounters with Muslims, it was he as a Hindu who spread the umbrella for Islam, and not the other way around.

The story of the Muslim scholar is the first of many that the author uses to demonstrate Swami Rama Tirtha's effortless understanding of India's needs. In yet another story which did not appear in earlier texts, the *RJC* reports that the Swami refused a lavish meal from a rich devotee, insisting that the food be given to the poor. Poverty in India, he explained, was a direct result of the nation's slavery to the British (*RJC:* 44). The author of the *RJC* uses this to illustrate that Swami Rama Tirtha always practiced what he preached, and that he understood that the British were responsible for many of India's ills. Rather than just talking about India's poverty, he was willing to make a personal sacrifice to help the poor. Whether intentionally barbed or not, the story serves as a critique of governmental ineptitude, a popular theme in hagiography. The Swami's willingness to put his ideas into action shows that he remains relevant in the present day: "That's why even today Rama's speeches and writings have an immediate effect on people's hearts. Rama knew everyone to be himself, and felt their sorrows as his own. This is Rama's Practical Vedānta" (*RJC:* 44-45). The humble farmer, the king, the militant Muslim, the rich man—none could resist the Swami's power. And it is a power which is still accessible in the present day to those who learn about the Swami's life. He spoke not only of the time in which he lived, but also knew what would happen in the future, and presented a better example for alleviating poverty than the leaders of independent India.

The *RJC* continually highlights Swami Rama's relevance to modern India by casting him as a "fearless social reformer" and a "spiritual patriot of the highest order" who made the prediction in 1900 that "India will achieve independence within the first half of the twentieth century, and will attain great honor, greatness and praise due to its ancient, fundamental glory" (*RJC:* 47). This prediction (examined in more detail in chapter seven) serves to strengthen even more the Swami's image as the *avatār* sent to bring knowledge to India. Everyone knows, the author points out, that this prediction came true in 1947. Since Swami Rama Tirtha knew forty-seven years before the fact that India would win independence from the British, whatever else he said about India must be relevant to issues currently facing the country. In the context of the author's contemporary independent India, Swami Rama Tirtha's statements take on new meaning, for example his request of Indians to imagine themselves as he did to be the whole country itself:

> I am India. India is my body. Ras Kumari is my feet, and the Himalayas are my head. The sacred Ganges flows from the locks of my hair. The Brahmaputra and the Sindh flow from my head. The Vindhya mountains are my loincloth. Coromandel is my right foot, and Malabar is my left. I am all of India. My hands are stretched to the east and to the west, I embrace the world with them. When I move, I know that all of India is moving, when I speak, I know that all of India is speaking, I am the soul of India. I am the form of India. (*RJC*: 48)

The Swami not only knew that India would become an independent nation, he knew that it would struggle to create a sense of national unity. His recommendation that Indians imagine themselves as India in its entirety seems today to address that very problem, and its importance is underscored by the echo of the quotation on the cover of the text. The author comments, "these were the lofty thoughts of Swami Rama in the sea of patriotism [*deś bhakti*], which every patriot should always remember. Only then can India remain free and move forward." Thus in the author's reckoning, Swami Rama Tirtha, who prophesied independence, had shown the way for India to be successful, and his doubts about becoming involved in the nationalist movement have been erased. Only the memory of his apparently pivotal role in it remains. The subsequent events in his life make even more clear his importance not just for India, but the whole world. Not only did he have a powerful effect on people from all walks of life in India, he earned the devotion of even the most stereotypically materialistic Americans.

Swami Rama Tirtha's Triumphant Travels

In its account of the Swami's travels in Japan and the United States, the *RJC* strays even further from the path laid by earlier texts. The *RJC*'s author continues to blend myth and history in relating the Swami's encounters overseas as he lengthens his list of people who came into contact with and were impressed by Swami Rama Tirtha.[19] The centrality of experience in the author's strategy to establish Swami Rama Tirtha's power is highlighted by one of the few direct quotes from an earlier hagiography, Puran Singh's statement about the effect that Swami Rama Tirtha had on him when he first met him in Japan. Taken from Din Dayalu's Hindi translation of *The Story of Swami Rama* (1982: 153), the quote is a paraphrase of the original English: "In my heart was a clamorous sense of joy, just like that of a young girl who comes under the power of the man of her dreams, and places him first above everything else. Rama pierced my heart." The author makes no reference to Puran Singh's own story of the Swami's life, from which the quote is taken verbatim; the quote is prefaced only by the phrase, "Puran Singh writes." What is important is Puran Singh's personal experience of the Swami, not that he too wrote a hagiography. The *RJC*'s subsequent narrative of the Swami's stay in Japan summarizes several pages of Puran Singh's text (again unattributed), reporting mainly the profound effect that the Swami had not only on Puran Singh, but also a Japanese Sanskrit professor, a group of Australian Buddhist Theosophists visiting Japan, and the Russian ambassador to Japan. Buddhists and Christians flocked to his lectures, and all the young Japanese girls wanted to marry him (*RJC:* 51-54). The details are no longer so important; what matters is that wherever he went, Swami Rama Tirtha could charm even the most resistant audience. Somehow, he knew the way to each person's heart, whatever their background.

In the *RJC* the Swami's brief stay in Japan serves as a prelude to his triumphal tour of the United States. The hagiographical tradition as a whole is vague about where the Swami went in the United States, further confirming that hagiographies are not driven by even the simplest historical research (even Narayan Swami, who did conduct some research, was unclear about Swami Rama Tirtha in the United States). It is quite easy to piece together a chronology of Swami Rama Tirtha's itinerary and activities in the United States simply by reading and noting the dates of his lectures and letters in *IWGR* which reveal that he lectured in a number of cities, but spent most of his time in northern California, attracted a fair amount of media attention (as evidenced by the newspaper articles his followers saved), and by his own account once had the chance to hand a copy of one of his lectures to President Theodore Roosevelt when his trained stopped in Shasta Springs. In his lectures, he spoke a great deal about Christianity and its relation to Vedānta and Hinduism. But the sketchiness of the early accounts allowed the *RJC*'s author to fill in the missing details, revealing himself at his most fanciful.

From the brief outline of the Swami's activities in the United States reported in earlier texts, the *RJC* spins an elaborate narrative which bears little resemblance to anything that came before it. The Swami, readers learn, struck fear in the hearts of the American Christian establishment, for ordinary Americans saw the Swami as an embodiment of Christ himself. When important Christian missionaries and priests came to see him, the Swami lovingly answered their foolish questions with his superior spiritual knowledge. Like Jesus, the Swami performed miracles: at each lecture, a special place was reserved for those in wheelchairs and on stretchers and they were healed simply by being in the Swami's presence (*RJC:* 64-65). As in India, the Swami won over both those in power and the ordinary folk, healing illnesses that Western medicine could not. Wherever he found himself, Swami Rama Tirtha became the spiritual ideal of the people—thus in the United States, he was like Jesus.

According to the *RJC*, the Swami's appeal to others stretched as far as the President himself, and his quick stop in Shasta Springs becomes a highly significant event. Like the Maharaja of Tehri, President Roosevelt was intrigued by the Swami, so much so that he followed the media accounts of the Swami's activities and made a special trip to Shasta Springs to present the Swami with flowers, offering to receive him as an official state guest. The *RJC* proclaims that the American president, despite his great power, was humbled before the supreme authority of the Swami (*RJC:* 57-58). This is yet another instance in which the *RJC* has embellished the events reported in earlier hagiographies and the Swami's own writings. In a lecture, Swami Rama Tirtha did describe having happened to see the President when his train came through Shasta Springs, but there is no evidence which confirms that the President traveled there specifically to meet the Swami.[20] Rather, his train stopped briefly at Shasta Springs, and Swami Rama Tirtha managed to hand him a copy of a pamphlet his American admirers had printed for him. The historical incident has been enhanced by the mythic motif of the great political leader humbled by the superior power of the saint.

The *RJC* narration of the meetings with Christian leaders and President Roosevelt echoes Swami Rama Tirtha's earlier meetings with Swami

Vivekananda and Maharaja Kirti Shah. Again, a religious leader and a political leader recognize and confer status upon the Swami, although in this case, the Christian leaders acknowledge the Swami's authority only grudgingly by perceiving him as a threat to their own power. Barely out of his twenties, the Swami's appeal extended even further as he dazzled American philosophers with his brilliant exposition of Indian philosophy. Readers discover that fourteen American universities decided to award Swami Rama Tirtha honorary doctorates (which he refused) because of the genius of his lecture, "Idealism and Realism Reconciled," which according to the *RJC* convinced every single American philosopher of the truth of the Vedantic point of view (*RJC:* 65). The Swami did indeed give such a lecture, though clearly he did not convert the entire American philosophical establishment to a Vedantic viewpoint.[21] The *RJC*'s target audience of young Indians may include some who are entranced by western (particularly American) ideas; the *RJC* attempts to show them that Indian ideas have always been superior.

The *RJC* further drives home its vision of the superiority of Indian thought through its depiction of a dramatic battle between the Swami and the leaders of American Christendom. While the Swami's letters suggest that he mainly had friendly, cordial discussions with Christian leaders, the *RJC* asserts that he was so successful in winning Americans over to a Vedantic perspective that Christian leaders from around the country met and conspired to discredit him so that he would leave the United States.[22] First, they tried sending beautiful young women to seduce him (there being no shortage of willing women in the United States, the author notes), but the Swami would not be trapped by this "net of illusion." Then, they threatened to have him killed (there being no shortage of hit men for hire). Finally, two ministers approached him, offering two briefcases overflowing with dollars if only the Swami would return to India (*RJC:* 72-73). But all their efforts were in vain, and ultimately many of the Christian leaders themselves turned to Vedānta on the basis of the Swami's masterful explanations. The author's portrayal of the Swami's rejection of the temptations of beauty and wealth echo similar tales from the lives of the Buddha and also Jesus.

The United States thus assumes the status of the ideal testing ground of the Swami's power. The tales of the Swami's American adventures rely upon the author's use of a stereotyped image of the United States as materially rich and spiritually impoverished. The important issue is not the actual details of his visit to America, but the imagined effect that his visit had. The experience of meeting Swami Rama Tirtha swayed not only the most committed Christians and prominent philosophers, but even the President himself. The message: young Indians who look to the west for inspiration should be chastened by the fact that the leaders of the United States were humbled before the Indian Swami Rama Tirtha, who was then barely out of his twenties. And once he had demonstrated the might of Vedānta to all America, the Swami was poised to return to India—but not without winning even more devotees along the way.

Homecoming

The *RJC* once again embellishes the basic details of the Swami's world travels. The author informs readers that Swami Rama sailed back to India on a German ship. After conversing with German passengers, he was within a few days able to give impressive lectures on Vedānta in fluent German. He even spent several days in Germany, convincing people there as in the United States that he was a messiah. And when his ship later stopped in Egypt and he spoke at a Cairo mosque, he was lovingly embraced as a true Muslim who genuinely understood the import of the *Qur'ān* (*RJC:* 76-82). The critical message is that the Swami won people over to Vedānta wherever he went. To convey this message, the *RJC* once again expands upon earlier tales. Swami Rama Tirtha did mention speaking with some German passengers on a ship he took, but nowhere did he describe actually visiting Germany or lecturing in German. He did stop briefly in Egypt en route to India, but no record of his lecture there survives.[23]

As in its telling of the Swami's American sojourn, the *RJC* version of Swami Rama's return to India is substantially different from that of the earliest hagiographies. The overarching goal of the *RJC* narrative is to demonstrate the Swami's critical role as an inspirational leader of the growing nationalist movement (India's subjugation by the British being one of the conditions that led to him being born as an *avatār*), and the incidents that the author of the *RJC* reports are all geared towards sustaining this image of the Swami as *avatār* and nationalist leader. Swami Shivagunacharya, the figure who was so controversial in earlier hagiographies (the suspicion being that he sought to profit from Swami Rama Tirtha's fame), is now cast as a completely benign character, and the discussion of Swami Rama Tirtha's apparent doubts about his mission is gone. Instead, Swami Rama Tirtha's return to India becomes high drama, for the fame he earned in his international travels became a matter of critical concern to the British government. British officials were so worried, in fact, that they planned to arrest Swami Rama Tirtha the moment he disembarked in Bombay and were dissuaded from doing so only on the basis of direct personal intervention from President Roosevelt (*RJC:* 83-84). Earlier in the *RJC* narrative, contacts with political leaders such as Theodore Roosevelt served as a means of further establishing the Swami's authority. Now, however, as the Swami returns to India, his authority is unassailable, and those with lesser power, such as the British, can only acquiesce as the Swami's mission as an *avatār* further unfolds.

Interestingly, the *RJC* devotes little attention at this point to the series of lectures that Swami Rama gave across north India after his return which directly addressed questions of social reform and nationalism. There is no mention of the Swami's doubts about the efficacy of social reform, or his own reluctance to adopt the role of a religious and political reformer. The *RJC*'s author neither explicates the Swami's statements of social reform and nationalism, nor does he present his own; instead, the concepts of social reform and nationalism remain vague and undefined, allowing readers to understand them in their own way. The focus continues to be on personal experience, not on teachings. And so the narrative jumps quickly to Swami Rama's late 1905 decision to find a secluded place to live in the Himalayas. Through the story of a bumbling Scotland Yard detective assigned to track the Swami's movements, the *RJC* illustrates the complete impotence of the British in the face of Swami Rama Tirtha's power.

According to the *RJC*, after Swami Rama Tirtha had decided to spend time alone in the Himalayas, Narayan Swami joined him briefly and was making arrangements for their meals when Swami Rama told him that there was a third person whom they would need to feed. He pointed out a deaf, mute man dressed in the garb of a renunciant, and told Narayan Swami that this man in fact was a famous Scotland Yard detective who had been shadowing the Swami ever since he left for Japan. Narayan Swami argued that they should let the man go hungry, but Swami Rama Tirtha insisted that they look after him. When Swami Rama Tirtha first spoke to the detective, the detective tried to maintain his disguise as a deaf, mute *sādhu*. But the Swami revealed that he had known the man's true identity all along:

> "When I was on my way to America from Japan, you were an American businessman. When Rama was in Shasta Springs, you kept coming to see me as a Christian minister. In Washington, you came to Rama as a Jewish rabbi. On the ship on the way back, you were a German Roman Catholic. In Egypt, you were an Arab businessman, and in Bombay you were a Parsi priest. Now you have revealed yourself to Rama in the form of an Indian *sādhu*. You keep showing up everywhere in new guises, giving your *darśan* to Rama, but all these different names and forms just seem the same to Rama, and besides, how can you hide yourself from Rama?" (*RJC*: 89)

The hapless detective was stunned, and began to weep. He revealed that he had long since realized that Swami Rama was god himself, and begged Swami Rama's forgiveness. This provoked a lengthy speech from the Swami on his determination to see India free. For India's freedom, he said, "Rama is ready to sacrifice his life. If the British so desire, they can cut Rama's body into little pieces, they can hang him, they can grind him into the dirt, but they can never change his opinions. . . . Go tell your British government that Rama is not the least bit afraid of their threats" (*RJC*: 88). The detective realized that his true duty was not to spy on others, but to spread the teachings of Vedānta, and he left the next day, planning to resign his position and teach Vedānta to his people. He also managed to convince British government officials that they should not arrest the Swami (the "truth" of which is confirmed by the fact that he never was arrested). This, coupled with President Roosevelt's further warning that the Swami's arrest would cause widespread protest not only in India but also throughout the United States, meant that the British stopped their intensive monitoring of his activities. Thus the *RJC*'s account of the Swami's return to India is yet another mythical tale woven upon a thin thread of historical truth, for Narayan Swami did once hear that Swami Rama Tirtha might be placed under surveillance by the British, but there is no clear evidence that he ever actually was. The basic idea provides the basis for yet another demonstration of the Swami's power. As the *avatār* whose role was to become an emperor of knowledge, he reigned over not only Indians, but even the British themselves, who mistakenly believed that they were the emperors.

To this point, the *RJC*'s author has related a steady stream of stories about the power of being in Swami Rama Tirtha's presence to make his case for the Swami as *avatār*. The Swami's power knew no bounds; he could overwhelm the arrogance of American Christians, make a humble farmer understand something about spirituality, convince an Indian king to adopt Vedānta—the list goes on and on. What is fascinating is that this power has not been specifically connected to the Swami's actual teachings other than by vague references to Krishna-devotion and Vedānta. Only after the tale of the Swami's vanquishing of the ace Scotland Yard detective do readers learn something about the lectures that Swami Rama Tirtha gave throughout north India when he first returned to India. The *RJC* shifts the stage to the city of Benares, bastion of Hindu orthodoxy, the ideal setting for the *RJC*'s portrayal of Swami Rama Tirtha as the quintessential modern religious leader. Huge crowds came to hear the Swami, including famous *paṇḍits* who were impressed by the Swami's flawless argumentation and his modern style of speaking. But the *paṇḍits* criticized him for not basing his arguments directly on ancient texts, insisting he could not hope to be taken seriously as an authority on Vedānta unless he actually knew the Vedas and the corpus of Sanskrit texts on Vedānta (*RJC:* 92-93). According to the *RJC*, it was this challenge (and not dissatisfaction with public life) that prompted Swami Rama Tirtha to take up residence in a Himalayan cave, where he spent the better part of a year mastering Sanskrit grammar, the Vedas, and Vedānta texts. Eventually, he would astound the traditional *paṇḍits* with his mastery of Sanskrit literature, but he was also saddened to realize that many of them gave incorrect or misleading interpretations of the texts to suit their own purposes.

The *RJC*'s report of the visit to Benares serves two purposes.[24] First, it establishes the Swami's authority over "orthodox" Hinduism, making him the leader ideally suited for modern India. He mastered the traditional form of learning, but used modern study techniques to do so, making his presentation of traditional learning accessible and relevant to modern audiences. Second, the Benares visit makes the Swami's withdrawal from public life fit into his overall mission as an *avatār*. He retired to the mountains to prepare further for his task of bringing knowledge to ignorant *paṇḍits*. They thought they understood the Hindu *dharma*, but it was Swami Rama Tirtha the *avatār* who would instruct them and restore genuine *dharma*—for it is the *avatār*'s task to reestablish *dharma* when it has degenerated. The Swami had no doubts, nor had he tired of public attention; he was simply working on his mission to bring knowledge. Yet the *RJC* is fairly vague about the precise nature of that knowledge.

In its discussion of the Swami's Practical Vedānta, the *RJC* emphasizes the Swami's method of study more than the actual substance of what he taught; the *RJC*'s presentation of the Swami's Practical Vedānta is in such vague terms that there is nothing sufficiently specific in beliefs or practices to challenge. Readers are free, then, to fill in the details for themselves. Consistent with his other narrative statements, when the *RJC*'s author presents doctrine or teaching, he focuses on the Swami's power, not the substance of what he taught.[25] Yet a crucial challenge remains for the author—how can he explain the sudden death of an *avatār* who, according to earlier accounts, was in the midst of preparing for his final mission? As was previously noted, the events leading to Swami Rama Tirtha's drowning were hotly contested in the earlier hagiographies. Was he depressed? Was he disillusioned? Did he want his life to end? The *RJC* removes all specific reference as well as allusions to these questions, mentioning only the Swami's declining physical health. Like earlier hagiographers, the author summarizes Swami Rama Tirtha's cook's account of what happened when the Swami decided to bathe in the Ganges on Diwālī in 1906, but he also adds new details that forge a stronger link between Swami Rama Tirtha's drowning and the Maharaja's return to the nearby town of Tehri.

According to the *RJC*, the cook frantically cried for help when he saw that the Swami was struggling against the current, but everyone was taking part in a procession honoring the Maharaja of Tehri on his return to his capital (a ceremony which itself took advantage of the symbolism of the Diwālī festival, which among other things marks Ram's return to the kingdom of Ayodhya). Just as the guns sounded to herald the Maharaja's arrival, Swami Rama Tirtha succumbed to the waters of the Ganges, releasing his soul from his transient body. And why did the guns really sound?

> Because Emperor Rama was giving up his limited physical body, and setting foot into the realm of limitlessness. And whatever the circumstances, it was not just simply one body of Rama's drowning in the Ganges, but hundreds of thousands of people in India and beyond were submerged in the sorrowful whirlpool of the Ganges river of separation from Rama. A shining life, like a flash of lightning, wandering in the darkness of ignorance, shining forth for just a moment, showing the way to tens of millions of seekers, completing with breathtaking efficiency its arduous task in the short period of just thirty-three years, became absorbed in the limitless expanse of the universe. (*RJC*: 98)

With this brief statement, the *RJC* concludes its account of Swami Rama Tirtha's life. Apparently, the Swami's mission was complete even though he was preparing to take on the traditional *paṇḍits*, for he had initiated a process that would continue even after his death. On the holiday celebrating the return of the *avatār* Rama to his kingdom in Ayodhya, Swami Rama Tirtha, himself an emperor and *avatār*, returned to his true realm, the "limitless expanse of the universe." Sharga's earlier interpretation of the Swami's death as the result of his status as a *jñānī* and the exhaustion of his *prārabhda karma* has been taken even further—it was not simply that the Swami's *karma* had been exhausted thereby allowing him to enter final liberation [*mokṣa*], but rather that he had completed his mission as an *avatār* and thus had no reason to continue leading an earthly life. Here, the *RJC*'s language is strongly evocative of that describing other *avatār*s in Indian tradition. Swami Rama Tirtha took a "limited physical body" in order to complete his mission not just to Indians but the entire world, and when it was finished, he shed that body to return to the source from which he came. That his life was so brief was not a sign of tragedy (and hence inexplicability), but rather his "breathtaking efficiency." His death brought sorrow to millions, yet his message lives on, and the *RJC* helps preserve it.

From "Bare Facts" to Avatār: Assessing the Changes

Thus in the *RJC*, Puran Singh's man of doubts and sadness became a triumphant *avatār*. How could the memory of Swami Rama Tirtha change so dramatically in less than a century? What logic is there to the *RJC*'s portrayal of the Swami as an *avatār*, a claim he himself never made? Why did the author include so many stories that seem to have no basis in the facts as they had been previously reported? While our first instinct might be to ask why the author "made things up," we must instead return to our definition of hagiography as recording not only the life of its subject, but also the author's experience of that life. Only through examining the changing nature of that experience we can begin to understand why the *RJC* took the form that it did.

The *RJC* is not, and never presents itself as a "historically" accurate account of the Swami's life. It is first and foremost an account of how people have continued to experience Swami Rama Tirtha long after his life had ended. As such, it stands in relation not to an ongoing tradition of historical research and interpretation, but an ongoing tradition of hagiographical presentation. That presentation began with Puran Singh, Narayan Swami, and Brijnath Sharga, who took the first steps in constructing an image of Swami Rama Tirtha, building their images on their direct experiences of a living, breathing human being. Their hagiographies became living memorials for others to experience the Swami—for obviously no one else could have that same direct experience as they. As we saw in chapter four, the hagiographical image of the Swami took precedence over even the image the Swami himself tried to create in his writings. The Swami thus lived on through an image of his hagiographers' making, not his own. Understandably, readers of a hagiography meet the image of the man his hagiographers have constructed, not the man himself. Virtually all hagiographies open their texts with the wish that readers will bring the subject into their own lives, which suggests that hagiographers in general write because they hope that the subject of their text will become a part of the readers' own spiritual experience. Ideally, each time someone reads a hagiography, there is yet another new experience of the subject; a successful hagiography is one that so moves readers that they themselves become his devotees. To meet Swami Rama Tirtha through reading about him is of course a very different experience than having actually known him. Since these hagiographies are at their core about experience, then it should come as no surprise that such new experiences generate new hagiographies.

It might seem that there could be nothing new to write if there has been no subsequent research into the Swami's life. But in fact there is something new: new experiences of the Swami, built upon what followers bring to and take away from their encounters with the Swami through his writings, the hagiographies about him, and the oral accounts of other followers. The inspiration for new hagiographies is those new experiences, which take place in new historical contexts, not new historical data about the Swami himself. The existing information about Swami Rama Tirtha is sufficient basis for experiencing him in some way, and thus no new research into his life is required. The specific details of Swami Rama Tirtha's life (so important for the earliest hagiographers) are now important only insofar as they illuminate present-day concerns. In the more recent hagiographies, the new experiences have become the basis for new images. The hagiographical tradition as a whole is thus a series of concatenated, but always new images, each building upon and modifying the earlier ones on the basis of new personal experiences, not new historical data. The 1989 *RJC* is like a palimpsest on which the historical figure of Swami Rama Tirtha is covered by layer after layer of new experiences of him, but not completely erased, for as we saw, the *RJC* consistently blended recognizable historical fact with mythical imagery. The mythical elements in the *RJC*, rather than signalling a degeneration into fiction or fantasy, actually reveal a fundamental truth about the nature of hagiography itself.

As always it is important to remember that hagiographers write because they want readers to make their subject a part of their own spiritual lives. The hagiography must convince readers of the worthiness and relevance of its subject. Its target audience is potential new devotees, not casual readers who skim through the text and never give it a second thought. The *RJC*'s author wrote to introduce young Indians to a man who had lived a century earlier, and he had to fashion an image of Swami Rama Tirtha that would be relevant to its audience, or as Ayodhia Nath put it, that would allow them to "become filled with Rama in a practical way." The *RJC*'s author thus had not only to create an image of Swami Rama Tirtha, he had also to bring that image to life in such a way that readers could experience him meaningfully.

When a deity's image is carved out of stone or wood, it may be viewed simply as a work of art; in order for it to become the object of worship in a home or temple, it must first be ritually empowered (typically through the rite of *prāṇapratiṣṭhā*). The hagiography is similar—readers may approach it as they would any story, and place it on the shelf with the rest of their libraries. But the hagiographer's goal goes beyond the mere telling of a story. If the subject is to become part of the reader's spiritual life, the reader has to be convinced that the subject is worthy. The hagiographer must convince the reader that his text is not just another book, but a book that describes an image worthy of devotion. To make this happen, the hagiographer relies not on the ritual that brings an image to life, but a rhetorical strategy that brings Swami Rama Tirtha to life through showing how those around him experienced his presence. For the author of the *RJC*, this meant that his task was to convince readers that Swami Rama Tirtha was not just another one of the many heroes from India's colonial past whose lives fill countless elementary textbook pages in Indian schools. He had to convince them that Swami Rama Tirtha was not just a relic from the past, but someone who could come to life in their own lives. The hagiographer had to muster the authority to convince readers to accept Swami Rama Tirtha through the power of his own rhetoric, but that rhetoric does not exist without context, nor is it without precedent.

The first hagiographers relied heavily upon their own authority in creating an image of the Swami as a spiritually powerful man. Their arguments rested upon the authority of their own experience, however difficult it was for them to convey it. In Puran Singh's *Story of Swami Rama*, for example, his own experience of the Swami lay at the heart of his text. It had affected him so deeply that he knew that whatever he wrote was true in some sense. Narayan Swami too rhapsodized about the power of the Swami's presence; even Sharga had heard the Swami speak, and had the additional authority of Narayan Swami's *imprimatur*. The "facts" that they wrote about—however jumbled or in some cases of no apparent significance—carried the weight of the authority of direct experience. But the later hagiographers did not have that authority. What they had to work with was the assemblage of "facts" that the earliest hagiographers had preserved, mediated by their own experience. How, then, could they give authority to their own experiences?

In the *RJC*, one of the author's primary sources of authority was the traditional imagery of myth. In the *RJC*, myth is not an extraneous element that makes the text less interesting, or somehow detached from historical reality. Myth serves two crucial purposes in the *RJC*'s rhetorical strategy. First, by linking Swami Rama Tirtha to the familiar mythical image of the *avatār*, the author establishes both his own (as one who recognizes and can demonstrate the Swami's true identity) and the Swami's authority. The second purpose that myth serves follows from its first. Once Swami Rama Tirtha has been linked to the class of *avatār*s, gaining their authority by association, the author then has the means to demonstrate Swami Rama Tirtha's relevance to his audience. As an *avatār*, he had a specific role to play in history. But the text is not purely a flight of mythical fancy.

The *RJC*'s author constructed the Swami's role as *avatār* from the vantage point of one who lives and writes in independent India. Consequently, he made it clear that Swami Rama Tirtha not only played a pivotal role in securing India's independence, but in doing so, showed Indians of the future how to live successfully as an independent nation. It is no accident that virtually all the episodes in the *RJC* that involved new stories or elaborations upon older stories were about people's experiences of Swami Rama Tirtha. In a story elaborating on basic facts, such as that of Tirath Ram's meeting with Swami Vivekananda, readers learn that Vivekananda, a figure very likely to be familiar to most young Indians, recognized young Tirath Ram as the man who would carry on his message of oneness or unity. In a story such as that of the Muslim scholar who planned to strike down the Swami with his dagger, readers learned that the

Swami had the power to diffuse the violence of a stereotypically angry Muslim. In every instance in which mythical elements seemingly intrude in the *RJC* narrative, they are in fact central to the rhetorical strategy of the text, for they always demonstrate something about what it was like to experience Swami Rama Tirtha—for a god such as Krishna, for a famous man such as Swami Vivekananda, for a powerful ruler such as the Maharaja of Tehri or the President of the United States, for an ordinary man such as the humble farmer who brought him food, even for snakes who befriended Tirath Ram in his decrepit Lahore room. More than anything else, it is the experience of being in Swami Rama Tirtha's presence that conveys his power—and when a hagiographer lacks direct experience, he weaves new experiences out of the threads of both fact and mythical "fiction." Those new experiences—the hagiographer's creation—are his authority, just as Narayan Swami's "wounded heart" was his. Indeed this may be why the author chose to remain anonymous, for he was relying less upon his individual authority than that of the experiences of others he wrote about.

It should come as no surprise that the resulting fabric is perfectly suited to the institutional purposes of the Swami Rama Tirtha Pratishthan and the Swami Rama Tirtha Mission; it is very common for hagiographical accounts to support institutional needs.[26] The *RJC*, after all, was a project of the Swami Rama Tirtha Pratishthan, and its message is a political one. The *RJC*'s newly constructed image of Swami Rama Tirtha as *avatār* legitimates the goals of the organized movement in Swami Rama Tirtha's memory. As *avatār*, Swami Rama Tirtha illustrated the importance of education, the necessity of social reform, and the true unity of all Indians. The Swami Rama Tirtha Mission, under the aegis of the Swami Rama Tirtha Educational Society, advocates both education and social reform through operating elementary schools in predominantly low-caste neighborhoods. The Mission holds regular health clinics for the poor. And in the many publications of both the Swami Rama Tirtha Mission and the Swami Rama Tirtha Pratishthan, the theme of Indian unity is stressed over and over again. The Swami's prediction that India would become independent and his other statements about India are printed in the Mission's flyers and pamphlets and emblazoned on stickers, magnets and key chains, while those same quotes are prominently featured on the covers and frontispieces of the publications of the Swami Rama Tirtha Pratishthan. The *RJC*'s new hagiographical image of the Swami as *avatār* generates an experience of Swami Rama Tirtha that is in accord with the institutional goals of the Swami Rama Tirtha Pratishthan and the Swami Rama Tirtha Mission. The Swami himself had serious doubts about the utility of organizations such as those that have since been founded in his name, but the aims of the institutions established in the Swami's memory, and the choices of their leaders, have come to outweigh his wishes. This does not mean, however, that the Swami Rama Tirtha Mission and Pratishthan have misunderstood the Swami or somehow sullied his name. They are, after all, organizations founded not *by* the Swami, but in his memory. When the Swami died in 1906, it was his followers who assumed the responsibility for preserving his memory, and their own changing memories illustrate their changing experiences of the Swami and what he means.

In his study of the master-disciple relationship, Wach argued that these developments are typical in the ongoing formation of the image of a leader no longer living. Although somewhat rigid in his distinction between history and myth, Wach described well what has happened to the image of Swami Rama Tirtha since 1906.

> With the exhaustion of the living fount, the process of the formation does not stop; but along with this continuing process, from now on, a petrification occurs under a different law of construction. Imagination and personal experience are replaced by productive fantasy, which continues to shape the further development of the image. The magical circle of individual life is broken through. In the interchange of dialogue and in the proclamation it becomes expanded. The "objective" character of the image, its social reception, demonstrates that it is on the way to becoming myth. With its reception it is modified in new ways: just as the individuality of the disciples was decisive for the selection, combination, and elaboration of the objective facts, so now the same conditions are effective in the contribution which everyone who seeks to perpetuate the image makes to its alteration. (Wach 1962: 19)

Narayan Swami may well have hoped that Sharga's *Life of Swami Rama Tirtha* would construct the definitive image of the Swami, but the "different law of construction" which produced other versions of the Swami's life has its roots in the nature of different, later experiences of the Swami. As we have seen, the *RJC* replaced personal experience with "productive fantasy" as new stories about Swami Rama Tirtha made their appearance. The individual life of Swami Rama Tirtha broke away from its historical moorings as his story was told and retold, embellished and augmented. The circle created by the Swami's direct interaction with his followers (and earliest hagiographers) was broken, and his image came to be wholly constructed by his followers. What Wach terms the "social reception" of that image may be more effectively characterized as people's *experience* of that image. In the intersection of their own lives and the object which the Swami's life has become, followers produce new images in much the same way that a text may be read and interpreted in different ways. The hagiographical image took on a life of its own, detached from the historical person of Swami Rama Tirtha. The followers' "individuality"—not just their preferences, but their own historical circumstances—meant that the image was necessarily altered as it was perpetuated. It was Puran Singh the poet who perhaps understood that this would happen when he wrote the introduction to his hagiography of the Swami; his words are worth recalling here.

> What can be the materials for the biography of a man who was silent on the secret of his joyous life. . . . And what can be his biography but that whoever happened to see him, a flower amongst men, stood for a while, looking at him, and having looked at him, went past him, deeply suspecting the existence of golden lands beyond this physical life, whose mystic glimpses shone on his smiling face. (*SSR*: v-vi)

Ultimately, the materials—Narayan Swami's "bare facts"—became irrelevant. To his followers, Swami Rama Tirtha's spiritual joy was like a secret he could not tell, however hard he may have tried. His true "biography" would lie not in the facts, but in the experience of those who saw him, and then went past him to create an image far removed from the details of his physical, historical life, but intimately connected with the details of their own. This very same process operates in hagiographical collections as well, texts which chronicle not one, but many saints' lives.

6

Many Saints, One Agenda
Hagiographical Collections

Analysis of the earliest hagiographies of Swami Rama Tirtha, his autohagiographical writings, and the 1989 *RJC* has suggested that the nature of the reporting of experience (the hagiographer's own as well as others') is a significant factor in understanding the dynamics of a modern hagiographical tradition. Thus far, the hagiographies we have considered were concerned with only one saint—Swami Rama Tirtha. However, collections of the lives of saints constitute a substantial portion of the hagiographical literature of India, from medieval collections such as Nabhadas' [Nābhādās] *Bhaktamāl* (c. 1600) to the numerous modern collections published in the regional languages of India and English, and are therefore worthy of attention in any attempt to understand the conventions of modern Hindu hagiography. What dynamics govern modern hagiographical collections, and how do they relate to single-saint hagiographies? Hagiographical collections differ from single-subject hagiographies in some significant ways. The accounts of the lives of the saints in hagiographical traditions are of course much shorter than those found in single-saint hagiographies. Rather than present a complete life-story, the authors of hagiographical collections generally present a series of vignettes or key incidents in each saint's life.[1] It is therefore especially important to consider why particular incidents are chosen over others, and how the incidents chosen for one saint's life may fit into the overall themes of a collection.

The hagiographical tradition about Swami Rama Tirtha began with texts written by people who had known the Swami personally; this was a major factor in distinguishing between the approach of the earliest hagiographers and that of later hagiographers who did not know the Swami. With collections, however, the situation is more complex. Often, collections cover a wide timespan, with accounts of lives of saints from the distant past as well as more recent figures—no author could have known them all, and this suggests that the role of experience, which is so critical in single-saint hagiographies, may be different in hagiographical collections.

Another important issue is the purpose of hagiographical collections. In single-saint hagiographies, the authors almost always intend for their texts to serve as devotional tools for readers; in the words of the *RJC*, reading the text itself becomes a way of experiencing *satsaṅg* with the saint. And in many hagiographies, such as the *RJC*, the text is designed not only to foster devotion to a particular saint, but to an institution connected to the saint as well. What, however, are hagiographical collections, which give accounts of many saints, meant to promote, if not devotion to a particular saint or institution? How and why do authors or compilers of collections choose the saints whom they include? This is a particularly intriguing question, given that so many hagiographical collections include accounts of saints with widely varying doctrinal positions, sometimes even saints from different religions.[2] What, if not doctrine, unites the saints in a collection? Given the wide range of saints covered in most collections, who might be the intended audience?

To explore these questions, we will here consider five twentieth-century hagiographical collections, with occasional reference to other recent collections as well. The five collections are a representative sample of twentieth-century texts available in bookshops and libraries in north Indian cities and towns in the late 1980s and early 1990s. Three of the collections are in English: *Ramanand to Ram Tirtha*, by an anonymous author, T.M.P. Mahadevan's *Ten Saints of India*, and Gopinath Talwalkar's *Some Indian Saints*. Two are in Hindi: S. Dube's [Dūbe] *Santõ kī Kahāniyā̃* ["stories of the saints"] and Prannath Vanaprasthi's [Praṇnāth Vānaprasthī] *Bhārat ke Mahān Ṛṣi* ["India's great sages"]. Each collection covers a wide range of saints; *Ramanand to Ram Tirath* and *Bhārat ke Mahān Ṛṣi* include accounts of Swami Rama Tirtha's life, allowing us to consider how he is portrayed alongside other saints. Each of the saints in these collections is also the subject of an extensive hagiographical tradition of his or her own. Here, we will focus on how the accounts of particular saints function within each collection, rather than considering the relation of the collections' accounts to each individual saint's own hagiographical tradition.

The Collections 1: the Anonymous "Ramanand to Ram Tirath"

The earliest collection of the five, *Ramanand to Ram Tirath: Lives of the Saints of Northern India Including the Sikh Gurus* (*RRT*) was published by G.A. Natesan and Company of Madras, the same publisher which brought out the first edition of Puran Singh's *Story of Swami Rama*. Natesan and Company had a wide list of publications on religious topics, such as a series entitled "The World Teachers," which included accounts of Ram, Krishna, Jesus, the Buddha, and Muhammad.

The first edition of *RRT* was apparently released sometime between 1910-1920; the second edition of *RRT* was released in August, 1947, the month India became an independent nation.[3] Like the author of the *RJC*, the author of *RRT* chose to remain anonymous. *RRT* covers a wide range of saints from north India: Ramanand, Kabir, Nanak, Ravi Das [Ravi Dās], Mirabai, Vallabhacarya [Vallabhācārya], Tulsi Das [Tulsī Dās], Nanak's successors, Swami Virajananda Saraswati [Swāmī Virājānanda Saraswatī], Swami Dayananda Saraswati, and Swami Rama Tirtha (whom the author knew). *RRT* unites this diverse group of saints by presenting each as some kind of reformer.

The underlying premise of *RRT* is that south India preserved the true heritage of India while north India struggled against Muslim invasions: "the Deccan kept ablaze the torch of Hindu civilization and became the rallying point of all that was true, beautiful, and of good report in our ancient heritage, while the rest of India was 'by darkness and dangers compassed round'" (*RRT*: 1). That which was most true and most beautiful, according to *RRT*, was the Vaiṣṇava tradition as set forth by the south Indian Ramanuja [Rāmānuja], whom the text dates to the thirteenth century CE. Through one of his successors, Ramanand, a Brāhmaṇ born in Allahabad, the glory of south Indian Vaiṣṇava tradition reached the spiritually impoverished north.

According to *RRT*, Ramanand's greatest contribution was that he cast aside the caste exclusivity of Vaiṣṇavism, and attracted disciples who included a Muslim, a Rajput, and even several women. By making himself accessible to the "degraded castes," Ramanand's work "rendered the Hindu religion all embracing in its sympathy, catholic in its outlook, a perennial fountain of delight and inspiration" (*RRT*: 4). Thanks to the efforts of Ramanand, caste restrictions were loosened, the status of women improved, and India became more humane and tolerant. Ramanand's religious reformation even went so far as to attempt a partial reconciliation with the Muslims of north India (*RRT*: 7). Thus, drawing his inspiration from the south, Ramanand became the conduit through which India's Vaiṣṇava heritage could be restored throughout northern India. Indeed, according to *RRT*, his influence was far-reaching, from the poet Kabir to Guru Nanak, the founder of Sikhism. The author's strategy is similar to that of the *RJC*, in which basic historical events were substantially embellished or modified to suit the text's agenda; in *RRT*, the generally accepted premise that the roots of the *bhakti* movement lie in south India becomes the basis for more far-reaching claims about the south's role in Indian culture overall.

RRT thus clearly reveals its biases in its first few pages. Indian heritage has been equated with Hinduism, specifically the Vaiṣṇava tradition as propounded in the south; Islam is portrayed as foreign, a threat to Indian heritage. Despite its glories, south Indian Vaiṣṇava practice suffered from the flaw of caste discrimination, and Ramanand began the task of eliminating it. Ramanand is the central figure in *RRT*, for it is through him that the great Indian "reformation" is carried out. In a note prefacing the first edition, the publisher explicitly compared this "reformation" to the Protestant movement of Europe. It was a reformation not of religious institutions, as had occurred in Europe, but of "caste superstition" (*RRT*: Publisher's Note to First Edition). The author suggests that India, therefore, required no inspiration from the west to identify and solve its problems. Ramanand, Hinduism's counterpart to Martin Luther, had done his work long before western Christians undertook their critique of Hinduism.

The saints who subsequently appear in *RRT* are explicitly linked to Ramanand and Vaiṣṇava tradition. In *RRT*'s account of Kabir, for example, Kabir becomes a thoroughgoing Vaiṣṇava, a portrayal which is at odds with much of the prevailing scholarly assessment of his work. In the hagiographical corpus that focuses specifically on Kabir, the saint's birth and caste status are hotly debated, along with the question of whether or not he was initiated by Ramanand.[4] According to the *RRT* (and indeed many other Kabir hagiographies) Kabir lay upon the steps of a bathing area one morning, awaiting Ramanand, and when Ramanand inadvertently stepped on Kabir, he muttered "Ram, Ram," which Kabir took to be his *mantra* of initiation. *RRT* notes the many legends about Kabir's birth and family, and concludes that "all legends considered, Kabir seems to have been of Hindu parentage, though adopted and brought up as a Mahomedan" (*RRT*: 14). The author does not explicitly indicate the grounds on which he reached that conclusion, but it is a conclusion which suits his purposes quite well. As one of the architects of the "reformation" of Indian heritage (to which Islam is foreign in *RRT*) Kabir of course had to be of Hindu birth. He also had to have a connection to the font of that reformation, and so the *RRT* presents as indisputable fact the story of Kabir's manipulating Ramanand into initiating him (a tale whose historical basis is contested). Thus the source of Kabir's creed, readers learn, was "current Vaishnavite philosophy and religion" (*RRT*: 21). In *RRT*, which treats Vaiṣṇavism as the essential form of Hindu and Indian culture, the connection to Ramanand, a Vaiṣṇava teacher, is critical.

The author's method thus far is akin to that of a revisionist historian. He makes explicit reference to the many legends about Kabir, and then accepts as authentic those which contribute to his overall agenda of tracing a north Indian reformation inspired by south Indian Vaiṣṇavism. *RRT*'s treatment of Guru Nanak is similar; the author notes that while some western scholars such as Ernest Trumpp have argued that Sikhism bears the influence of foreign thought (i.e. Islam), "nothing however could be farther from the truth" (*RRT*: 45).

Anyone who studies the religious history of Nanak's period "would find that the doctrines and teachings of Nanak, like those of the other great reformer Kabir, to whom he bears a great similarity in character and teaching alike, were chiefly derived from the contemporary Vaishnava schools of thought" (*RRT*: 45). While the author's rhetoric suggests some of the conventions of critical scholarship, he makes his final assessments not on the basis of a sustained argument, but on the basis of his underlying premise about the reformation brought from the south. In *RRT*, Sikhism is assumed as a part of the Hindu heritage of India; as such, it can have no connections with "foreign" traditions such as Islam, and any scholar (such as Trumpp) who argues such is simply wrong.

Ravi Das and Mirabai, the next two subjects of *RRT*, are fit into the author's scheme as well. He declares Ravi Das the untouchable to be a follower of Ramanand, and Mirabai a likely disciple of Ravi Das, thereby asserting south Indian Vaiṣṇavism as the source of their inspiration. His subsequent accounts of Vallabha, Tulsi Das, and the successors of Guru Nanak similarly highlight their connection to south Indian Vaiṣṇavism, as well as their opposition to discriminatory caste practices. For example, Guru Gobind Singh, the tenth guru of the Sikh tradition, "appealed to the eternal instincts of equality, liberty, and brotherhood, broke forever the caste prejudices and received into the Khalsa people of all classes who had hitherto been debarred from bearing arms and participating in religion" (*RRT*: 144-145). He links Guru Gobind Singh's founding of the Khalsa to its purported Vaiṣṇava roots, disregarding its implications in eventually making Sikhism a tradition separate from Hinduism.

RRT's revisionist religious history reaches new heights in the author's rendering of Swami Virajananda Saraswati and his disciple Swami Dayananada Saraswati, the founder of the Arya Samaj. The author's account of the life of Swami Virajananda is brief; he notes triumphantly that it may have been a south Indian Brāhmaṇ who first introduced Virajananda to the study of Sanskrit grammar. The south once more is shown as the source of all things good. Through his promotion of the Vedas, Swami Virajananda rendered "yeoman service" to the cause of Hindu nationality (*RRT*: 169). Swami Dayananada Saraswati he terms the "Indian Luther"; his picture of the Swami is fascinating given that Swami Dayananda was so critical of precisely the Vaiṣṇava tradition that the *RRT* espouses (Swami Dayananada Saraswati argued that Hindu practices which arose after the period of the war chronicled in the *Mahābhārata* are debased and must be rejected). But in *RRT*, the actual teachings of the Arya Samaj are not to be found; instead, Swami Dayananda emerges as a champion of the true Indian culture of the Vedas, though the author does not go so far as to declare him a Vaiṣṇava outright. According to *RRT*, he sought to purge Puranic

Hinduism of the evils that had crept into it in northern India (the land depicted as defiled by Muslim invaders), and fought against the evils of the caste system. In the *RRT*, the nuances of the Swami's actual argument about the caste system as one of merit, not birth, are lost so that Swami Dayananda may better suit the author's purposes.

Finally, the *RRT* introduces readers to Swami Rama Tirtha in an account largely based on the 1912 publication (evidently by the same anonymous writer) *Swami Rama Tirath: A Sketch of His Life and Teachings*. The Swami was an "explosive personality" who occasionally "burst out like a volcano" to "give out his thoughts in a wild manner" (*RRT*:217). Indians, be they Hindu or Muslim, saw him as a great saint, as did the Japanese and Americans. He impressed people the world over with his fervent devotion. The Swami's intense emotion was not that of a philosopher; "this passion was that of a Vaishnava bhakta" (*RRT*: 228). Here, the primacy of the author's Vaiṣṇava bias is laid bare, for we know that Swami Rama Tirtha championed Practical Vedānta, believing that Vaiṣṇava devotion was but a lesser elementary stage through which he had passed. Presumably the author knew this as well, because he had spent time with Swami Rama Tirtha during the last months of his life. His recasting of the Swami as a Vaiṣṇava reflects the centrality of his agenda in promoting Vaiṣṇavism; it is his experience of Swami Rama Tirtha as a Vaiṣṇava that governs his telling of the Swami's life.

Indeed in the *RRT*, every saint has been remolded into a Vaiṣṇava of some variety—or at least made into a supporter of Vaiṣṇava ideals. The source of those ideals was south India, which preserved India's heritage so that it might be restored in the troubled north. And so the Vaiṣṇava saints of north India constituted a "protestant" reformation of sorts, fighting against inappropriate image worship, caste discrimination, and promoting true Indian culture over the debased culture of the north. While the author's method clearly was to select only those aspects of the saints' lives which fit into his model of the Indian reformation, he nonetheless couched his efforts in the rhetoric of critical historical scholarship, a common strategy in modern hagiographies.

The Collections 2: Mahadevan's "Ten Saints of India"

T.M.P. Mahadevan's *Ten Saints of India* (*TSI*) was first published in 1961; by 1990, it was in its fifth edition, with translations in Tamil, Telugu, Kannada, and Malayalam. The text includes accounts of the lives of Campantar, Appar, Sundaramurti [Sundaramūrti], Manikkavacakar [Māṇikkavācakar], Nammalvar

[Nammālvār], Antal [Āṇḍāl], Sankara, Ramanuja, Ramakrishna, and Ramana Maharshi [Ramaṇa Maharṣi]. Its author, T.M.P. Mahadevan, was a noted south Indian scholar at the University of Madras who published extensively on Vedānta and Indian philosophy. *Ten Saints of India* is a publication of the Bharatiya Vidya Bhavan ["house of Indian knowledge"], a publishing house which seeks to promote "Bharatiya Shiksha," or "Indian education." The Bharatiya Vidya Bhavan has its headquarters in Bombay, with branches throughout India, as well as a number of constituent institutions.[5] *Ten Saints of India* is part of the Bhavan's Book University, which "publishes books, ancient and modern, at low price to make available the best literature and classics of India and the world to the common man in an easily understandable form" (*TSI*: inside back cover). The goal of "Bharatiya Shiksha" is to reintegrate "Bharatiya Vidya" [Indian knowledge] through "a study of forces, movements, motives, ideas, forms and art of creative life-energy through which it has expressed itself in different ages as a single continuous process" (*TSI*: inside front cover). Thus the underlying premise of the Book University is that there is and always has been a fundamental unity to Indian culture, though it has expressed itself in different ways. A proper presentation of this culture will "reintegrate" the disparate forms it has taken.

> The ultimate aim of Bharatiya Shiksha is to teach the younger generation to appreciate and live up to the permanent values of Bharatiya Vidya which is flowing from the supreme art of creative life-energy as represented by Shri Ramachandra, Shri Krishna, Vyasa, Buddha, and Mahavira have expressed themselves in modern times in the life of Shri Ramakrishna Paramahamsa, Swami Dayananda Saraswati, and Swami Vivekananda, Shri Aurobindo and Mahatma Gandhi [*sic*].[6] (*TSI*: inside front cover)

To study the lives of saints such as those listed above then is an important means of rediscovering the "permanent values" of Indian culture. There is no mention of Hinduism specifically; the list of saints advocated by the Bharatiya Vidya Bhavan includes not just Hindu figures but also the Buddha and Mahavira [Mahāvīra], who were Indian. Mahadevan's text must be read within the context of the Bharatiya Vidya Bhavan's overall agenda.

In his preface, Mahadevan advocates meditation on saints' lives as "a potent means to elevating our own lives" (*TSI*: ix). He believes there is a message to be learned from the saints; given that this is a publication of the Bharatiya Vidya Bhavan, one has a hint of the kind of message that will emerge. Mahadevan defines sainthood as a universal phenomenon, with India being unique among nations for having an unbroken saintly tradition (*TSI*: 1, 2). Thus the saints have something to teach not just India but the entire world, and the best place to find their message is India. It is a message which cannot be confined to any particular religious tradition: "the saints are truly citizens of the world; they belong to all mankind; they have no narrow attachments" (*TSI*: 3).[7] Nor are the differences of time and place important; saints are "witnesses to one and the same spirit." Indeed they all proclaim the same message of the spiritual unity of all beings (*TSI*: 9). To bolster his argument about the universality of sainthood, Mahadevan makes curious use of the work of psychologists, arguing on the one hand that "unknowing scholars" see saints as abnormal or even psychotic, yet also citing approvingly William James' analysis of the mystic (*TSI*: 6, 9). Just as did the author of *Ramanand to Ram Tirath*, Mahadevan makes use of whatever information supports his underlying agenda, disregarding any that does not fit.

The first three saints Mahadevan considers are from among the great saints of the Tamil devotional movement. First, he surveys some of the Śaiva Nāyaṉmārs: Campantar, Appar, Sundarar, and Manikkavacakar, and then turns to the the Vaiṣṇava Āḻvārs Nammalvar and Antal. His renderings of each highlight their numerous miracles and fervent devotion transcending all worldly conventions; they do not diverge from the traditional Tamil sources Mahadevan cites, nor are they explicitly linked to any modern concerns. Indeed, Mahadevan presents them with virtually no commentary. It is in the following section on the great Advaita Vedānta philosopher Sankara that Mahadevan begins to connect the saint's life to a modern agenda, devoting more space to Sankara than any other figure. Mahadevan explicitly compares Sankara's time to the present day: "the age which saw the advent of Sankara was not unlike our own. It was an age of unrest and strife, of spiritual bankruptcy and social discord" (*TSI*: 76). There was hostility among different religious groups: "the people forgot the ancient Vedic teaching that the Real is One; clinging to their narrow conceptions of the Godhead and swayed by fanaticism, they used religion as a weapon of aggression instead of finding in it the solace of life" (*TSI*: 76). Mahadevan's words seem intended to elicit immediate recognition from a twentieth-century reader all too aware of India's social and religious strife. Sankara, he makes clear, offered a solution to problems that are very much like those of the present day when "fanatics" have made a weapon out of religion.

Not surprisingly, Mahadevan carefully chose stories of Sankara's life that address issues related to the general themes of his text as well as the mission of the Bharatiya Vidya Bhavan. He acknowledges that there are only legendary accounts of Sankara's life, and then much like the author of the *RRT* establishes the standard of his own agenda as a criterion of trustworthiness. If a tale fits the image of Sankara he wishes to construct, then it among the myriad legends must be reliable. For example, the fact that some accounts contradict one another provides justification for Mahadevan to reject one of the most common stories about Sankara's life, that of Sankara's decision to enter the body of a deceased king so that he might experience the physical pleasures he had renounced. For Mahadevan, this story is "an unnecessary interlude introduced by Sankara's biographers" (*TSI*: 84) because it does not fit within his understanding of Sankara's character. He does not argue that switching bodies is implausible, and therefore the story should be rejected; rather, he argues that a man of Sankara's character would have no interest in pursuing physical pleasure. Other tales, however, are acceptable because of the message they convey. For example, Mahadevan relates the tale of Sankara meeting an untouchable man; when Sankara tried to shoo him away, the man asked whether his body or his self should leave. Only then did Sankara realize that the man was in fact the god Shiva in disguise. As a result, Sankara learned that anyone could realize the truth of non-duality, regardless of caste status, a message that is still valid (*TSI*: 81). And, as a teacher of non-dual Vedānta, he showed Indians a way to overcome their apparent differences. "At a time when false doctrines were misguiding the generality of people, and orthodoxy had nothing better to offer to counteract the atheism of the heterodox than a barren and outmoded ritualism, Sankara recaptured the heights of the Upanisadic philosophy and brought from there for the benefit of humanity the waters of eternal life" (*TSI*: 86). For Mahadevan, modern India's woes stem from false doctrines and dry ritualism which can be combatted only by the cleansing waters of the philosophy of the Upaniṣads as expounded by Sankara. Unlike the myriad false doctrines, Sankara's philosophy encompassed all others, and was therefore a unifying force. "The higher does not contradict the lower, but conserves what is of value in it and sublimates it. As one does not quarrel with one's own limbs, so Advaita can have no disputer with the philosophical systems" (*TSI*: 86). Advaita Vedānta is presented as the highest doctrine; it is the standard whereby whatever good there is in other philosophies may be extracted. It is Advaita Vedānta alone which can bring together India's disparate religious traditions, be they high or low. The Śaiva and Vaiṣṇava saints whose lives were introduced earlier are thus implicitly lumped together under the larger umbrella of Vedānta, any debates between them erased. To Mahadevan, their teachings are not contradictory, but rather lower forms—lower "limbs"—of the body of religion whose head is Vedānta.

To drive home this point further, Mahadevan sketches the atmosphere of religious debate which prevailed among teachers of Mīmāṃsa (one of the six systems of classical Indian philosophy), Buddhists, and adherents of other kinds of worship in Sankara's lifetime. Sankara alone brought them all together through Advaita, rescuing them from their futile bickering. Mahadevan's message is loud and clear once more—the situation in India today, where adherents of various sects are at odds with one another, is similar. Sankara's teachings, as presented by Mahadevan, could be a remedy. Various Hindu groups, Sikhs, Buddhists, and Christians are all limbs of the same body; Advaita Vedānta alone demonstrates that they are intimately connected.

Mahadevan's subsequent presentation of Ramanuja, the philosopher of Viśiṣṭādvaita Vedānta (qualified non-dual Vedānta) is half the length of his account of Sankara. Mahadevan is considerably less enthusiastic about Ramanuja than was the author of *RRT*, for whom Ramanuja was the ultimate source of the north Indian reformation. In Mahadevan's eyes, Ramanuja preached a "lower limb" of Vedānta and thus had little to say that might be useful to a contemporary audience. Mahadevan's interest is rekindled, however, by the account of Ramakrishna [Rāmakṛṣṇa] (1836-1886) which follows, his only treatment of a saint from the north (Bengal). Like Sankara nearly a thousand years earlier, Mahadevan reports, Ramakrishna was born into troubled times when the Indian intelligentsia were abandoning Indian culture wholesale for the enticements of the west. It was Ramakrishna's destiny to be born near Calcutta, the metropolis of the British empire in India, so that he might reach the intelligentsia who were forsaking their own heritage. Calcutta was an ideal place for him to demonstrate the value of the ancient way of life of Indian sages and saints, a clear antidote to the élite's flirtation with the west (*TSI*: 103). Mahadevan details Ramakrishna's far-ranging experimentation in Tāntrik and Vaiṣṇava disciplines, depicting them as brilliantly conceived experiments which were subsequently eclipsed by his experience of non-duality.

> Having gained the transcendent experience of the supreme Spirit, Ramakrishna came down to the plane of relativity and turned to the practice of alien faiths such as Islam and Christianity. The Advaita-realization which he had had, had enabled him to look upon all faiths as but different paths to the same destination. His universalism was not the result of a process of rationalization; it was a conviction born of experience. . . . In his experience we have an authentic evidence of the supremacy and identity of the truth taught in all faiths. (*TSI*: 133)

Thus in Mahadevan's account, Ramakrishna brought Sankara's truths to light in such a way as to convince westernized Indians of their value; he confirmed the truths of Advaita Vedānta, which subsume the truths of all other religions. Ramakrishna further illustrated the method of realizing truth through social service, and thereby set a shining example for Indians to follow. They could look to the west, but Ramakrishna had already done just that, giving its religions a fair hearing by trying them for himself, only to find that the highest truth was to be found in India all along. Those who realized that Advaita Vedānta was the highest truth were obligated to help those of lesser realization, not only through religious instruction, but also social service. Mahadevan is equally enthusiastic about the silent saint whose life closes his book, Ramana Maharshi; his philosophy was "the same as that of Advaita Vedānta," and "to inspire even the lowliest of us with hope and help us out of the slough of despond, is the supreme significance of such illustrious exemplars as the Maharshi" (*TSI*: 136).[8]

Out of ten saints, then, Mahadevan has explicitly presented three as exemplars: Sankara, Ramakrishna, and Ramana Maharshi. It is they who illustrated the efficacy of Advaita Vedānta, providing an example for "even the lowliest." Mahadevan's strategy was clever; he began by arguing that all saints and sages teach essentially the same thing. Those saints and sages who actually had something to teach his audience, however, were those who advocated Advaita Vedānta. His unstated assertion is that the other seven saints taught lesser versions of the one truth; Advaita Vedānta could conserve whatever was of value in their doctrine and practice. Mahadevan's blasé treatment of their messages serves to emphasize his unbridled enthusiasm for the message of Vedānta followers. For Mahadevan, only Advaita Vedānta can show India a path to unity amidst its social and religious diversity. For the author of *RRT*, it was south Indian Vaiṣṇavism which epitomized Indian culture; for Mahadevan, it was Advaita Vedānta as propounded by the south Indian Sankara.

The Collections 3: Talwalkar's "Some Indian Saints"

The third English collection, Gopinath Talwalkar's *Some Indian Saints* (*SIS*) was first published by the National Book Trust of India in 1977, and reprinted in 1989. It forms part of the Nehru Bal Pustakalaya [Nehru Children's Library], named after Jawaharlal Nehru, India's first prime minister, who is remembered as a great advocate for children.[9] The comic-book style text is geared towards older children, and includes accounts of Nanak, Basaveswar [Basaveśwar], Cakradhar, Eknath [Eknāth], Candidas [Caṇḍīdās], and Kabir. As a publication of the National Book Trust, it promotes government-sanctioned values, particularly the eradication of caste discrimination and expensive rituals.

In the narratives about both Guru Nanak (founder of Sikhism) and Basaveswar (founder of the Lingāyat sect), Talwalkar stresses their resistance to caste discrimination and their respect for all faiths, noting that Basaveswar was even willing to sanction intercaste marriage. Talwalkar presents Cakradhar (founder of the Mahānubhav sect) in a similar vein; he highlights Cakradhar's resistance to Brāhmaṇ orthodoxy and his challenge against mindless performance of rituals. Beheaded for his challenge to the orthodox,

"Chakradhar may well be called the Gandhi of the thirteenth century" (*SIS*: 34). In an interesting twist on a familiar theme, Talwalkar has sought to legitimate an earlier saint through the more recent figure of Mahatma Gandhi and his agenda for modern India (typically, such comparisons are reversed, with an older saint legitimating a more recent one). The Maharashtrian saint Eknath too is singled out for his opposition to caste discrimination and elaborate rituals; Talwalkar repeats a common story about Eknath giving water to a dying donkey rather than saving it to use as part of a ritual offering (*SIS*: 41-43). Similarly, the Brāhmaṇ Candidas, who worshipped with a low-caste washerman's daughter, is championed as an exemplar of caste-free living (*SIS*: 46).

Kabir, a perennial favorite in hagiographical collections, serves a special purpose in Talwalkar's text. Talwalkar favors the legend according to which Kabir was born of Hindu parents but raised by Muslims (*SIS*: 55). He does so, however, not to claim Kabir as a Hindu (as do many who subscribe to this version of Kabir's life, such as in the *RRT* rendering of Kabir) but rather to paint him as the saint who showed the way to Hindu-Muslim unity. Because he was born Hindu but raised Muslim, he knew both Hindu and Muslim ways and saw their fundamental unity. Talwalkar's reading of Kabir's message is clearly targeted at modern India. Thus Talwalkar similarly accepts the story of Kabir's initiation by Ramanand, but does not use it to demonstrate Kabir's impeccable Hindu credentials; instead, he uses it to demonstrate Kabir's ability to annoy Hindus and Muslims alike with his effortless switching between the two faiths. Ultimately, what readers may learn from Kabir's example is that everyone should work for a living, as he did; that rites and rituals are of little use, and that the caste system is inherently flawed. For exemplifying such ideals, Talwalkar reports, Kabir earned the love of the common people.

Talwalkar has thus marshalled stories about the lives of Indian saints for yet another agenda—not south Indian Vaiṣṇavism, or Advaita Vedānta, but that of the secular Indian state. He finds in the lives of saints from the past the ideals that the nation of India strives for in the present: an end to caste discrimination and elaborate ritual observances, unity among Hindus and Muslims, and acceptance of the equality of all people. By choosing saints associated with particular Hindu sects, Talwalkar highlights not only the unity of Hinduism and Islam, but also disparate forms of Hinduism. Talwalkar further implies that all those ideals may be found in India's past, and need not necessarily come from the west. Nonetheless, it is significant that none of his "Indian" saints is Muslim (despite Kabir's connections to Islam). As is so often the case, "Indian" and "Muslim" are seen as somehow mutually exclusive terms.

The Collections 4: Dube's "Santõ kī Kahāniyā̃"

Sukdev Dube's Hindi *Santõ kī Kahāniyā̃* ("Stories of the Saints"; *SKK*) was published in 1970 by the Sahitya Bhavan of Allahabad. Dube's collection is the longest of the five, with accounts of Kabir, Mirabai, Ramanuja, Namdev [Nāmdev], Jnanesvar [Jñāneśvar], Vallabhacarya, Tulsi Das, Surdas, Caitanya, Eknath, Tukaram [Tukārām], Bhakta Nandanar [Nandanār], Tyagaraja, and Nanak. In his introduction, Dube addresses one of the more interesting characteristics of hagiographical collections, the fact that they so often include accounts of the lives of saints with radically different doctrinal positions. Dube explains that he chose to include saints whom he terms both *nirākār* and *saguṇa* devotees (those who worship a formless god, and those who conceive of god with qualities) because "ordinary people consider them alike" (*SKK*: Do Śabda). In Dube's view, then, ordinary people believe that there is something about saints that unites them into a single group despite any apparent doctrinal differences. Saints, Dube argues, have played a substantial role in forming and maintaining "our culture." Although he does not specify precisely whose culture he means, Dube notes that he sought to include representative saints from all regions of India, choosing in particular those who composed poetry (*SKK*: Do Śabda). Like Mahadevan, Dube implies that there is a fundamental Indian culture, and that one way to illustrate the unity of that culture is by considering the lives of saints from different regions of the subcontinent. The Education Department of the Government of Madhya Pradesh gave Dube's text an award, which suggests that it found its message compatible with the goals of government-sponsored education.

That Dube's text won an award is somewhat puzzling, however; the award was likely not an acknowledgement of the text's literary merit. Dube's Hindi prose lacks grace, and his accounts of individual saints' lives are often hard to follow, with no apparent connections between the incidents he describes. Though he chose saints who wrote poetry, Dube very rarely addresses their poetry other than listing the titles of works attributed to particular saints. His list of saints includes more north Indian than south Indian saints, and more Vaiṣṇavas than Śaivas, but beyond their numerical dominance, there is no clear north Indian or Vaiṣṇava bias (unlike those that emerged in the earlier collections). The text in fact has no clear message, though it does occasionally offhandedly champion Hindu-Muslim unity, patriotism, and the eradication of caste discrimination.

Throughout the text, Dube casually adopts the rhetoric of critical historical analysis, noting the many legends and traditions about particular saints and the need to determine their accuracy. The critical analysis, however, goes no further than this, for Dube simply describes legends and then proclaims particular ones true without offering any compelling reasons why. For example, Dube asserts that Surdas was blind because there is a poem attributed to Surdas in which he makes reference to his blindness. Dube then expresses pity for the poor scholars who still argue about whether Surdas indeed was blind when the proof that he was is staring them in the face (*SKK*: 58). Despite adopting some of the rhetoric of a critical scholarly approach, Dube in fact dismisses (or is unaware of) critical textual scholarship and the possibility that not all the poems attributed to Surdas are indeed the compositions of the historical figure by that name. Nor does he cite his sources; they appear to range from original hagiographical texts to comic book versions such as those of the *Amar Citra Katha* series. Despite his oft-repeated skepticism about legends and tradition, Dube's accounts are replete with miracles and other fantastic happenings. The language of critical scholarship is apparently meant to lend an air of scholarly legitimacy to his efforts, but *SKK* is not a scholarly work.

The ever-popular Kabir is the first saint Dube presents in *Santõ kī Kahāniyā̃*. After Dube considers the various traditions about Kabir's birth, he finally settles upon a story (similar to Talwalkar's) involving Ramanand meeting a young Brāhmaṇ widow and her father. In Dube's version, Ramanand gave the woman the blessing of a child, not realizing that she was a widow. She miraculously became pregnant and gave birth to a son, but fearing condemnation as a widow with a newborn, she hid the baby in a lake, where he was found and adopted by a Muslim weaver couple. Dube expresses some uncertainty about this story, but suggests that it is possible that Kabir was raised by this couple, and that he was indeed a member of the Julāhā caste of weavers (*SKK*: 8-9). For Dube, then, the possibility that something might have happened is sufficient reason to assume that it did happen. Dube's tentative acceptance of Kabir's mother as a Brāhmaṇ widow paves the way for him to accept unquestioningly the story of Kabir's initiation by Ramanand, the great Brāhmaṇ Vaiṣṇava teacher. Kabir, born Hindu but raised by Muslims, realized that there was no difference between Hinduism and Islam. Thus he "laid the foundation for Hindu-Muslim unity" (*SKK*: 11). The status of Islam in such a unity, however, is questionable. The story of Kabir's original Hindu birth makes his Muslim identity but a thin veneer, and the implication is that Indian Muslims should realize that in fact they are more Indian (Hindu) than Muslim, and their acceptance of that fact would be the road to unity. Dube's presentation of the Kabir birth and initiation stories thus does not accept Islam as an independent (much less Indian) entity. For Dube, Hindu/Muslim unity is essentially Muslim submission to Hinduism, which he portrays as the true Indian heritage.

Finally, Dube concludes: "Kabir was an ideal leader for us, a true reformer, and showed us the true path. Centuries ago, he raised the call for the equality of humanity and unity, which nearly all the nations of the world today attempt to achieve" (*SKK*: 14). What kind of ideal leader was Kabir, what kind of reformer? What true path did he lay before his followers? Beyond the problematic call for Hindu-Muslim unity, nothing in Dube's account answers those questions. Readers, presumably, must supply the answers themselves. Dube's vagueness is significant, and indeed such vagueness permeates the entire text. Dube's saints' lives reveal messages that never rise above such platitudes as the need for unity, the folly of discrimination, and the value of hard work.

What makes this an award-winning text, given that it lacks literary merit and presents questionable scholarship? It may well be that the book's apparent weakness—its vagueness and inconsistency—is in fact its strength. While *SKK* could be challenged as a scholarly text on any number of grounds, it is in one crucial way utterly uncontroversial: it favors no one particular theological position, it advocates no particular practice, nor rejects any others. Rather, Dube presents a grab-bag assortment of saints in such a way as to make it possible for readers to supply the substance of their messages. The range of saints in the text is sufficiently wide that most readers would find someone familiar for whom they could supply further details. Perhaps this is why the Madhya Pradesh Education Department deemed it a worthy text for students and even gave it an award. Who could argue with a call for unity, for less discrimination, for patriotism and hard work? Such calls for unity are at the heart of much Indian political rhetoric; they are sufficiently vague that they may be addressed to virtually any community. Nonetheless, there is a telling omission—the saints Dube chose are all closely associated with Hinduism (though Kabir and Guru Nanak's status vis-à-vis Hinduism is debatable). The saints of Islam in India are denied any status as representatives of "Indian" ideals; true Indian culture, in Dube's construction, requires that Indian Muslims recognize (as did Kabir) that their true identity is Indian, not Muslim; it is as if the two cannot be reconciled. Other than relegating Islam to secondary status, there is no substantive content to Dube's "unity."

The Collections 5: Vanaprasthi's "Bhārat ke Mahān Ṛṣi"

Prannath Vanaprasthi's *Bhārat ke Mahān Ṛṣi* ["The Great Sages of India"; *BMR*], published in Delhi in 1963, addresses the lives of Valmiki [Vālmīki] (the reputed author of the Sanskrit *Rāmāyaṇa*), Sankara, Canakya [Cānakya], Guru Nanak, Swami Dayananada Saraswati, Ramakrishna, and Swami Rama Tirtha.

The text, part of a series of biographies for young people [*bālopayogī jīvaniyā*] is written in simple, straightforward Hindi prose. Other titles in the series include studies of political figures such as Lokamanya Tilak, Jawaharlal Nehru, and the king Ashoka [Aśoka]; religious leaders such as Swami Vivekananda, Guru Gobind Singh, and the Buddha, and gods such as Krishna and Hanuman [Hanumān]. Vanaprasthi's text has no introduction, but his title and selection of saints (as well as the subjects of other titles in the series) suggest some of the aims of this collection. As in other texts, Vanaprasthi makes no mention of Hinduism, but rather of India, suggesting that his choice of subjects serves to convey something not of Hindu culture specifically, but a unified Indian cultural heritage. "Indian" is effectively equated with "Hindu"; all the saints in Vanaprasthi's book are associated in some way with Hinduism, including Guru Nanak.

Vanaprasthi's opening account of the life of Valmiki and his transformation from a robber into a master poet and devotee of Ram does not vary from other legendary accounts of Valmiki's life; Vanaprasthi presents it without any comment. Like Mahadevan, he presents some saints without explicitly connecting them to a particular theme or agenda while highlighting others as exemplars for the present age. Indeed Vanaprasthi's treatment of Sankara in *Bhārat ke Mahān Ṛṣi* is very similar to Mahadevan's. Vanaprasthi explains that Sankara lived at a time when the Buddhist *dharma* was in decline, when many people no longer believed in god, and immorality reigned supreme. Vanaprasthi's presentation of Buddhism is somewhat vague; he implies that there is an ideal form of Buddhism which is perfectly acceptable, and indeed a part of Indian culture (therefore Hindu) but that its practice had become debased. At a time when the religious leadership of India was in decline, it took the leadership of a Hindu to rescue India from this fallen form of Buddhism. To do this, Sankara mastered the Vedas and Śāstraṣ and then traveled throughout India, defeating morally bankrupt Buddhists in debate. Sankara thus revived true Vedic religion throughout the subcontinent and people once again believed in god, so that they could then reject the debased form of Buddhism that they had been practicing. Sankara continued to spread true Vedic religion throughout India, and when his mission was complete, died at the age of thirty-three on the night of Diwālī, the festival of lights (*BMR*: 10-14).

In their accounts of Sankara's life, both Mahadevan and Vanaprasthi place primary emphasis on the role that Sankara played in assuaging the spiritual ills of his time, and draw an explicit connection between those ills and the problems of the present day. Both authors presume that there is an ideal form of Indian religion (though they are vague about what precisely it is) which became obscured by sectarian divisions. Sankara, they argue, through his deep understanding of traditional Indian religious literature, was able to restore that ideal religion. And now, many centuries later, India is faced with a similar situation—people have lost a sense of the true unity of the Indian people. For Vanaprasthi, Sankara's message is just as relevant today as it was in his own lifetime. All these collections have asserted that India's true unity can be found in its Hindu heritage, with no suggestion that examples of unity might be found in Islam.

Vanaprasthi highlights that theme in his tale of the Brāhmaṇ sage Canakya who became a political leader: after his mother's death, Canakya lived the life of a renunciant, but when he saw that Alexander had come to India and was swallowing up territory in the north, he realized that Indians, the descendants of Ram and Krishna, were suffering. Then, through the force of his superior intelligence, he effectively seized control of India's then most powerful kingdom by becoming minister to King Candragupta in his capital city of Pataliputra. Using his wisdom, he was able to unite India under one flag, and despatched Candragupta's army to free the nation from foreigners, pushing the Greek kings of the northwest back west across the Sindh river. Once the foreigners had been humbled and expelled, Canakya resigned his ministerial position and resumed the life of a renunciant Brāhmaṇ (*BMR*: 15-17). While the historical details of Vanaprasthi's tale here may be somewhat suspect, the underlying message is unmistakable. Vanaprasthi suggests that to be successful, India must expel foreigners. True Indians, the descendants of Ram and Krishna, suffer when foreigners rule. At such times, even solitary renunciants must take up arms to expel the foreigners. If this message is applied to modern India, its ramifications are chilling, for Vanaprasthi's implied modern analog to the Greeks and Egyptians is the Muslims, descendants of invaders who made Indians suffer. Again, "Indian" and "Islam" have become mutually exclusive (and the fact that many Indian Muslims are not descendants of invaders, but descendants of native Indian converts to Islam, is not acknowledged).

The idea that India had nothing to gain from Islam is subsequently highlighted in Vanaprasthi's opening tale about Guru Nanak, an account found in much of the hagiographical literature surrounding Nanak which details his travels to distant lands. Guru Nanak and some followers had undertaken a pilgrimage to Mecca and Medina, the holiest cities of Islam. Reaching Mecca, they had stopped to rest when a Muslim scholar came across them and angrily asked why Nanak's feet were pointed towards the *ka'bah*, sacred site of the Muslims. Nanak lovingly requested that the scholar turn his legs in whichever direction the *ka'bah* couldn't be found. Each time the scholar moved Nanak's legs, the *ka'bah* would follow.[10] Trembling, the scholar went to his superiors to tell them what had happened. They quickly realized that a great man had come to Mecca, and fell at Guru Nanak's feet, whereupon he preached the *dharma* to them and won thousands of devotees. In Vanaprasthi's second story about Guru Nanak, readers learn that on his way back to India Nanak stopped in Kabul, where the Mughal Babur [Bābur] was preparing to invade the Indian subcontinent. Hearing that a teacher of great renown was in his city, Babur called Nanak to his court and asked him if he would be successful in seizing power in India. Nanak assured Babur that he would, but that his power would last only if his descendants considered India to be their own country. In reply, Babur offered Nanak a glass of liquor, which he declined with the reply, "I have drunk that wine which never intoxicates" (*BMR*: 19-22).

These two stories teach that an Indian teacher could go into the very heartland of Islam and convert the highest Muslim officials with his wisdom. The Muslim scholars are portrayed as fools, slavishly devoted to the *ka'bah* at Mecca, not realizing that its essence could be found in any direction. And Babur, the founder of the Mughal empire in India, was intoxicated not only with wine, but with his own power. Nanak however had the greater power; he knew that Babur could conquer northern India, but he also knew that his power would last only if Babur's descendants made India their own country. The Mughal empire, as readers would surely know, after years of glory eventually went into a long decline, finally coming to an end with British rule. Vanaprasthi's implication is that this happened because Babur's descendants, the Muslims of India, did not consider India their own country. Instead, they looked westward to the sacred sites of Islam, just as had the scholars in the first story. To Vanaprasthi, they were incapable of being Muslims and Indians at the same time.

After these two tales of Guru Nanak's triumph over Muslims, Vanaprasthi turns to Nanak's early life with stories familiar from the Sikh hagiographical tradition; Vanaprasthi emphasizes Nanak's devotion to one god, his respect for the poor, and his willingness to work hard, but does not comment on Nanak's subsequent renown as the founder of Sikhism. Similarly, Vanaprasthi detaches his next subject Swami Dayananada Saraswati from the tradition he founded, the Arya Samaj. Vanaprasthi chronicles the events typically found in accounts of Swami Dayananda (the ultimate source of which is in many cases Swami Dayananda's own autobiography): his questions about the worship of images, his debates with traditional pandits, and the attempts on his life. It is only in his last paragraph on Dayananda that Vanaprasthi names his as the founder of the Arya Samaj; there is no discussion of the specific teachings of the Arya Samaj other than Vanaprasthi's earlier recounting of the Swami's opposition to image-worship (*BMR*: 23-29).

In Vanaprasthi's collection, then, Swami Dayananada Saraswati is noteworthy not because he propounded a radically revised form of Hindu *dharma* (which Vanaprasthi ignores) but because of his membership in the class of "great Indian sages." As such, his life is of interest; the specific details of his life pertaining to his establishment of the Arya Samaj fall away. Vanaprasthi's treatment of Ramakrishna is much the same; he portrays Ramakrishna as a great *sādhu*, indifferent to worldly wealth and his own health, fully dedicated to God in all forms (though not the teacher of Advaita Vedānta that Mahadevan styled him). He was so humble that he would sweep the goddess Kali's [Kālī] temple himself, and eat the leftovers of food that had been served to beggars. Like Swami Dayananda, he is situated within the generic class of great Indian sages. His specific teachings, closest followers (e.g. Swami Vivekananda), and the institution founded in his name, the Ramakrishna Mission, all fall by the wayside (*BMR*: 30-34).

The final saint depicted in Vanaprasthi's collection is none other than Swami Rama Tirtha, and Vanaprasthi introduces him to readers through a conversation set on Swami Rama Tirtha's America-bound ship.

> "Where are you going?"
> "America."
> "Aren't you a Hindustani *sādhu*?"
> "Yes."
> "Will you go there in these clothes?"
> "Yes."
> "You have plenty of money, don't you?"
> "None at all."
> "You don't have anything?"
> "Rama doesn't even touch money."
> "Well! Where are you going to stay?"
> "Wherever I find a place to rest my feet."
> "Do you know anyone there?"
> "Rama belongs to the entire world, and the entire world belongs to Rama."
> "I've never seen a man as unusual as you. You're going to such a huge country, and you haven't made any arrangements at all. You're going to end up starving there."
> Swami Rama listened to the man and roared with laughter. The ship continued on its way, and after a couple of days, Swami Rama began talking to the same man again. As they spoke, the man realized that this was the very same Swami Rama Tirtha who had proclaimed the greatness of ancient Indian civilization in Japan. He bowed his forehead in reverence, then quickly scurried off to send telegrams to various eminent Americans informing them of the Swami's impending arrival. And so when the ship arrived at New York's port, there were countless people gathered to receive this great man. They welcomed him with open hearts. Swami Rama smiled at his companion and said,
> "Will I still end up starving here?" (*BMR*: 35-36)

In Vanaprasthi's account, just as Guru Nanak showed Muslims the futility of their fixation on the *ka'bah*, so Swami Rama Tirtha showed Americans their unnatural attachment to material wealth. The basic story of Swami Rama Tirtha arriving in the United States with no luggage or provisions is common throughout the hagiographical tradition (e.g. *LSRT*: 250); Vanaprasthi's introduction of Swami Rama Tirtha with this tale in many ways recalls the style of the *Rām Jīvan Citrāvalī*.[11] It is based on a historical event—Swami Rama Tirtha's visit to America—but with a fair amount of embellishment and the occasional factual error (Swami Rama Tirtha's ship from Japan landed in Seattle, not New York City; given that in much contemporary Indian thinking, New York epitomizes America, the mistake is not surprising). Swami Rama Tirtha emerges as the all-knowing Indian *sādhu* who understands that his needs will be met wherever he goes. His American acquaintance is typically preoccupied with mundane details—money, food, clothing—but also becomes the agent of Swami Rama Tirtha's grand reception in the United States. Just as in the *RJC*, the Swami's travels are a triumphal tour—he earned worldwide renown after news of his visit to Japan spread, and Americans thronged to greet this champion of ancient Indian civilization. The Swami had known all along that everything would fall into place as he brought his message of India's glory to materialistic Americans.

Subsequently, Vanaprasthi produces a brief sketch of the Swami's life: his mother died soon after his birth, and her son soon revealed his innate spirituality, crying to be taken to the temple when its bells sounded. He became a brilliant student and a gifted poet. First entranced by his love for Krishna, he later was "dyed in the color of Vedānta." Vanaprasthi next charts the Swami's short stint as a math professor, his vows of renunciation, and efforts to spread *dharma* throughout Japan, America, and every corner of India: the Swami always advocated hard work and simple living, himself wearing nothing but a sheet in the dead of the American winter. Then, at the young age of thirty-three, he drowned in the Ganges. "And so this great man who raised the flag of *dharma* forever sleeps in the holy waves of the Ganges" (*BMR*: 50). And so too ends Vanaprasthi's book. As in his lives of other saints, there is not much discussion of specific teachings, but rather the glorification of the values of hard work and simple lifestyles.

Vanaprasthi's agenda is much like that of the other collections: to promote a particular view of Indian culture, one that reserves the land of India for the descendants of Ram and Krishna. Vanaprasthi highlighted Sankara, Canakya, and Guru Nanak in particular, which at first glance seems an odd combination. Yet each of the three represents a crucial part of Vanaprasthi's overall message. For him, Sankara was a man who in his brief lifetime was able to restore true Vedic religion and unite the various sects of India (including those who consider themselves Buddhists). Just as in other collections, he emerges as someone whose message is still urgently needed in India. Unlike other collections, however, Vanaprasthi does not emphasize Sankara's Advaita Vedānta specifically; rather, it is his general knowledge of the Vedas that is most important. Canakya is an especially interesting inclusion, for Vanaprasthi lauds him not for his religious achievement, but his political triumph in expelling foreigners from India, suggesting that Vanaprasthi believes that India's political salvation lies in the inspiration not of her politicians, but her religious leaders. It took Canakya, a Brāhmaṇ sage, to realize that the descendants of Ram and Krishna (whom Vanaprasthi styles the true citizens of India) were suffering at the hands of outside invaders; King Candragupta could do nothing without the sage's advice. Vanaprasthi's tales about Guru Nanak, which immediately follow the story of Canakya, show that India was to suffer at the hands of foreigners again, in the form of Muslims in Nanak's time. In Vanaprasthi's presentation, Nanak demonstrates the spiritual superiority of Hinduism over Islam (Vanaprasthi does not treat Sikhism as a separate religious tradition but as a part of the larger Indian culture). Like Canakya, he is a religious leader who nonetheless understands the political situation, for he could foresee that Babur's empire would only be temporary. Vanaprasthi's renderings of Swami Dayananda Saraswati, Ramakrishna, and Swami Rama Tirtha carried no similar message; rather, they served almost as generic figures with no clear teachings other than the value of hard work and the rejection of western materialism. Their presence in the text serves primarily to legitimate the overall agenda of the text. For Vanaprasthi, India's proper political course of action must be set by its religious leaders, and it must involve a purging of those who are not part of the true Indian culture. Like the authors of the other hagiographical collections, Vanaprasthi used the lives of saints to promote a particular agenda.

The Dynamics of Hagiographical Collections

In the single-subject hagiographies considered in earlier chapters, the hagiographers used either their own or others' experiences of Swami Rama Tirtha to demonstrate his power; that reporting of experience is a fundamental tool of the hagiographer's rhetoric, the means whereby the hagiographer convinces readers that they too should become the saint's follower. In the first phase of that tradition, hagiographers (Puran Singh in particular) used direct personal experience in constructing their images of Swami Rama Tirtha; in the second and third stages, that personal experience was replaced by accounts of others' experiences and an increasing reliance on mythical images. Each of the hagiographers from all three phases of the tradition expressed the wish that readers should learn something from the Swami's life and be changed through the experience of reading the hagiographies themselves. What the hagiographers hoped readers could learn from Swami Rama Tirtha's life varied depending upon the hagiographer's concerns. Narayan Swami urged readers to look around them and find that his "Emperor Rama" was everywhere; the *RJC* urged readers to become "filled with Rama in a practical way," a way which the *RJC* defined according to the institutional agenda of the SRTP.

The purpose of hagiographical collections, however, is somewhat different. None of the authors explicitly sought to promote devotion to all or some of the saints in the texts, nor were there exhortations to make each and every saint in the collection a part of one's spiritual life. Indeed this would be a considerable challenge, given that each collection covers such a wide range of saints representing different sects and different social strata. In the collections, however, there was the same idea as in single-subject hagiographies that there is something to be learned from saints' lives, and the collections are grounded upon the assumption that all saints teach something similar. The collection authors' portrayals of different saints reveal that their primary goal is not to promote devotion to all those saints, but instead to promote a specific agenda (whether social, political, religious, or some combination thereof), and these agendas are all rooted in a particular view of a unified Indian culture exemplified by its many saints. For the author of *RRT*, south Indian Vaiṣṇavism epitomizes that culture; for Mahadevan, it is the Advaita Vedānta of Sankara; for Talwalkar, it is a "secular," anti-caste form of Hinduism; for Dube, it is a vaguely conceived India of unity and caste equality; for Vanaprasthi, it is an India free from foreigners governed on the authority of her wise sages. Rather than promoting devotion to a particular saint or institution, the collections use the legitimating authority of the saints to promote acceptance of their agendas.

The collection authors employ the saints' lives and teachings selectively to construct the saints' images so that they in some way exemplify or legitimate the collections' agendas. In some cases, the authors did so explicitly by highlighting their accounts of particular saints who best suited their purposes, such as Mahadevan's use of Sankara as the exemplary teacher of Advaita Vedānta. In other cases, the authors either downplayed or seemingly misrepresented the teachings of particular saints in order to make them fit their program. Swami Dayananada Saraswati's complete detachment from the teachings of the Arya Samaj in several collections is the most clearcut example of this strategy; *RRT*'s portrayal of Swami Rama Tirtha as a Vaiṣṇava is another. In still other instances, the authors include brief accounts of saints whose stories had no explicit connection to the agenda. Those accounts were well-known stories likely familiar to most Indian readers, such as Vanaprasthi's brief recounting of the life of Valmiki, or Mahadevan's stories of the saints of the Tamil devotional tradition. In single-saint hagiographies, for followers it was the presence of the saint which was most important, not what the saint taught; it is the same in the collections. Even if certain saints' teachings are mischaracterized or omitted entirely, the power of the presence of multiple saints lends power and authority to the author's agenda.

Single-saint hagiographers assemble the pieces of the saint's life (and accounts of how others perceived the saint) so that readers are led to the inexorable conclusion that the saint earned membership in the larger category of great saints throughout history, and is therefore worthy of devotion. In contrast, the collections seem designed to lead readers to the inexorable conclusion that their agendas are correct. It is crucial to note, however, that the collections are predicated on readers' previous experience and acceptance of the power of the saints. Without that previous experience, the collections' strategy of legitimation through the saints' power would not work.

While the single-saint hagiographer must make choices about how to select and present the significant events in a saint's life, the collection author must first choose the saints the collection will include. As the collections show, the saints need not necessarily come from the same era, or region, or caste, or sectarian tradition. In fact, diversity is a critical part of the collection authors' rhetorical strategy, for more saints mean more legitimating support. In the collections considered in this chapter, all of which promoted a particular vision of Indian culture, a diversity of saints was especially critical for authors as a way to demonstrate that the ideals they promoted were indeed pan-Indian. Many of the authors justified their inclusion of saints of different sectarian traditions, however, by asserting that sainthood itself is a universal phenomenon which transcends apparent boundaries of region, caste, and creed.

Yet when collection authors proclaim the universality of the saints and that the saints all teach essentially the same thing, they are not necessarily arguing for the fundamental unity of all religious traditions. None of the authors actually demonstrated that all the saints shared some fundamental characteristics or taught the same things; rather, they highlighted the teachings of particular saints, modified the teachings of some, and ignored the teachings of still others outright. The concept of the universality of sainthood is a rhetorical device which allows authors to lend authority to their agendas from as many disparate sources as possible. If an author can show every saint in a collection to be supportive of his agenda in some way, then his or her case is strengthened; that saints from diverse backgrounds appear in collections is thus not illogical or inconsistent. Including a wide range of saints also helps target a potentially wider audience, because readers may already be familiar with some of the saints in the collection (a function of their prior experience of saints), and therefore more willing to accept what the author claims on those saints' behalf.

In hagiography, stories about how people experience a saint—from Puran Singh's gushing love to the *RJC*'s Muslim scholar who dropped his dagger and became a lifelong devotee of Swami Rama Tirtha—are a means of establishing the saint's power, a power rooted not in specific teachings, but in the presence of the saint himself. In the collections, that power is assumed from the very beginning. The collections, after all, are not accounts of the entire lives of the saints, but rather brief sketches. They thus presuppose some prior familiarity with the saints' lives, and this may be why the collections include relatively few stories about the experiences people had in the presence of the saints. Without readers who have had some experience of the saints in the collection, the author can derive little power from those saints for his own agenda. Experience is thus important in hagiographical collections, but it is the presupposition of prior experience rather than the recurrent highlighting of experience found in texts such as the *RJC*.

In the first stage of the Swami Rama Tirtha hagiographical tradition, the hagiographers chronicled and preserved their memories of the Swami's power; later hagiographers had to establish not only the Swami's power, but also his relevance to a later age. In this regard, the rhetorical strategy of third phase hagiographies such as the *RJC* most closely resembles that of the collections; in both cases, the authors could not rely upon the authority of their own firsthand experience of the saints whose lives they reported. The *RJC*'s author sought to legitimate his account of Swami Rama Tirtha through multiple accounts of how people responded to the Swami's presence; these accounts took basic facts from the earlier hagiographical tradition and elaborated upon them (often using mythical imagery) to portray Swami Rama Tirtha as an *avatār*. Similarly, the authors of collections select certain components from the hagiographical traditions surrounding particular saints, and then refashion those components to suit their purposes, appropriating mythical imagery in much the same way as texts such as the *RJC*. In both the hagiographical collections and the later hagiographies from the Swami Rama Tirtha tradition, the saints have been detached from their own specific historical contexts so that the hagiographers may show their lives to be most important insofar as they are relevant to contemporary concerns. Sankara, for example, was a key figure in several collections not so much because of what he did in his own era, but more importantly because he set an example that is presented as applicable to the present age.

While the mediating role that saints play between followers and divinity beyond is well-recognized, the hagiographer's role as mediator between the saint and readers of the hagiography is equally important. Hagiographies are much more than simple accounts of the "lives of saints." As the collections and the Swami Rama Tirtha hagiographical tradition have shown, it is the hagiographer who constructs an image of the saint and presents it to readers; that image is intricately bound up with the hagiographer's own purpose, whether it is to attract new devotees to a saint, or convince others of some religious or political agenda. The saint may show the way to what Puran Singh called "golden lands beyond this physical life" (*SSR*: v), but it is the hagiographer who first sets out the path that readers may follow. The path itself, as we have seen, may change course from one hagiography to another, and what hagiographers hope that readers bring back from their journey on the path to the saint's life changes as well, from the acceptance of the political agendas promoted in some of the collections, to the *RJC*'s image of Swami Rama Tirtha as the *avatār* who set the stage for independent India. To learn more about hagiography's mediating role, we will now turn to specific images that recur throughout the Swami Rama Tirtha hagiographical tradition: the Swami as a poet, the Swami as a nationalist, and finally, the Swami as a "supersaint."

7

Swami Rama Tirtha as Poet, Nationalist, and Supersaint

Reflections on the Role of Experience in Hagiography

The authors of modern hagiographical collections carefully selected images of saints to legitimate their own agendas; now, to highlight further how Swami Rama Tirtha's image has been constructed and reconstructed by his followers in his hagiographies (images which also support particular agendas), we will revisit the tradition as a whole (including not only the hagiographies described in chapter two, but also briefer passages in a hagiographical vein included as introductory material in *IWGR*) to consider two key issues: the Swami as a poet, and as a nationalist. The goal is not to produce a critical assessment of Swami Rama Tirtha as a poet (which is of course to a certain extent a subjective judgement), but rather to examine how the hagiographical tradition itself has assessed his poetry. Similarly, we shall consider how hagiographers have understood the Swami as a nationalist. In this regard, the record of what Swami Rama Tirtha himself wrote about nationalism and patriotism provides a useful basis of comparison for the later interpretations of his stand. The chapter concludes with some final thoughts about the role that the reporting of experience has played in the Swami Rama Tirtha hagiographical tradition.

"Grass and Dry Pebbles": Swami Rama Tirtha's Poetry

In addition to his many essays and lectures, Swami Rama Tirtha composed poems in Urdu, Persian, and English throughout his life,[1] many of which are quoted approvingly in the hagiographical tradition. Yet there is a challenge to overcome for those who praise the Swami's English poetry. When the first edition of *In Woods of God Realization* was published in 1909, Narayan Swami asked C.F. Andrews, a former Anglican missionary (also a disciple of Rabindranath Tagore, and later an admirer of Mahatma Gandhi), to write the introduction. Andrews on the one hand wrote glowingly of the Swami's reputation and further confirmed the importance of the experience of being in Swami Rama Tirtha's presence:

> Many of those with whom I have conversed about him have told me of the innate power which he possessed, a power which moved them profoundly whenever they met and talked with him, a power which took their thoughts away from material things and made them feel, if only for a moment, the reality of spiritual experience. (*IWGR* 1:xxxiii-xxxiv)

But at the same time, Andrews' assessment of Swami Rama Tirtha's lectures and poems was more guarded.

> The Lectures unfortunately have not had the revision of the author himself. He would undoubtedly have altered much, and possibly abbreviated much. He would have corrected also the metrical form of some of his poems, which have clearly been put down on paper as the inspiration to write came to him, without any laboured correction. But while there is considerable loss to the reader on this account, there is also considerable gain; for what is lost in finish and correctness is gained in freshness and vitality. I cannot doubt that the friends of the author were right in tenderly and piously preserving every word of the manuscript before them. The readers will gladly make allowance for repetition and lack of finish, when the individuality of the Swami himself is brought so vividly before them by his manuscript notes. We seem to be talking with him, as we read, and he seems to be talking to us. We feel the Swami himself still present in his words, and can almost picture him speaking. (*IWGR* 1:xxxiv)

Of the Swami's English poems, Andrews commented:

> He is full of happiness himself which he wishes to give to the world, and he is never so happy as when happiness is his subject. It is this also which bubbles over in his poems, waking in others an echo of his own laughter. The outward setting of these poems, as I have already said, may often be crude and even grotesque, but the inner spirit may be caught by the sympathetic reader beneath the imperfect vehicle of expression. (*IWGR* 1:xxxvi)

Andrews continued with a critique of the Swami's Practical Vedānta (*IWGR* 1:xl-xliii); overall, however, he praised the Swami's poetic spirit and his openness to diverse religious beliefs. Yet Andrews chided the Swami for his careless repetition, and termed the setting of his poems "crude and even grotesque." If Andrews' generally positive statements about Swami Rama Tirtha add prestige to his memory, then presumably his critical remarks must be taken seriously as well. Narayan Swami and Amir Chand, the original publishers of *IWGR*, perhaps hoped that Andrews' comments would lend added prestige to the volume, and indeed Andrews' remarks have been included in all subsequent printings of *IWGR*. Though neither Andrews nor subsequent writers set forth in any great detail the specific nature of the perceived flaws in the Swami's poetry, the general criticism seems to have been aimed at metrical inconsistencies, unidiomatic use of English, and repetition, characteristics which are evident to a certain extent in one of the Swami's most frequently quoted poems, "Peace Like a River Flows to Me" (*IWGR* 1:352):

> Peace like a river flows to me,
> Peace as an ocean rolls in me,
> Peace like the Ganga flows,
> It flows from all my hair and toes
> O fetch me quick my wedding robes
> White robes of light, bright rays of gold,
> Slips on, lo! once for all the veil to fling!
> Flow, flow, O wreaths, flow fair and free,
> Flow wreaths of tears of joy, flow free.
> What glorious aureole, wondrous ring.
> O nectar of life! O magic wine.
> To fill my pores of body and mind!
> Come fish, come dogs, come all who please
> Come powers of nature, bird and beast.
> Drink deep my blood my flesh do eat.
> O come, partake of marriage feast
> I dance, I dance with glee
> In stars, in suns, in oceans free,
> In moons and clouds, in winds I dance,
> In will, emotions, mind I dance
> I sing, I sing, I am symphony.
> I'm boundless ocean of Harmony.
> The subject which perceives,
> The object—thing perceived,
> As waves in me they double
> In me the world's a bubble.
> Om!

As the hagiographical tradition has developed, hagiographers have adopted different strategies for dealing with the criticism of the Swami's poetry preserved in his printed works. In the earliest stage of the tradition, the hagiographers took seriously Andrews' negative assessment of the Swami's poetic style. The anonymous author (1912: 18) of the 1912 *Swami Rama Tirath: A Sketch of His Life and Teachings* essentially concurred with Andrews, noting that while there is much that seems uninteresting in the Swami's lectures and poems, those who wade through the "grass and dry pebbles" will nonetheless be rewarded. Like Andrews, he further noted that Swami Rama Tirtha himself had not intended to publish the material in *IWGR*, and most likely would have revised it had he lived longer. Similarly, S.R. Sharma, whose *Swami Rama Tirtha: The Poet Apostle of*

Practical Vedanta was published in 1921, cited Andrews' critique after quoting one of the Swami's poems and further observed (1921: 93-94):

> This is no doubt lacking in the perfection of outward form, as all his writings sadly do; but the soul of poetry is there, and again, as Mr. Andrews has remarked, "what is lost in finish and correctness is gained in freshness and vitality." Had Swami Rama lived a little longer, he would probably have revised all his works that betray the want of a second reading.[2]

Nonetheless, Sharma highlighted the Swami's poetic spirit, and went on to assert that many of his poems are more powerful than some of the greatest classics of Western poetry (1921: 92), e.g. "Tennyson's 'Charge of the Light Brigade' is as nothing when compared with this thunderbolt of poetry."

Both Narayan Swami and Sharga quoted extensively from the Swami's poems; Sharga also translated many of his Urdu poems into English, but in keeping with their allegiance to "bare facts," neither author made any particular comment on the quality of the poetry or Andrews' criticisms. However, in *The Story of Swami Rama*, Puran Singh, himself a highly regarded poet, also concurred with Andrews that the setting of many of the Swami's poems was "crude and grotesque" (*SSR*: 226). Elsewhere he noted that the Swami's thought was "scattered and fragmentary" and that readers would have to be patient when they were unable to follow the Swami's ideas (*IWGR* 1: xix-xx). Nonetheless, Singh clearly thought poetry was a central facet of the Swami's work—the subtitle of his hagiography, after all, is "The Poet Monk of India"—and he added that when he first met the Swami, he "did not know any defect in the form of his poems then" and "drank them literally as draughts of sunlight" (*SSR*: 226). Earlier, in his preface to the first edition of *IWGR* published in 1909, Singh wrote of the Swami, "In these volumes, he appears before us by no means as a literary man and has no desire to be judged as an author, but he comes before us with the majesty of a teacher of the spiritual laws of life" (*IWGR* 1: xx). For Puran Singh, the Swami's immense spiritual power overshadowed any external flaws in his compositions.

In the first stage of the hagiographical tradition, those authors who commented upon the Swami's poetry were willing to be somewhat critical of his poetic style, while nonetheless emphasizing the soaring "poetic nature" that was revealed despite outward defects. To Sharma, the Swami was a "poet apostle" and to Singh he was a "poet monk," yet it was possible to be critical of one aspect of the Swami's work but still present him as a highly accomplished religious leader. Interestingly, no one pointed out that Andrews' comments referred exclusively to the Swami's English poems; English was not the Swami's native tongue, and composing poetry in a foreign language is not easy.

The texts from the second, transitional phase of the hagiographical tradition split in their appraisal of Swami Rama Tirtha's poetry. S.R. Sharma highly praised the Swami's English poetry, and included an entire chapter of his poems in his 1961 *Swami Rama Tirtha* (1961: 66-74). D.R. Sood, however, in his 1970 *Swami Ram Tirth*, followed the assessment of the earlier texts, noting the poor metrical quality of the poems despite their uplifting content (1970: 101). In the hagiographies written in English in the third phase of the hagiographical tradition, however, guarded assessments give way to unabashed encomia as Swami Rama Tirtha emerges as one the greatest poets in Indian history. Nonetheless, the shadow of Andrews' criticism still looms large, as is well-illustrated by two English texts from the third phase, Satish Kumar's 1977 *Swami Rama Tirtha: Great Mystic Poet of the Modern India* (*GMP*), published by the Swami Rama Tirtha Pratishthan, and Prem Lata's 1993 *Life, Teachings and Writings of Swami Rama Tirtha* (*LTW*).

In a brief introductory note to Kumar's study, R.K. Lal, then the Assistant Secretary of the Swami Rama Tirtha Pratishthan, commended the text to "the lovers of Rama's works" and expressed the wish that it would create further interest in the Swami's poetry "which by all standards, is of very high order from literary standpoint" (*GMP*: i). Kumar himself presented his work as a corrective, arguing that the Swami's "poetical aspect" had not been sufficiently highlighted. The cover of the text includes not only Kumar's name, but his position as a professor of English at K.N. Government College in Varanasi, thereby lending authority to his assessment of the Swami's English poems (which are the primary focus of his work). In his preface, Kumar wrote:

> In this monograph, I have made a humble attempt to bring to light the beauty and sublimity of his charming lyrics which were composed in the tranquil atmosphere of the Garhwal Himalayas. His poems, composed both in English and Urdu, are words of infinite religious passion and are pregnant with the precious pearls of his wisdom. Indeed, he is one of the greatest mystical poets of India. (*GMP*: iii-iv)

Throughout his brief text, Kumar lavished praise on the Swami's poetry, asserting that "he composed poetry as easily and as effortlessly as birds sing" and "possessed the gift of communicating his emotions and feelings to his readers in lucid, clear, graceful and highly effective language" (*GMP*: 3-4). Kumar termed the Swami's poems "sublime," exhibiting a "matchless freshness and spontaneity" that made him comparable to western poets such as Shelley. While Kumar did not directly challenge the assessment of earlier hagiographers such as Puran Singh, he made clear that he believed there had not as yet been a proper appreciation of the Swami's poetry, and R.K. Lal's introduction supported this contention. While the earlier hagiographers' assessment of the Swami's poetry was confined to general terms and did not address specific poems, Kumar highlighted particular passages such as the following, with the comment, "how artistically he uses oxymoron in the following lines":

> The soundless sound, the flameless light
> The darkless dark and wingless flight
> The mindless thought, the eyeless sight
> The mouthless thought, the handless grasp so tight.
> Am I, am I, am I. (*GMP*: 21)

Kumar's relatively detailed study of the Swami's poetry is not a critical analysis as such; rather, as in the above example, he quoted particular passages and made assertions about them. Kumar was fully aware of C.F. Andrews' critique of the Swami's poetry, and indeed he quoted Andrews' statement about the "crude and grotesque" setting of some of the poetry. While Kumar acquiesced to Andrews's critique, everything else about his narrative suggests that in fact he did not agree with it. Rather than directly challenging Andrews, his strategy was to present evidence that he believed would in and of itself belie Andrews' assessment. Kumar concluded with the bold assertion that "the poetic vision of Swami Rama Tirtha can save humanity and human civilisation from the ruin, utter and irretrievable which has been staring at them . . . He is a poet not for an age, but for all ages" (*GMP*: 25). In a brief introductory essay for the ninth reprinting of the second volume of *IWGR* in 1978, Radha Kamal Mukherjee was equally effusive (with no reference to Andrews' comments): "Swami Rama is modern India's greatest poet-mystic . . . How beautifully he has expressed himself":

> It is I that appear as beautiful flowers in the garden. It is I that smile with the bewitching face of all the fairies. It is I that make the muscles of the warriors that fight. I am the all. I shine in the lightning; I roar in the thunder; I flutter in the leaves; I hiss in the winds; I roll in the surging seas; I am in the throbbing breast of the lover; I am also in the smile of the proud beloved. (*IWGR 2*:xxiii)

After quoting these lines, Mukherjee noted, "these are words of infinite passion and bliss, reminiscent of the profound poetry of the Upanishads and yet possessing a freshness and spontaneity that make these a remarkable contribution to the religious experience of humanity" (*IWGR* 2: xxiii). For both Kumar and Mukherjee, the Swami's poetry clearly ranked among India's finest religious expression, its vision capable of no less than saving civilization from utter ruin.

In her *Life, Teachings and Writings of Swami Rama Tirtha* (*LTW*), Prem Lata was more openly critical of Andrews as she glowingly praised the Swami's poetry. Opening her chapter on the Swami's poetry by quoting Andrews' comments, she went on to assert that Puran Singh had disagreed with Andrews's criticisms, thereby implying that the criticism of the Swami came only from a misguiged outsider, and not from followers of the Swami. This is a misreading of Singh; he had argued that when he first heard the Swami's poems, he did not notice the defects in meter because he did not then know any better, and it was only later that he realized (like Andrews) that the poems had formal problems. Despite this misreading, Lata's overall defense of the Swami's poetry is more sophisticated than Kumar's. To counter the challenge that Swami Rama Tirtha's poems were metrically flawed, she wrote:

> Rama Tirtha's poems were mostly written in Urdu while he was in India. While in America he wrote them in English. He made use of rhyme and metre. But this was rare, and could not be long continued, for the effusions of his heart could not be confined within any rigid frame. So later he wrote in Urdu in free verse without rhyme and metre. Thus he was a versatile poet writing in the old style of Keats and Shelley as well as in the modern one like that of Walt Whitman, T.S. Eliot, Robert Frost and so forth. The main difference between the old and the modern style is that while in the former there is rhyme and metre, the present trend is to dispense with both. (*LTW*: 144)

Thus for Lata, when Swami Rama Tirtha wrote rhymed English poetry, he attempted to stay within the rigid boundaries of metrical consistency, but his poetic spirit broke free from such artificial constraints. As such, his poetry exemplified a more modern style comparable to that of noted Western poets such as Walt Whitman and Robert Frost. Placing the Swami among modern poets noted for their departure from traditional styles, Lata artfully maneuvered around Andrews' criticism of the Swami's metrical inconsistencies, hinting that Andrews did not recognize the modern nature of the Swami's poetry and instead judged it against outdated standards. Lest anyone counter that the Swami sought only to match the works of Western poets, Lata subsequently argued that the Swami expressed himself even better in his Urdu poetry (a further challenge to Andrews, who wrote only about the Swami's English poetry) (*LTW*: 48). Thus while the earliest hagiographers were comfortable with the idea that not everything about Swami Rama Tirtha was perfect, later hagiographers clearly were not, and made increasingly grand assertions about his poetic gifts.

Narayan Swami, who was so uneasy with Puran Singh's characterization of the Swami as a man of doubts, was nonetheless willing to publish C.F. Andrews's remarks which included his critical assessment of Swami Rama Tirtha's poetry and other writings. Similarly, the Swami Rama Tirtha Pratishthan has not in any way edited those remarks in subsequent English editions of *IWGR*. Interestingly, the assessment of the Swami's poetry is the only issue on which the English hagiographies and the Hindi and Urdu hagiographies differ. Nearly all the English hagiographies which make any mention of the Swami's poetry address Andrews' comments in some fashion. With one exception,[3] however, the authors of the Hindi texts of the later phase of the hagiographical tradition make no mention of Andrews' comments, even though many of them clearly used some of the English hagiographies, as well as the Swami's English writings, as source material for their works. This may well reflect the authors' perceptions regarding their intended audiences; while readers of the English texts might either already be aware of Andrews' comments in the English *IWGR*, or be likely to encounter them if the hagiography itself inspired them to study the Swami and his works further, many Hindi readers would be less likely to know that Andrews found the Swami's poetic style lacking. Indeed in Din Dayalu's Hindi translation of Puran Singh's *Story of Swami Rama*, the chapter on Swami Rama Tirtha's poetry is the only one in which Dayalu did not closely follow Singh's text. Whereas Singh's original English chapter opened with several lengthy quotations from Andrews' critique, Dayalu's rendering of the chapter begins not with Andrews' remarks, but by expressing how rare it is for an individual to be talented not only in scientific pursuits, but also literary arts such as poetry. Only after several such paragraphs (which bear no relation to Singh's English text) did Dayalu (1982: 310-311) introduce Andrews, reducing what in Singh's English were two full pages of quotation to a few lines that paraphrase Andrews, highlighting his admiration for the Swami's poetic spirit which shone through even occasional defects in outward form. The poems which follow were selected from among Swami Rama Tirtha's Urdu poems, and are not Hindi translations of his English poems. Thus Dayalu's translation of Puran Singh, presumably the most likely avenue for the critical assessment of the Swami's poetry to enter the Hindi hagiographical tradition, muted any hint of criticism.

On the whole, the hagiographical tradition's treatment of Swami Rama Tirtha as a poet follows the same trends that are evidenced in its treatment of the events of his life. Hagiographers from the earliest stage of the tradition such as Puran Singh and S.R. Sharma freely acknowledged problems with Swami Rama Tirtha's poetic style, and noted reasonably enough that it was perhaps unfair to judge the Swami too harshly since he never had the opportunity to revise his works for publication. Such flaws did not in any way diminish their perception of him as a remarkable saint. While both the earlier and later hagiographers could conceivably have ignored C.F. Andrews' criticisms of Swami Rama Tirtha's poetry, all the hagiographers writing in English included Andrews' remarks in their own characterizations of the Swami's poetry. It is quite possible that criticism of the Swami's poetic style would have made its way into the tradition even if Andrews had not written what he did; Sood, for example, one of the hagiographers from the second phase of the tradition, commented upon problems with Swami Rama Tirtha's use of meter without making direct reference to Andrews' similar critique.

In both the English and Hindi/Urdu hagiographies of the third phase of the tradition, hagiographers presented Swami Rama Tirtha in a more mythical framework, effacing any hints of doubts or imperfections in the Swami's life; similarly, they were reluctant to suggest any imperfections in the Swami's poetry and other compositions. The Hindi and Urdu texts from the third phase simply left aside the question of the Swami's English poetry (and his tendency towards repetition evidenced throughout all his writings), but the English texts from this phase take Andrews to task. Satish Kumar and Prem Lata both saw the need to explain a reference to an apparent imperfection—flawed poetry—in the Swami's life, an imperfection seemingly acknowledged by the Swami Rama Tirtha Pratishthan itself, which has reprinted Andrews' introduction many times.

None of the assessments of Swami Rama Tirtha's poetic style from any of the phases of the hagiographical tradition is based upon a sustained analysis of the poetry itself; rather, the assessments are largely impressionistic. The authority on which the authors base their critiques is their own reactions—their own experiences in reading the Swami's poetry and other works. While we may distinguish between the nature of the experience of the Swami's life by those who knew him personally, and those who met him only through the medium of hagiographies, the Swami's writings present the opportunity for a direct experience of sorts, although that experience is filtered through the tradition as a whole. Kumar and Lata did not simply react to the Swami's poetry; their assessment of it was tempered by the various preexisting interpretations of the Swami's poetry in the hagiographical tradition. Still, Kumar's and Lata's assessments of Swami Rama Tirtha's poetry were built upon their own reading experiences, and those experiences served as their ultimate authority, which allowed them to challenge implicitly the authority of the earlier assessments of writers such as Singh and Sharma, and create new images of the Swami as a great poet. Their strategy stands in contrast to that of the *RJC*, which used the earlier hagiographies as a base but did not directly challenge their reporting of events (though of course the dramatically different portrayal of the Swami in the *RJC* constitutes an indirect challenge). Writing about their own experiences reading the Swami's poetry, Kumar and Lata used the authority of that direct experience to question the earlier hagiographers, and cloaked their pronouncements with the further authority of their position as citizens of modern, independent India. From that perspective, C.F. Andrews, a Christian missionary, serves as an example of the western colonial critique of Indian culture. What Kumar and Lata suggest is that Singh, Sharma and others writing during the colonial era could not help but be swayed by Andrews' influence, but are redeemed by their clear devotion to the Swami. It remained for authors such as Kumar and Lata to make what they considered definitive assessments from the vantage point of independent, modern India; we may recall that Kumar termed Swami Rama Tirtha the great mystic poet of "modern India." Just as the *RJC* showed that the Swami was an *avatār* whose life could be relevant to young Indians in the late twentieth century, so too did Kumar and Lata suggest that his poetry was still relevant and worthy of attention, even more than his earlier hagiographers could recognize.

Thus the hagiographical tradition has continued to employ a dynamic interaction between "history" and "myth" not only in its narratives about the Swami's life, but also in those about his compositions. The tradition itself has recorded that many of the Swami's earliest followers found his English poetry awkward and his lectures repetitive and even difficult to follow; their assessment constitutes a "historical fact" about followers' perceptions of the Swami. The later hagiographical tradition, however, has moved towards making Swami Rama Tirtha into an idealized, flawless figure, a portrayal grounded in the authority of mythical imagery (as exemplified by the *RJC*). The idealized Swami Rama Tirtha could not have composed "bad" poetry (nor would he have wanted to revise his work, as earlier hagiographers suggested); indeed to Kumar he was one of the greatest poets of all time. This mythicization of the Swami as great poet, however, is built in part upon a critique of the historical circumstances which led to the negative assessments of his work. A product of colonial India who traveled to the English-speaking United States, Swami Rama Tirtha often expressed himself in English, and was thereby constrained by the formal conventions of English poetics. Yet for his hagiographers, his expansive poetic spirit could not help but break free from such artificial constraints, and he produced poetry which on the surface might seem flawed by conventional standards (those of the English-speaking west), but would reveal itself as completely transcending such conventions only to later hagiographers such as Kumar and Lata who wrote not as colonial subjects (such as Puran Singh), but as citizens of independent India who had made English their own and had their own standards for assessing English poetry.

None of the later hagiographers could challenge the fact of the earlier hagiographers authoritative, first-hand personal experience of Swami Rama Tirtha, but the fact that the Swami's published works create the opportunity for ongoing direct experience (although that experience is mediated by the tradition as a whole) has meant that later writers such as Kumar and Lata could directly critique the earlier hagiographers (who were critical of the Swami's poems) in a way not possible when they wrote about particular events in the Swami's life. It is also worth noting the genre of hagiography in late twentieth-century India has appropriated the rhetoric of other genres as well. Lata and Kumar both adopted the language and some of the trappings of scholarly analysis, even though their presentations of the Swami's poetry were not methodologically rigorous from a scholarly standpoint. Clearly, however, these authors believed that a "scholarly style" itself would lend further authority to their work, even though the primary basis for their work was still their experience of the Swami's poetry, which they presented as assertions rather than sustained arguments. A similar tendency was exhibited in hagiographical collections, in which a pseudo-scholarly style of presentation served as part of the authors' rhetorical style. Just as new images of Swami Rama Tirtha's life in the hagiographical tradition were based upon followers' changing experiences of that life, so too the new image of him as a master poet came not from new insights into the form of the poetry itself, but from new experiences of it. Those experiences themselves were likely shaped by the new hagiographical images of Swami Rama Tirtha; an *avatār*, it seems, simply cannot write bad poetry.

Swami Rama Tirtha as Nationalist and Prophet of Independent India

If Swami Rama Tirtha's transformation from a less-than-perfect poet into the greatest poet-mystic of modern India is striking, then even more remarkable is the later hagiographical tradition's transformation of the Swami into not only a great Indian nationalist, but into the figure who first prophesied and set in motion the forces that led to India's independence from the British, a trend earlier exemplified in the *RJC*. Radha Kamal Mukherjee (affiliated with the SRTP) directly linked these two trends by relating the Swami's status as a poet to his nationalism: "The poet-mystic, as he turns to the affairs of men, shows a clarity of vision for the future and stress of the fundamentals for ethical and social renovation which the country must lay to heart" (*IWGR* 2:xxv). By suggesting that Indians imagine themselves at one with their country, Mukherjee argued, Swami Rama Tirtha added a new dimension to nationalism; his poetic "vision for the future" made him into a prophet. "Such is the spiritual transformation of Indian nationalism rooted in God-consciousness which is the poet mystic's great contribution to India's political consciousness" (*IWGR* 2:xxv). In Mukherjee's reckoning, Swami Rama Tirtha was one among a class of great poet-mystics who added a necessary spiritual dimension to India's political life. While Mukherjee's presentation of the Swami was based on the idea that his nationalist sentiment was a natural outgrowth of his poetic nature, other hagiographers have made even grander claims about the nature of Swami Rama Tirtha's role in the Indian independence movement.

The Swami lived during the early days of the Indian independence movement, though he died long before India became an independent nation in 1947. As noted in chapter three, his position on Indian nationalism was a source of contention between Puran Singh and Narayan Swami, and it has since become the most important question in the hagiographical tradition. Since 1947, many Indians have viewed the history of much of the nineteenth and all of the twentieth century through the lens of nationalism, and India's attainment of independence on August 15, 1947 stands as the defining moment in its recent history. Modern Indian historiography champions those who fought for independence. As fundamental issues in twentieth-century Indian consciousness, nationalism and independence inevitably came into play in the hagiographical tradition as well.

Yet just as was the case with his poetry, there are potential problems with Swami Rama Tirtha's record on Indian nationalism. In his personal notebooks (in which the Swami wrote primarily in English, but also Urdu, Persian, Hindi, and Sanskrit), there are a number of entries (unfortunately undated) which suggest that he was quite skeptical of the nationalist movement and particularly the efficacy of the leaders of the Indian National Congress:

> Timid, prudent National Congress people! The cruel death of one of the speakers in the name of nationality can do far more to unite the nation than thousands of lectures by all the members put together. (*IWGR* 7:228)

In other notebook entries, he was even more cynical:

> The political agitators of India have practically the following position:—"The English are making fools of themselves, why should not we follow the example?" (*IWGR* 7:90)

> The fall of a family man is to sensuous life and that of a God-man is to patriotism. (*IWGR* 7:248)

To be sure, Swami Rama Tirtha often spoke publicly of his desire to see his country free, yet he chose not to become directly involved in any sort of organization, including those with political goals; he did not want to "fall" to patriotism. His followers, however, have downplayed the Swami's misgivings. Only Puran Singh suggested that when the Swami spoke of nationalism, it "rang hollow," but such comments were among the reasons that Narayan Singh commissioned a new hagiography, for Narayan Swami saw Swami Rama Tirtha as a patriot of the highest order. And despite the ongoing popularity of Puran Singh's *The Story of Swami Rama*, the one area in which subsequent hagiographers have challenged him has been his statements about the Swami's indifference to the nationalist cause.

The Prediction: Swami Rama Tirtha's Nationalism and the Swami Rama Tirtha Pratishthan

The impulse to make the Swami into a nationalist may be dated even earlier than the first hagiographies, and it has been a persistent theme throughout the publications of the Swami Rama Tirtha Pratishthan. In his 1913 English introduction to what was originally the fourth volume of *IWGR* (its contents are now part of the third volume), Amir Chand sought to correct what he saw as an oversight in many of the comments about Swami Rama Tirtha that appeared in the press after his death: the fact that no one had noted that the Swami was not just a spiritual teacher, but a great patriot as well.

> But the striking personality of our Rama does not appeal to me only as a great spiritual teacher. He appeals to me, impresses me, forcibly strikes me as a genuine, sincere and devoted patriot, a true lover of 'India, the Motherland,' a true and worthy son of *Bharat*, the *janmabhumi* [homeland] of great sages, seers and savants, of *Rishis* and *Munis*, ascetics and *yogis* as well as of the greatest warriors, rulers, and heroes; a devoted and faithful *Sevak* [servant] of the holy *Aryavarta* and a martyr to the cause of the country. He has clearly taught us our National *Dharma* and his utterances inspire us with a sense of the great responsibility we owe to our Motherland as the inheritors of a great and historic past. (*IWGR* 3:xv)

Soon after writing this introduction, Amir Chand, who had never met Swami Rama Tirtha (but learned about him from Narayan Swami), was hanged for his alleged role in a bombing plot against Lord Hardinge, then the Viceroy of India. Subsequent writers have not commented directly upon Amir Chand's portrayal of the Swami as a patriot and martyr to the cause of his country, or his linking of the Swami not only to sages and savants, but also warriors and rulers. But Amir Chand was by no means the last commentator to see in Swami Rama Tirtha not only a religious leader, but a patriot as well.

Many of the hagiographical portrayals of the Swami as a patriot hinge upon a crucial prediction attributed to him. The prediction, dated January 1, 1900, opens the ninth edition (1978) of the first volume of *IWGR*[4] :

> Whether working through many souls or alone, Rama seriously promises to infuse true life and dispel darkness and weakness from India within ten years; and within the first half of the twentieth century, India will be restored to more than its original glory. Let these words be recorded. (*IWGR* 1:iii)

Various other versions of the prediction appear in other publications of the Swami Rama Tirtha Pratishthan, including the version in the *RJC*. The source of this prediction (and whether it was originally in English or Urdu) is unclear. Early in 1900, Swami Rama Tirtha was still known by his family name of Tirath Ram (although the quote is attributed to "Swami Rama"); he was then becoming increasingly interested in Vedānta. Narayan (not yet a Swami) had become a close friend, and indeed he later provided the only firsthand account in his Urdu narrative of this phase of the Swami's life, when he "almost always stayed with him night and day" (*KeR* 2:207). If anyone were likely to know what Tirath Ram might have said on January 1, 1900, it is Narayan Swami. According to him, Tirath Ram fell gravely ill with fever at the end of 1899, and as we saw in chapter three, when Tirath Ram finally regained consciousness, he made a portentous statement to Narayan which Narayan later recorded. Narayan's full Urdu account of Tirath Rama's statement is worth considering here; it is not fully quoted or translated in any of the subsequent hagiographies.

> "Look Narayan, India's fortune may soon awaken, now that health has shown its face to Rama once more. My mind is full of countless issues and opinions. Who knows, maybe I've recovered so that these issues and opinions should be put in writing [*qalamband*]. If I write all these things, but they don't reach the public, then it is possible that this body [i.e. Tirath Ram's body] will once more take to bed, and instead of serving the people of India [*bhāratvarṣ ke nivāsiyõ*], make its way to the next world. So it is better that we make some sort of arrangements to put my thoughts into writing and reach people." (*KeR* 2:207)

This request led to the publication of the journal *Alif*; according to Narayan Swami, the first issue appeared early in 1900. In neither Narayan's account, nor the original Urdu essay entitled "*Ānand*" (*KeR* 1:3-65; translated in *IWGR* 5:82-119 as "Anand or Eternal-Bliss") which was the first issue of *Alif*, does any sort of prediction for India's freedom appear. Rather, according to Narayan Swami, Tirath Ram had concluded that he needed to make his thoughts known publicly in order to help Indians, but not necessarily to secure political independence.

If Tirath Ram indeed made on January 1, 1900 the prediction that the SRTP attributes to him, it seems likely that Narayan Swami would have either been present for it, or at least heard about it, and included some report of it in his own text. However, the prediction does not appear within the body of any of the Swami's published essays, lectures, or notebooks, and it is not found in any of the earliest hagiographies. Of course for the earliest texts, published before 1947, such a prediction would not have had the same resonance. A further inspiration for the prediction may have been a brief anecdote Puran Singh related from the last months of Swami Rama Tirtha's life in 1906. The Swami had apparently received a letter warning him that the Indian police were after him, "suspecting him to be a great nationalist who wished to subvert the British Government." Puran Singh's tone suggests that he found such suspicions unconvincing; according to him, Swami Rama Tirtha's response to the letter was:

> "Tell them I do not defend myself. They may treat me as they like. I cannot be other than what I am. I wish as an Indian that my country should be free. Free it shall be one day, but whether this Rama secures its freedom or a thousand other Ramas, no one knows." (*SSR*: 164)

Narayan Swami did mention rumors regarding possible police surveillance, but not Swami Rama Tirtha's response (*KeR* 2:288); Sharga's account (*LSRT*: 375) of the same period directly cited Puran Singh. Din Dayalu's Hindi translation of this passage of Puran Singh's text is fairly literal (1982: 229), so the prediction was not introduced through translation. Perhaps the reference in Puran Singh's text to either "Rama" or a "thousand other Ramas" became the basis for the notion of the Swami "working through many souls or alone" and the passage that Puran Singh dates to 1906 was somehow transformed into the prediction of January 1, 1900. Surely the choice of date is not insignificant; it leaves us to imagine a young Swami Rama Tirtha regaining consciousness at the end of the nineteenth century to make a momentous prediction to usher in the twentieth. Whatever its source or authenticity, however, in the publications of the SRTP, the prediction was to become a central feature of subsequent portrayals of Swami Rama Tirtha as a nationalist.

Rameshwar Sahai Sinha cited the prediction in his 1957 English introduction to the third volume of *IWGR*, "Lessons from Rama's Message." Sinha was a close follower of Narayan Swami, was long associated with the SRTP, and was also active in politics. Sinha dated the prediction to 1901, and his quotation of it reads slightly differently than the one that appears in *IWGR* 1, which suggests that multiple versions of the prediction may have circulated orally among the Swami's followers. His interpretation of the prediction marks the beginning of a trend to see Swami Rama Tirtha not simply as one of many great Indian nationalists, but as the figure primarily responsible for independence.

> He was a Vedantin, he was Jiwan-Mukta [liberated in life], but with all that he was a patriot to the core of his heart. But his method of service was unique. As

> early as 1901, he exclaimed, "Whether working through many souls or alone, Rama seriously promises to infuse true life and dispel darkness and weakness from India within ten years; and within the first half of the twentieth century, India will be restored to more than its original glory. Let these words be recorded." Now this promise, singular as it is, is not certainly the foresight of a politician, nor the prophecy of a sooth-sayer, nor the figment of a mystic mind. It was the serious promise of a realized soul and hence executed with full responsibility to the very letter thereof according to his own viewpoint. (*IWGR* 3:x)

Sinha's interpretation of the prediction serves two purposes: first, it makes Swami Rama Tirtha the primary mover behind India's independence, and second, it explains why nonetheless he apparently did not participate actively in the independence movement. Sinha suggested instead that as a realized soul, Swami Rama Tirtha could not only foresee but could also effect the future, and fully confident in his abilities, he made the promise that India would become free within fifty years. Those who actually took part in political organizations and other mass movements were working at a lower level; beyond them, Swami Rama Tirtha orchestrated the entire process. Sinha's presentation of Swami Rama Tirtha's nationalism thus follows the trend typical of the later hagiographical tradition. His characterization is based on the historical reality of the fact that the Swami had little to say on the subject of nationalism, but his interpretive mechanism for explaining that fact involves mythicization as exemplified by his assertion that it was Swami Rama Tirtha himself who actually brought about India's independence. Sinha further linked this interpretation to the paucity of specific religious instructions in Swami Rama Tirtha's Indian lectures, another potentially troubling "fact":

> Thus we find in his American lectures on India suggestions from his own Vedantic view-point practically on every walk of life which hold good even to-day. But when he returned home from his foreign tour he did not lay very much stress on them. Who knows why? Perhaps he saw with his clear vision that unless and until the country was not made free from foreign yoke, nothing substantial could be achieved in any sphere of life by way of real progress. (*IWGR* 3:ix)

According to Sinha, so great was Swami Rama Tirtha's desire to bring about independence that he placed it above providing instructions to his devotees in India. Sinha thus answered the critic who might comment that for an inspirational religious leader hailed as a great exemplar, Swami Rama Tirtha had little by way of specific instructions for his followers. Sinha's comment illustrates wonderfully the tendency for a saint's devotees to place more emphasis on the saint's person rather than his teachings, for the simpler answer to the question of why Swami Rama Tirtha gave so few specific instructions may be found in the Swami's teachings themselves—the notion that people must find their own paths rather than blindly follow someone else's instructions was a major tenet of his Practical Vedānta. That Sinha chose not to interpret the Swami's lack of instructions in a way that would be consistent with the Swami's own writings further demonstrates that the hagiographical image of Swami Rama Tirtha as a great nationalist had long since eclipsed the image the Swami himself presented.[5]

In 1957, Rameshwar Sahai Sinha's reading of the alleged prediction was the basis for his characterization of Swami Rama Tirtha as the guiding hand behind the entire independence movement; more recently, Ayodhia Nath (author of the introduction to the 1989 *RJC*) took that line of reasoning even further. In a 1979 English preface to a reprinting of the third volume of *IWGR*, Nath cited yet another version of the prediction:

> [Swami Rama Tirtha] had said, "I wish, as an Indian, that my country should be free and free it shall be one day, without doubt, within the first half of the 20th century." His order that India shall be free by the middle of this century was implicitly obeyed by Nature and, as we all know, India did achieve freedom from the bondage of the foreign rulers within the period, as ordered by Rama. (*IWGR* 3:xxxiv)

Then, in a 1982 English preface to a reprinting of the fourth volume of *IWGR*, Nath further extended the range of Swami Rama Tirtha's influence:

> To my mind, it is due to the stirring and inspiring works of Rama and his Divine-Wish that not only India but also other subject nations of the world have been winning freedom from year to year and developing a broader outlook of universalism, as compared to their earlier narrow parochialism. In this connection, I feel pleasure in inviting our readers' attention to the fact that India was more or less the first nation to achieve political independence, exactly within the stipulated period, as was ordered by Rama, half a century before her actual freedom from the bondage of the British rule or misrule. (*IWGR* 4:i-ii)

Nath thus directly linked not only Indian independence, but the end of colonial rule in other nations to the Swami's "divine wish" or prediction.

According to a 1988 publication of the Swami Rama Tirtha Pratishthan, the Hindi *Swāmī Rāmtīrth kī Saṅkṣipt Jīvanī* [A Brief Life of Swami Rama Tirtha] by Din Dayalu, Swami Rama Tirtha was in Darjeeling in 1900 when he made the prediction [*bhaviṣyavāṇī*], although in 1900 Swami Rama Tirtha was still known as Tirath Ram, and he did not go to Darjeeling until several years later.[6] The prediction, though its form and date vary, has become a central feature of the Swami Rama Tirtha Pratishthan's presentation of the Swami.[7] The officials of the Swami Rama Tirtha Pratishthan have actively promoted the image of Swami Rama Tirtha as the primary force behind India's independence in their introductions to the various volumes and reprintings of *IWGR*, the Swami's collected works, and their other publications. From the perspective of the SRTP, the accuracy and precision of the Swami's prediction (he did not simply predict that India would someday become free, but that it would become free within fifty years) lends credence to their assertion that it was Swami Rama Tirtha alone who showed the proper path to success for independent India.

Skepticism in the Second Phase of the Hagiographical Tradition

Officials of the Swami Rama Tirtha Pratishthan apparently first cited the Swami's prediction of independence in the 1950s (the first decade of India's independence), and have continued to elaborate on it. However, not all of Swami Rama Tirtha's hagiographers have accepted this image of the Swami as the chief architect of Indian nationalism. The two texts of the second phase of the hagiographical tradition (neither of which are publications of the Swami Rama Tirtha Pratishthan) make much less dramatic claims. In his 1961 *Swami Rama Tirtha*, published by Bharatiya Vidya Bhavan, S.R. Sharma painted Swami Rama Tirtha as a patriot, but made no reference to the prediction. More important for Sharma was the assertion that Swami Rama Tirtha's patriotism dated to his teen years, and was not the result of Japanese or American influence, a position he documented with direct quotes from the Swami's writings (1961: 57). He further criticized Puran Singh for mistrusting the Swami's nationalist fervor (1961: 54-55). Even more skeptical about Swami Rama Tirtha's nationalism was D.R. Sood, whose 1970 *Swami Ram Tirth* was published as part of the National Book Trust's "National Biography Series." In his foreword to the text, B.V. Keskar proclaimed Swami Rama Tirtha a "modern yogi and Sufi" whose life was included in the National Biography Series because of his message of national brotherhood, even though he was "not great in political or national activities." Sood constructed an image of the Swami which highlighted his regard for all religions, rather than making any claims about his role in the nationalist movement. In his account of the Swami's life, like Sharma, he explicitly steered away from "mythicizing" claims. In discussing the various claims about Tirath Ram's horoscope, for example, he noted (1970: 1-2), "sometimes the events in the life of a great man are read back and given the shape of legends or astrological predictions." Later, he pointed out (1970: 61) that while one of Swami Rama Tirtha's admirers had once suggested that he establish an organization for nation-building, the Swami had no desire to do so.[8] Both Sharma and Sood were skeptical about increasingly "mythical" portrayals of the Swami that were then circulating. Writing in 1961, Sharma (1961: 89) recognized the general tendency among saints' followers to claim their saints as *avatārs* and miracle-workers. He believed that Swami Rama Tirtha's followers would not claim him as a prophet or *avatār* because "there was no equivocation or ambiguity in whatever he said." Yet Sharma also indicated (1961: 91-92) that already there were those who considered the Swami to have been a great healer, even though this came about through "no fault" of the Swami himself.

The texts from this second, transitional phase of the hagiographical tradition indicate that the "mythologizing" tendency was already at work in people's memories of Swami Rama Tirtha (and that some, even avowed followers of the Swami such as Sharma, resisted it). Sood was aware of embellished versions of the predictions surrounding Tirath Ram's horoscope, and Sharma knew that people considered Swami Rama Tirtha a miraculous healer. Yet both Sood and Sharma rejected such claims. The second phase of the hagiographical tradition, then, seems in part to have addressed traditions circulating among Swami Rama Tirtha's followers that had not yet appeared in hagiographical texts. Thus before the resurgence of interest in Swami Rama Tirtha and the flurry of new hagiographies in the 1970s and 1980s, there were two disparate trends in the hagiographical tradition. The publications of the Swami Rama Tirtha Pratishthan included increasingly elaborate claims about the Swami's role in the Indian nationalist movement, and reflected a tendency towards mythicization. In contrast, Sharma's text published by the Bharatiya Vidya Bhavan, and Sood's contribution to the National Biography Series instead attempted a more sober assessment of the Swami as nationalist. That Sood and Sharma both challenged the mythicization that was already taking place suggests that it is not necessarily an automatic development in a hagiographical tradition, and that hagiographers themselves are to some degree aware of the process of mythicization. Arguably, Sharma and Sood may well have been making an attempt to arrest the mythicization process, and move instead towards historically oriented critical biographies. Sood, for example, clearly relied heavily upon Narayan Swami's untitled Urdu hagiography (a compendium of "bare facts"), to which few other hagiographers had referred either before or since. While both Sood and Sharma referred to the power of being in Swami Rama Tirtha's presence, neither highlighted experience in quite the same way as Puran Singh had done earlier, or as the *RJC* did later. Yet both texts relied primarily upon the earlier hagiographies for their information (although with some skepticism), and used an organizational model which presented the Swami's life as the life of a saint whose greatness was evident from his earliest childhood.

Each text reflects the institutional agenda of its publisher: the Bharatiya Vidya Bhavan, which promotes a particular version of "Indian" culture, and the National Biography Series, which chronicles figures deemed important for the modern Indian nation, agendas which are both different from that of the Swami Rama Tirtha Pratishthan, whose primary goal is to attract new followers of the Swami. To what extent Sharma's and Sood's books contributed to the resurgence of interest in Swami Rama Tirtha in the 1970s and 1980s in unclear; in any case, their "demythologizing" approach did not persist.

India's Heritage of Sainthood: The Third Phase of the Hagiographical Tradition

The Swami Rama Tirtha Pratishthan was by no means unique in its increasingly grand claims about the Swami's role in the Indian nationalist movement. The hagiographies from the third phase of the tradition, composed mostly in Hindi, are based upon an implicit conception of the heritage of the Indian nation, a heritage which is understood to be primarily Hindu though it may incorporate Buddhism, Jainism, and sometimes Islam or Christianity. Although the current independent Indian state dates only to 1947, this notion of Indian heritage views all prior Indian history as the history of the Indian nation. In the third phase hagiographies, saints serve as an important part of the heritage of India. Though they came from different regions, different eras, and held different theological positions, as saints they helped bind together the diverse Indian nation. Hagiographers in this phase place Swami Rama Tirtha amidst a constellation of other saints associated with Vedānta ranging from the ninth century Sankara to Ramakrishna and Swami Vivekananda. These saints are also identified by their region (Swami Rama Tirtha from Punjab, Ramakrishna and Swami Vivekananda from Bengal), suggesting that each state in modern India contributed something to the national heritage. The hagiographers explicitly link these saints' ideas (including Sankara's) about Vedānta to nationalism, suggesting that India has for centuries maintained a tradition of nationalism based in Vedānta which may now serve as the basis for the independent Indian state.

The third phase hagiographers most commonly compared Swami Rama Tirtha to his better-known contemporary Swami Vivekananda, who addressed the World's Parliament of Religions in Chicago in 1893, and founded the Ramakrishna Mission to perform social service in memory of his teacher Ramakrishna. Some hagiographers simply noted that Swami Rama Tirtha was like Swami Vivekananda[9]; others made more detailed comparisons. In his 1974 *Jīvan Carit Swāmī Rāmatīrtha* (published both in Hindi and in Urdu), Sivanath

Ram Taskin [Śivanāth Rāy Taskīn] (1974: 121-122) argued that while Swami Vivekananda was a more important nation-builder than Swami Rama Tirtha, Swami Rama Tirtha nonetheless had all the qualifications to become a great nation-builder and would have done so had he lived longer. Similarly, according to Raj Kumar Arora's 1978 English text, *Swami Ram Tirath: His Life and Works* (1978: 108):

> The two Swamis, Vivekananda and Ram Tirtha, the great conquerors and the athletes of God expounded the universal and eternal principles of Indian philosophy, called the Vedānta, in India as well as abroad. The son of Bengal utilised logic and the force of his irrefutable reasoning to captivate his audience, while the mystic of Punjab let loose fountains of divine love to cast a magnetic spell on his hearers.

Thus to Arora both Swami Vivekananda and Swami Rama Tirtha were teaching the same philosophy, though with different methods. Especially important is the fact that both taught not only in India, but abroad, spreading the "universal and eternal principles of Indian philosophy." Travelling to spread Vedānta also links these two swamis to Sankara, who, according to the hagiographical tradition surrounding him, traveled to each corner of India to establish Vedantic learning. Inderjit's Urdu text, *Swāmī Rām Tīrtha* (1976: 3), explicitly compared Sankara's tours through the Indian subcontinent to Swami Rama Tirtha's travels: both lived only thirty-three years, and both traveled to spread Vedānta, but while Sankara confined his activities to India, Swami Rama Tirtha traveled to Japan, the United States, and Egypt.

Hagiographers not only linked (and thereby legitimated) Swami Rama Tirtha to earlier propagators of Vedānta, they also cited his influence on those who came after him. Jayaram Misra [Jayarām Miśra] (1979: 288), for example, rhapsodized about the confluence of the three rivers of patriotism [*deśbhakti*], concern for national welfare [*rāṣṭrahit*], and service to humanity [*mānav sevā*] in Swami Rama Tirtha's heart (the three rivers, or *triveṇī* is an allusion to the city of Allahabad/Prayag, where according to Hindu mythology not only the Ganges and Yamuna rivers flow together, but also the invisible Saraswati river). To Misra (1979: 288), Swami Rama Tirtha was unique in that he combined nationalism and patriotism with a life of renunciation; his patriotism was part of his Vedānta, and it later influenced Bal Gangadhar Tilak, Mohandas K. Gandhi, Aurobindo, and others. Similarly, Rameshwar Sahai Sinha cited the 1910 publication of Swami Rama Tirtha's American lectures as laying the groundwork for Mahatma Gandhi's later work:

> It is needless to mention here that this publication of Swami Rama's lectures was warmly greeted by the educated Indians of the time, for in them was a

> distinct note of national service interpreted according the highest knowledge of Vedanta. No doubt a large number of educated Indians was inspired by Swami Rama's teachings for the self-less service of Mother India, who later willingly offered themselves as the faithful soldiers of Mahatma Gandhi's Satyagraha movement. (*IWGR* 1:xv-xvi)

While the image of Swami Rama Tirtha as a great nationalist reflects his increasing mythicization, at the same time the new mythical image is firmly grounded in a specific historical context as hagiographers have assigned the Swami a particular place in the history of Indian nationalism, and argued that his message is still timely and relevant. As Arora (1988: 46) put it, "Let us hope that the present day political and social reformers who are tired and timid, selfish and slumbering, imbibe this new and ever fresh spirit of Rama and bring India back to its original place, its spirituality."

To explain the fact that there is little specifically political content in Swami Rama Tirtha's works, Misra (1979: 297) used the quasi-historical argument that the Swami's writings on the subject were seized in 1913 when Amir Chand was charged in the bombing attack on Lord Hardinge. This is a powerful argument, for it suggests that Swami Rama Tirtha's political statements were so compelling that India's British rulers perceived them as a direct threat that had to be suppressed (even though there is no surviving record of the actual content of any writings that may have been lost).[10] In contrast, Prem Lata suggested that Swami Rama Tirtha "did not take any active part in the freedom struggle despite the charge against him brought by the Indian police, acting on the instructions of the British administration that he was trying to subvert the government" (*LTW*: 241). Instead, he sought to remove the weaknesses in Hindu society which had led to India's subjugation by the British in the first place, weaknesses which were "the canker in Hindutva" (*LTW*: 241).[11] Lata thus argued that India's current social and political problems (such as communalism and debates about secularism) were the direct result of Indians not having adopted Swami Rama Tirtha's ideas—so although he did not take an active role in the independence movement, he showed Indians a path that could have led them to even greater success as an independent nation, which in effect made him a nationalist of a higher order than others who might be better known for their role in the nationalist movement.

These new images of the Swami as poet and nationalist contradict information from the earliest hagiographical tradition and the Swami's own writings, but they are nonetheless not completely ahistorical; rather, the historical emphasis has shifted to the hagiographers' own era. The earliest hagiographers were contemporaries of the Swami, living within the same historical context; the third phase hagiographers bring to their texts a very different historical perspective. Now that nationalism is the lens through which most nineteenth and early twentieth century Indian history is viewed, Swami Rama Tirtha's place within that history must be established. There were several different strategies for accomplishing this—the Swami Rama Tirtha Pratishthan used an apocryphal prediction which made the Swami the prime mover behind Indian independence. Others created means of explaining why there is so little discussion of nationalism in the Swami's writings—Misra attributed it to the loss of those materials, while Lata argued that Swami Rama Tirtha saw the potential flaws in the dominant form of nationalism which would lead to communalism and other problems, and therefore instead addressed the root problem of weaknesses within Hinduism which would prevent India from gaining strength as an independent nation.

While the centrality of nationalism in current Indian thought explains why creating an image of the Swami as nationalist should be so important, the reasons behind the Swami's portrayal as a master poet are perhaps not as immediately evident. The reasons lie both within both the mythical and the historical dimension of the hagiographical tradition. First, as hagiographers increasingly mythicize the Swami, it becomes impossible to portray him as having been flawed in any way—and therefore he simply must have been a good poet in English and other languages. Second, from a historical perspective, C.F. Andrews' comments presented a real challenge. A Christian missionary, perhaps one of the most potent symbols of British imperialism, dared to criticize Swami Rama Tirtha's poetry. Yet the fact that Narayan Swami asked him to write an introduction to the first volume of *IWGR* demonstrates that his participation in the venture lent it authority. Indeed a central feature of the hagiographers' rhetorical strategy is to highlight the Swami's appeal to everyone, everywhere, as is suggested by the common trope "to Muslims he seemed as Muhammad, to Buddhists as the Buddha, to Christians as Jesus, etc." Andrews' appreciation of the Swami's "poetic nature" thus serves that rhetoric well, but it leaves hagiographers with the challenge of explaining his criticisms of the Swami's poetry. The explanations of the hagiographers writing in English reveal a profound ambivalence about the western world and the fact that Swami Rama Tirtha was so comfortable in it. Yet the later hagiographers were keen to show that the Swami was in no way influenced by the western world (e.g. Arora's claim that his patriotism derived from his teen years, and not his travels abroad). It became important to claim that when Swami Rama Tirtha wrote in English, he did so even better than Westerners (e.g. Lata's argument that Andrews did not understand the style in which the Swami was working). Thus for the hagiographers it was not that Swami Rama Tirtha was influenced by western culture; rather, he approached it from a position of superiority, and used whatever parts of it he deemed useful. Whatever he did in an apparent western context far surpassed the efforts of westerners themselves. With such arguments, his hagiographers have effectively constructed a new image of Swami Rama Tirtha. While it is different than that of the earliest hagiographers, and the Swami's own image of himself, it is important to note that this image is still rooted within the basic parameters of his life. Whether Swami Rama Tirtha really was a great poet and a great nationalist is no longer so important as the fact that his followers understand him to have been such.

Hagiography and Experience: Concluding Reflections

The development of the Swami Rama Tirtha hagiographical tradition has given us a window into the processes at work in the ongoing creation and preservation of a saint's memory. In less than a century, Swami Rama Tirtha's followers have radically transformed his image through hagiography, and as the image of Swami Rama Tirtha has become increasingly mythicized, the tradition as a whole has developed along lines typical of many hagiographical traditions. Such changes in the Swami's image have occurred in an environment in which many of the hagiographers are aware of the standards of critical historical biography, and indeed so-called "modern" standards such as objectivity and documentation have made their way into the hagiographies, from Narayan Swami's quest for "bare facts" and "cool observation" to the *RJC*'s argument for the plausibility of miracles. Many studies of pre-modern hagiography (both in the west and elsewhere) have described the genre as a kind of "pious fiction" for the uneducated, attributing the tendency for hagiographical traditions to become increasingly far removed from historical truth in part as the result of the needs of a populace unaware of historical standards. That Swami Rama Tirtha's hagiographers are aware of such standards, but still write hagiographies that conform to traditional patterns emphasizes the fact that there are distinct conventions to the genre of hagiography which distinguish it from other forms of biographical writing. Those aspects of hagiography which some critics have found simple and unsophisticated are often in fact integral parts of a complex rhetorical strategy.

The difference between critical biography and hagiography is perhaps best understood as one of degree rather than complete difference. Both are concerned with accounts of lives, as well as how others have assessed and remembered those lives. In biography, other people's "experience" of the subject may be important as well, and critical biographies may serve a didactic purpose, just as hagiographies do. What is distinctive about hagiography, however, is its religious dimension. The experience of the saint (the reporting of which is such a critical element in the Swami Rama Tirtha hagiographical tradition) is first and foremost a religious experience. And according to his followers, Swami Rama Tirtha, though he is no longer living, is in some sense eternally present[12]; we may recall yet again Narayan Swami's declaration that Swami Rama Tirtha is still "everywhere" for those who will "just look," or Ayodhia Nath's introduction to the *RJC* in which he hopes that readers of the text will become "filled with Rama in a practical way." While the subject of critical biography may be shown to have had a direct effect on events in his or her own lifetime (and of course influence extending beyond that lifetime), this is not the same as the direct effect on events after his death which Swami Rama Tirtha's followers understand him to have (e.g. Nath's claim that the Swami has been directly responsible for not only India's independence, but that of other former colonies as well).

While it is no longer possible to have the direct, personal experience of Swami Rama Tirtha that Puran Singh and Narayan Swami did, it is possible to "experience" the Swami through perceiving his effect on the unfolding of history. Sometime in the distant future, Swami Rama Tirtha's followers may well see his hand in the course of events in their own lives. What makes this ongoing relationship with Swami Rama Tirtha possible is in part the mythical images of him constructed by later hagiographers. Mythical images such as the Swami as an *avatār* were defended by accounts of other people's experiences of him as such, for experience itself is one of the most important ways of conveying Swami Rama Tirtha's power as a saint. Tracing the changing nature of the reporting of experience (*satsaṅg* with Swami Rama Tirtha) has allowed us to describe not only how the image of the Swami has changed, but also to suggest why it has changed. The centrality of the followers' experiences allowed followers themselves to define what was most meaningful about the Swami, and deflects attention from the actual content of the Swami's teachings. In Puran Singh's words,

> Even without talking to him you would feel that you could not help loving him. (*SSR*: xxix)

What he said was not so important as the fact that just being around him made a person love him. Many years later, Ayodhia Nath would attribute that ability to Tirath Ram even as a baby by describing his effect on others in his village:

> The baby was the centre of attraction for the entire village, Hindus, Muslims or Sikhs alike, because he was not only extremely beautiful and charming but was also a rare specimen of extraordinary intelligence. His radiating smiles were simply bewitching. (*IWGR* 1:v-x)

His strength to affect others only grew, so that as a triumphant world traveler:

> The Christians called him the living Christ, the Buddhists saw in him the renunciation of Lord Buddha, the Mohamedans visualised in him the spark of prophet Mohammed and the Hindus considered him to be the very incarnation of Adi Guru Shankaracharya. (*IWGR* 1:vi)

Thus Swami Rama Tirtha did not create a new ideal for people through his teachings, but instead affected people in such a way that they saw him as exemplifying their own diverse religious ideals (so that he could simultaneously be as the Buddha, Muhammad, and Jesus). Even when he taught, it was his "charm" and "exalting presence" which exerted the most influence on people:

> He kept spell bound the vast audience of heterogeneous shade through the magnetic charm of his eloquence. He had an attractive aura of peace intermingled with divine ecstasy which unconsciously influenced all who came in the fragrant sphere of his exalting presence. (*IWGR* 1:vi)

It mattered not whether he taught, or just remained silent; of the days before the Swami left for Japan, when he lived in Tehri, Taskin (1974: 82) wrote:

> He usually remained silent, but those who came to meet him caught a whiff of the sweet scent of *paramātmā* [supreme self].

Prem Lata expressed similar sentiments in 1993:

> More than anything else, it was the Swami's personality which instantly impressed everyone who met him. . . Millionaires came to him and realized the vanity of wealth. An American whom he merely touched on the shoulder instantly became his admirer. His mere presence comforted people. That indeed is the touchstone of saintliness. . . . It is the saints who can bring us closer to the good. It is they who are the real teachers, for they speak not to the mind but to the soul. . . . Rama Tirtha was one of such men. He had seen the Truth. And therefore his words, his voice, his very presence was enough to convey that truth to others. (*LTW*: 14-15)

Such examples from all phases of the hagiographical tradition could be multiplied endlessly; what the hagiographers have stressed again and again was that Swami Rama Tirtha's presence in and of itself (even when he was silent) was powerful and transformative.

The earliest hagiographers used their own experiences of being in Swami Rama Tirtha's presence as part of their evidence for his sainthood, and one of the stated aims of those earliest hagiographies was to convey something of that experience so that readers would want to "experience" the Swami for themselves. The earliest hagiographies themselves became a way to continue to experience Swami Rama Tirtha even though he was no longer alive. The nature of such later experiences, however, was of necessity quite different. Once the Swami was no longer alive, followers could encounter him through his writings, through writings about him, through oral tradition, and through the Swami's successors and other admirers. Such experiences were all filtered through the experiences of others.[13] Yet even these "filtered" experiences were powerful enough that people continued to want to convey them, often through the medium of new hagiographies.

Those new hagiographies then sought to tell the story of the Swami's life, but through the lens of their new experiences. Later hagiographies lacked the authority of direct personal experience, but they legitimated their efforts both through reports of others' experiences of the Swami (e.g. the *RJC*'s stories of the tailor and the cloth merchant, the Muslim women begging, the mountain farmer), and through constructing an image of the Swami that linked him to the mythical model of the *avatār*. Such new images of the Swami as *avatār* became the basis for increasingly grand claims about his role in history as the prophet and even architect of Indian independence.

In summary, the following model may be used to explain the development of the Swami Rama Tirtha hagiographical tradition:

1. Hagiography is an account of a saint's life, and a crucial part of conveying the saint's status as a saint is the reporting of the experiences people have in the saint's presence. It is the saints' followers who recognize him as such; their perceptions are more powerful than even the saint's own presentation of himself.

2. The reporting of direct personal experience of the saint's presence lends authority to the hagiography (e.g. Puran Singh's *SSR*).

3. Authoritative hagiographies themselves become the basis for new experiences of the saint; such experiences are necessarily different when the saint is no longer alive, and the historical context of those new experiences is different.

4. New experiences become the basis for new hagiographies as people relate the saint to their own concerns.

> 5. New hagiographies require authority, but cannot draw upon direct experience; they therefore rely upon extensive reports of others' direct experiences (which may be "inventions"), and link the saint to mythical images such as that of the *avatār*.
>
> 6. The recourse to mythical images (particularly the *avatār* model) provides the opportunity to make the saint relevant to a later historical period; the new mythical images thus link the saint to a specific historical context (e.g. Swami Rama Tirtha as exemplar for life in independent India), and they may also be connected to institutional agendas (e.g. the *RJC*'s promotion of the goals of the SRTP).[14]

An especially important lesson from the Swami Rama Tirtha hagiographical tradition is that mythicization in a hagiographical tradition does not necessarily mean that the tradition has become ahistorical. While the hagiographies from the third phase of the tradition may not evidence much interest in the specific details of the historical context in which Swami Rama Tirtha lived, they are deeply concerned with their own historical context, and the ways in which Swami Rama Tirtha may be shown to affect it.[15] The new mythical images of the Swami further reflect the advantage of the increased historical perspective on his life afforded by the passage of time. The later hagiographers' understanding of both their own historical situation and the Swami's governed the mythical images that they fashioned; the hagiographers related those aspects of the past which they deemed relevant to their own context. Mythical images thus served to link discrete historical events (e.g. the 1900 prediction attributed to Swami Rama Tirtha, and India's independence in 1947). If his followers believe that he set in motion the processes that led to India's becoming independent, obviously only his followers in independent India could confirm this and make it a central part of their portrayal of him. The passage of time also allowed his followers to gauge his position amongst other saints from India's history. That the Swami's memory has endured proved to them that he was indeed a member of a larger class of great Indian saints, something which the earlier hagiographers could not assert so confidently. Puran Singh, for example, described the saints who influenced Swami Rama Tirtha:

> . . . He was undoubtedly in the company of a galaxy of saints and prophets and poets before he came to be a poet and an apostle himself. He was a constant companion of the Sufis of Persia, notable of Hafiz, Attar, Maulana Room and Shamstabrez. The saints of India with centuries of their religious culture informed his spirit. Tulsi Das and Sur Das were undoubtedly his inspirers. (*IWGR* 1:xxiv)

Puran Singh did not go so far as to place Swami Rama Tirtha among the saints he named as his influences (though he certainly hinted at it); later hagiographers would not be so restrained. In the words of Ayodhia Nath the Swami became not just a saint, but a "supersaint" whose power was greater than that of ordinary saints:

> Saints may come and saints may go, but the spiritually surcharged supersaint and highly talented adepts, like Swami Rama Tirtha, who come to this earthly vale at the critical period of human history to dispel the darkness of ignorance and to liberate the human beings from agonising miseries, continue to be enthroned on the hearts of millions of their admirers, even after the death of their mortal bodies. Verily, Swami Rama was such a super-saint. (*IWGR* 2:xix)

And so Swami Rama Tirtha, the man who resisted all attempts to found an institution in his name, the man who fled to a lonely mountain cave to escape the adulation of his admirers, sending away even his closest disciple, is now an *avatār* and supersaint whose memory lives on in ways he could not possibly have imagined. Amir Chand's words in 1913 would prove correct:

> It is clear from all the above that Swami Rama's influence belongs more to the Future than to the Past and that he will exercise a more prominent and powerful influence over the future course of events in this country than is now known or realized, as he would have done, had he not prematurely left us so suddenly. His worth will be better known, understood and realized now that he is no more with us in the flesh. (*IWGR* 3:xix)

APPENDIX
A Chronological, Annotated List of the Hagiographies

The list below includes not only full-length hagiographies, but also texts which include brief hagiographical accounts of Swami Rama Tirtha's life. In addition to those texts listed below, there are brief hagiographical passages throughout the introductory material in the seven volumes of *IWGR*, some of which are discussed in chapter seven.

Phase One: The Earliest Hagiographies

Anonymous. 1912. *Swami Rama Tirath: A Sketch of His Life and Teachings.* Madras: G.A. Natesan and Company. A very brief account of Swami Rama Tirtha's life which forms part of the publisher's "National Biography Series"; according to his account, the anonymous author of this text spent some time with Swami Rama Tirtha. This text was apparently not widely circulated, and there are few references to it in the later hagiographies.

Sharma, Shripad Rama [1]. 1921. *Swami Rama Tirtha: The Poet Apostle of Practical Vedanta.* Mangalore: Dharma Prakash Press. Sharma, who believed that he was writing the first account of the Swami's life, consulted with Swami Rama Tirtha's younger son Brahmananda in compiling his hagiography. The text is still available from the Swami Rama Tirtha Mission in New Delhi, but there are few references to it in the later hagiographies.

Puran Singh. 1937 [1907]. *Swāmī Rāmtīrth Jī Mahārāj kī 'Ilmī Zindagī par Tāirāna Nazar.* Originally published in the journal *Sat Upadesh*; reprinted in *KeR* 3. Urdu.

———. 1924. *The Story of Swami Rama: The Poet Monk of India*, 1st ed. Madras: Ganesh and Company Publishers. This version of the text included Puran Singh's original analysis of Swami Rama Tirtha's death.

———. 1974. *The Story of Swami Rama: The Poet Monk of India,* 2nd rev. ed. Lucknow: Rama Tirtha Pratisthan; Ludhiana: Kalyani Publishers. Puran Singh's *The Story of Swami Rama* (an expanded version of his earlier "brief sketches" in Urdu and English) is the most important text in the hagiographical tradition. It was translated into Hindi by Din Dayalu, an officer of the SRTP, and is cited (sometimes with attribution, sometimes without) in virtually all future hagiographies.

———. 1978 [n.d.]. *Life Sketch of Swami Rama* in *IWGR* 2: vii-xxii. Lucknow: Swami Rama Tirtha Pratishthan. This edition includes Puran Singh's revised analysis of Swami Rama Tirtha's death.

Anonymous. 1929. *Swami Ram Tirath: His Life and Teachings.* Madras: Ganesh and Company Publishers. The first section of this text is a reprinting of Puran Singh's "Life Sketch of Swami Rama" originally published in *IWGR* 1. The bulk of the text contains material from *IWGR* with occasional editorial commentary.

Narayan Swami. 1944. Untitled life of Swami Rama Tirtha, published in *Kulliyāt-e-Rām*, vol. 2. Lucknow: Swami Rama Tirtha Publication League. Paginated separately from the rest of the volume. Although Narayan Swami's Urdu text was first published in 1935, it was apparently written earlier. Narayan Swami's narrative is built around lengthy quotations from Swami Rama Tirtha's own writings; it also includes Narayan Swami's firsthand accounts of events in the Swami's life.

Sharga, Brijnath. 1935. *Life of Swami Rama Tirtha.* 2nd ed. 1968. Lucknow: Swami Rama Tirtha Pratishthan. Narayan Swami commissioned Sharga to write this text to counter what he believed to be misrepresentations in Puran Singh's *SSR. LSRT* is a lengthy, extremely detailed text with extensive quotations from the Swami's writings. Although Narayan Swami intended it to be the official account of Swami Rama Tirtha's life, it is no longer in print and was never as popular as Puran Singh's *SSR.*

Tara, Pandit Ram Lal. 1943. "The Late Swami Ram Tirath." In *Punjab's Eminent Hindus: Being Biographical and Analytical Sketches of Twenty Hindu Ministers, Judges, Politicians, Educationists and Legislators of the Punjab by some well-known Writers of this Province.* Lahore: New Book Society, 120-126. A brief account whose portrayal of the Swami, particularly his visit to the United States, exhibited some of the mythicizing tendencies that were criticized in the texts from the second phase of the hagiographical tradition.

In addition to the texts listed here, S.R. Sharma (1961: 96) refers to a 1922 Marathi biography by Govind P. Bhave, published by Triambak Prabhakar Bhave and a 12-volume Marathi translation of his works published by Bhaskar Vishnu Phadki. I have not been able to locate these works.

Phase Two: Skepticism and Reassessment

S.R. Sharma [2]. 1961. *Swami Rama Tirtha.* Bombay: Bharatiya Vidya Bhavan. English. Sharma first read about Swami Rama Tirtha while he was a student, and considered him a profound influence on his life. His hagiography relied heavily upon Puran Singh's *SSR.* Sharma argued that Swami Rama Tirtha's writings were very straightforward and unambiguous, and predicted that as a result, his followers would never claim him as an *avatār* or prophet. His prediction would soon be proven false.

Sood, D.R. 1970. *Swami Ram Tirth.* New Delhi: National Book Trust. English.

———. 1974. *Swāmī Rāma Tīrtha.* Urdu translation by Muhammad Jalandhari. New Delhi: National Book Trust. Sood took a somewhat skeptical approach to many of the stories about Swami Rama Tirtha's life, challenging, for example, stories about young Tirath Ram's astrologer having warned that he should be careful around water between the ages of thirty and forty.

Phase Three: Mythicization

Vatsya, Santarām. 1973. *Swāmī Rāma Tīrtha.* Delhi: Sanmarg Prakashan. Reprinted in 1985 in New Delhi by Subodh Publications. Hindi. Vatsya relied heavily upon Puran Singh's *SSR*, and emphasized Swami Rama Tirtha as a shining example for young Indian students. Vatsya argued that Swami Rama Tirtha was a great saint on a par with Ramakrishna and Swami Vivekananda, and a great nationalist as well.

Aggarwal, Harikishandas, and Eric Francis. 1974. Divinity Trail. Bombay: Tulsi Manas Prakashan. English. A brief comic book account of Swami Rama Tirtha's life, with some minor factual errors; the authors particularly focused on Swami Rama Tirtha's struggles as a student and his triumphant travels in Japan and the United States.

Taskīn, Śivanāth Rāy Jī. 1974. *Jīvan Caritra Swāmī Rāmatīrtha.* Delhi: Chand Book Depot. Hindi and Urdu editions published simultaneously. Taskin borrowed heavily from Puran Singh (often without attribution). He portrayed Swami Rama Tirtha as a great nationalist, but argued that the Swami's contact with the west had brought about occasional "looseness" or "laxity" in his actions.

Bhārdvāja, Kailāś Nāth, ed. 1976. *Swāmī Rām Tīrth: Jīvan, Darśan aur Sandeś.* Phagwara: Navodaya Sahitya Sangam Prakashan. Hindi. An anthology of short essays by and about Swami Rama Tirtha written by college professors and high school principals in India, this text highlights the relevance of Swami Rama Tirtha's thought to modern India.

Inderjīt. 1976. *Swāmī Rāma Tīrtha.* Delhi: Hari Kranti Enterprises. Urdu. A short text which terms Swami Rama Tirtha a great Vedānta philosopher and Sufi poet, and compares his travels around the world to Sankara's travels around India teaching Vedānta.

Kumar, Satish. 1977. *Swami Rama Tirtha: Great Mystic Poet of the Modern India.* Lucknow: Rama Tirtha Pratisthan. A brief text in which the author argued that Swami Rama Tirtha's genius as an English poet had not been sufficiently appreciated (see chapter 7).

Arora, Raj Kumar. 1978. *Swami Ram Tirath: His Life and Works.* New Delhi: Rajesh Publications. Arora relied heavily on Puran Singh's *SSR*; he emphasized Swami Rama Tirtha's Punjabi heritage and the Punjab's overall contribution to Indian spirituality, portraying Swami Rama Tirtha as a great patriot whose message is desperately needed in contemporary India.

Miśra, Jayarām. 1979. *Swāmī Rāma Tīrtha: Jīvan aur Darśan.* Allahabad: Lok Bharati Prakashan. Hindi. More detailed than many of the other Hindi hagiographies, Miśra's text is based on both Puran Singh's *SSR* and Brijnath Sharga's *LSRT.* Miśra included lengthy quotations from young Tirath Ram's letters, and portrayed Swami Rama Tirtha as a great nationalist whose life is a lesson for modern India.

Sultānpurī, Śaṅkar. 1981. *Swāmi Rām Tīrtha (Bālopayogī khaṇḍ kāvya).* New Delhi: Arya Book Depot. Hindi. Sultānpurī's text, aimed at young children, portrayed Swami Rama Tirtha as one of a class of great Indian saints, an *avatār* whose life provides a leadership example for young Indians.

Singh, Randhīr. n.d. *Jīvan Swāmī Rām Tīrth.* Hardwar: Randhir Book Sales. Hindi. Written in relatively simple Hindi, Singh's text portrayed Swami Rama Tirtha as one of India's greatest twentieth-century saints, and a fine example of a young man who overcame poverty and other obstacles to become a great Indian leader.

Dīn Dayālu. 1988. *Swāmī Rām Tīrth kī Saṅkṣipt Jīvanī.* Lucknow: SRTP. Hindi. Dīn Dayālu, a disciple of Narayan Swami, served for many years as head of the Swami Rama Tirtha Pratishthan. In this brief text, he portrayed Swami Rama Tirtha as a great Indian nationalist who set in motion the forces that brought about India's independence from the British.

Rama Tirtha Pratisthan. 1989. *Rāma Jīvan Citrāvalī.* Lucknow: Rama Tirtha Pratisthan. Hindi. A text which portrayed Swami Rama Tirtha as the *avatār* of the colonial era sent to teach Indians how to gain freedom from the British; discussed in detail in chapter 5.

Lata, Prem. 1993. *Life, Teachings and Writings of Swami Rama Tirtha.* New Delhi: Sumit Publications. Lata adopted the rhetoric of critical scholarship to address Swami Rama Tirtha's contributions to Indian history; her critique of contemporary Indian society is biting, and she argued that Swami Rama Tirtha's message could provide the answers to many of India's ills.

Other Hagiographies

Shastri, Hari Prasad. n.d. *Ram Tirtha: Scientist and Mahatma.* London: Shanti Sadan. As noted above, Shastri was at odds with Puran Singh and Narayan Swami; in this text, he highlighted his own relationship with Swami Rama Tirtha and was strongly critical of some of the Swami's other devotees.

Alston, A.J. 1983. *Yoga and the Supreme Bliss: Songs of Enlightenment by Swami Rama Tirtha.* New Delhi: Heritage Publishers. First published by Shanti Sadan in London in 1982.

———. 1991. *Songs of Enlightenment: Poems of Swami Rama Tirtha.* Reprint with title change. London: Shanti Sadan. Alston knew Hari Prasad Shastri; his translations of some of the Swami's Urdu poems are preceded by a brief biographical sketch which builds upon Shastri's text.

Prabhakar, Kedarnath. 1983. *Rām Bādshāh.* Saharanpur: Ram Tirth Kendra. Urdu.

———. 1984. *Yugsant Rāmtīrth: Tathyātmak Jīvan Caritra.* Saharanpur: Ramtirth Kendra. Hindi.

———. 1986. *Ahal-e-Islām kī Nazarīn Swāmī Rāma Tīrtha.* Deoband: Mahboob Printing Press. Urdu. Prabhakar was an official of the Rama Tirtha Kendra in Saharanpur, Uttar Pradesh. His family was from the same area as Swami Rama Tirtha, and his father and other relatives knew Swami Rama Tirtha's family. Prabhakar began writing Urdu texts after meeting someone from Pakistan who had heard about Swami Rama Tirtha but knew little about him. Prabhakar established contact with residents of Muraliwala, Swami Rama Tirtha's home village, and his texts include photographs of the family's former home there. *Ahal-e-Islām kī Nazarīn Swāmī Rāma Tīrtha* [Swami Rama Tirtha in the views of Muslims] details Swami Rama Tirtha's relationships with Muslims, and includes comments from Muslim writers who knew him. *Yugsant Rāmtīrth* includes information about Swami Rama Tirtha's past lives not found elsewhere in the hagiographical tradition.

Notes

Chapter One

1. For an introduction to Swami Rama Tirtha's Practical Vedānta, see Rinehart 1998. The term "Practical Vedānta" was first coined by Swami Vivekananda, an earlier contemporary of Swami Rama Tirtha, who sought to move the philosophy of Vedānta out of the abstract realm and into everyday life.

2. David N. Lorenzen has noted that hagiography apparently did not play a significant role in Vedic religion; there is little evidence for interest in life histories in the Vedas, Brāhmaṇas, or Upaniṣads. The earliest surviving hagiographical material concerns the Buddha, Mahavira, and Krishna. See Lorenzen 1976: 89. For a discussion of Vedānta hagiography with particular focus on miracles, see Granoff 1985. One of the most important early Vaiṣṇava hagiographical texts from north India is Nābhādās's *Bhaktamāla* (c. 1600) with Priyadāsa's commentary, the *Bhaktirasabodhinī* (1712). For a partial English translation of the text and commentary, see Grierson 1909 and 1910. A very useful introduction to the saints of south India is Dehejia 1988. A general introduction to hagiography in India is Callawaert and Snell 1994, which includes essays on various Vaiṣṇava and Śaiva hagiographical traditions, as well as Jaina, Marathi, and Sufi hagiography.

3. In the case of medieval Hindu poets, the poems attributed to them may not necessarily all be the poets' original compositions. However, hagiographers often use biographical information from spurious poems to establish information about the poet's life. See Hawley 1988 and 1993. There are similar problems in Indian Sufi hagiography; see Rinehart 1999.

4. The Greek term was originally applied to the last portion of the Hebrew Bible; its application later changed in Christian usage.

5. This edited volume provides a useful cross-cultural survey of the phenomenon of sainthood, with essays on Christianity, Judaism, Islam, Hinduism, Theravada and Mahayana Buddhism, and Confucianism. See also Cohn 1987 for another helpful analysis of cross-cultural applications of the term saint. Cohn highlights some of the central issues related to sainthood, such as the role of the saint as exemplar, particularly the tension between "imitability" and "inimitability."

6. There are of course significant political and historical factors affecting conceptions of sainthood in each religious tradition as well. For example, the development of the process of canonization in the Roman Catholic church, with its standards for official recognition of a saint, makes the recognition of sainthood very different from that of the Hindu tradition, which has no formal organizational body to regulate the recognition of those deemed holy. On the process of canonization in the Roman Catholic church, see Vauchez 1981.

7. For a brief introduction to some of the terms linked to the broad category of "sainthood" used in Vedic Hinduism, as well as Buddhism and Jainism, see White 1988; see also White 1972; 1981; 1974 for further discussion of terminology.

8. For example, many of the English pamphlets of the Swami Rama Tirtha Mission use the heading "Great Saint Rama Tirtha."

9. The Hindi word *sant* (literally, good person) is often translated into English as "saint"; there is no etymological connection between the two words although they sound similar. The term *bhakta* [lit. "devotee"], frequently applied to medieval Hindu figures, is also sometimes translated as "saint." The terms used for followers of saints vary as well; in English, admirers of Swami Rama Tirtha refer to themselves both as "followers" and "devotees"; in Hindi, they use the terms *bhakta* [devotee] and *premī* [lover].

10. In his study of Christian hagiography from the Middle Ages, for example, Thomas Heffernan (1988: 16) writes, ". . . the perfectly suitable term *hagiography* is now virtually impossible to read except as an epithet signifying a pious fiction or an exercise in panegyric." Heffernan therefore chooses the term *sacred biography* over hagiography. More recently, Coon (1997: xiv-xv) has used the term "sacred fictions" to designate hagiographical accounts of Christian women's lives in an effort to focus not on the historical lives of the subjects of hagiographies, "but on the theological and didactic agendas of their authors," whose motifs are "driven not by historical fact but by biblical *topoi*, literary invention, and moral imperative."

11. Alternatively, in his entry "Biography" in the *Encyclopedia of Religion*, William LaFleur (1987: 220-224) combines hagiography and sacred biography under the single heading "sacred biography," which he defines as "the written accounts of lives of persons deemed to be holy."

12. There are several terms used in Hindi which are typically translated into English as "biography" including *jīvan carit*, ("life acts"; less frequently *jīvan caritra*; *carita* and *caritra* being formations from the same Sanksrit verbal root) or simply *jīvanī* ("life"). Medieval Hindi biographies of religious figures are sometimes referred to as *bhakta-carita*s ("biographies of devotees"), but this term is not used in the Swami Rama Tirtha tradition. There is a small body of Hindi scholarship on biography; it typically makes no distinction between biographies and texts which in English would be designated as either sacred biographies or hagiographies. See, for example, Bhāradvāj 1978, which examines biographical writing in Hindi; see also two texts which take the *Bhaktamāl* as their starting point for studies of biography in Hindi: Jhā 1978, especially chapter 3, and Śarma 1983, especially chapter 8, "*Jīvanī Sāhitya aur Bhaktamāl ki Paramparā*." A useful study in English is Sen 1979, which contains essays on biographical traditions from different regions of India.

13. For a useful critique of various historicist approaches to the study of hagiography see Heffernan 1988, chapter 2, "Sacred Biography as Historical Narrative: Testing the Tradition, Gibbon to Gadamer."

14. Delehaye was well aware that his critical enterprise—which he termed "scientific hagiography"—ran the risk of offending the faithful; indeed he noted that his critics within the church often expressed their discontent "in somewhat violent terms" (Delehaye 1907: vii).

15. Karl J. Weintraub (1975) has noted a similar tendency in critical assessments of autobiographical writing; he argued that since the Renaissance, individuality has been highly regarded in western culture, and autobiographies are therefore valued according to the degree to which they describe a unique life, rather than a life which conforms to an ideal.

16. A well-known example of this phenomenon is the stories of the lives of the saints Barlaam and Iosaph found in Christian hagiography; their stories are now recognized as adaptations of accounts of the lives of the Buddha.

17. Similarly, Michel de Certeau (1988: 274) suggests that hagiographies of Christian saints create an area of "vacation" because unlike canonical texts which present dogma, the stories of saints' lives "oscillate between the believable and the marvelous, advocating what one is at liberty to think or do."

18. McLeod of course recognized that the substantial portion of the *janam-sākhī* literature which is largely legendary or mythical in character is nonetheless important in Sikh devotion; however, his approach to the *janam-sākhī* literature was governed by standards of critical historical biography. See also McLeod 1994.

19. See Lorenzen 1991, especially 3-22. Winand Callewaert (1988: 31) describes a similar attempt to downplay possible Muslim origins in the biographical tradition surrounding Dadu Dayal.

20. Ramanujan (1982: 318-319) created a flow chart indicating the typical stages of life for women saints; his primary examples were from the Vīraśaiva tradition, with the addition of other female saints such as Lallā, Bahiṇābāī, Mīrā, and Āṇḍāl. He also noted distinctions between the life patterns of male and female saints, as well as distinctions between upper-caste and outcaste saints. Ramanujan argued that female saints invert the traditional ideals of womanhood found in figures such as Sita [Sītā] and Savitri [Sāvitrī]; he found male saints harder to typify, but did suggest the following characteristics: an early life of ease and pleasure, abasement, loss, and subsequent awakening, conversion or initiation at the hands of a guru, defying of orthodox authority and social norms, the converting or defeating of people of other religions or sects, the founding of his own sect, and merging with god.

21. White outlined some of the central events in Swami Muktananda's life as reported by his devotees, e.g. his pious mother, his relatively easy birth, his keen intelligence as a young boy, his initiation into *sannyās*, etc.

22. The twelve motifs are: a miracle of origins, initiation and aid from a *sannyāsin*, learning from an extraordinary guru, trial and vision, contempt of court, endangered musician sings and is rescued by the Lord, a loss of something such as divine images, miraculous recovery, manifestation of the power of music, the Lord's response to song, the musician as an *aṃsa*, or partial descent of a divine being, and foreknowledge of death.

23. Snell listed the following typical formulae found in Indian hagiographies: miracle stories, dream interventions, precocious erudition, conquests in debate with established scholars, conversions, adventurous journeys, credence-stretching longevity, and formulaic sacred numbers.

24. Lorenzen identified the major elements of the typical pattern in *nirguṇī* saints' lives as: unusual birth; display of religious vocation, supernatural power, or outright divinity at a young age; life-changing encounter with first guru and/or celestial voice or vision; marriage or celibacy (with earlier accounts describing saint as married, later accounts emphasizing celibacy); encounters with people of different categories; stories about the saint appointing a successor or giving instructions to followers; unusual death.

25. For discussion of life patterns in South Asian Islam, see Lawrence 1982.

26. Rank argued for a universal pattern which included elements such as the hero's difficulty in conception, his being surrendered to the water in a box, his achievement of rank and honors, etc. Lord Raglan's pattern included the mother of the hero as a royal virgin, the hero's unusual conception, his marriage to a princess, his mysterious death, etc. In *The Hero with a Thousand Faces,* Joseph Campbell argued that there was a universal biographical pattern (which he termed the "monomyth") in the lives of heroes, a pattern based upon a three-stage process of separation or departure, initiation, and return. Segal 1990 includes the full texts of Otto Rank's *The Myth of the Birth of the Hero*, Lord Raglan's *The Hero: A Study in Tradition, Myth, and Drama, Part 2,* and Alan Dundes' "The Hero Pattern and the Life of Jesus," as well as an introductory essay by Segal. For a very interesting study of the applicability of the hero pattern to the life of Caitanya and the construction of community by his followers, see Stewart 1997.

27. The reduction of legendary tales to set patterns reached its extreme in the folklore studies of Vladimir Propp (1975), who argued that using a relatively extensive cataloguing of typical situations and incidents found in a folk tradition, one could take even a fragment of a folktale and reasonably reconstruct its full parameters on the basis of the patterns extrapolated from the tradition as a whole.

28. A further difficulty in assessing the use of patterns in hagiography is determining the extent to which saints themselves may consciously or unconsciously pattern their own lives on existing models (what Ernst Kris termed "enacted biography"), versus the extent to which hagiographers later impose a pattern upon saints' lives.

29. For a more detailed discussion of hagiographical models in Christianity, see Coon (1997: 1-27), "Hagiography and Sacred Models." Coon describes how Christian hagiography made use not only of the life of Jesus as a model, but also the lives of other biblical figures (e.g. Eve and Mary as models for female saints).

30. Reynolds and Capps (1976: 28) noted a general tendency among scholars to separate myth from history in the study of sacred biography and hagiography (rather than considering their interaction), with those interested in biographical images focusing on myths, and those studying individual lives highlighting historical information.

31. This presentation of miracles for a scientifically-minded audience is by no means unique to the Swami Rama Tirtha hagiographical tradition. It is especially apparent in the Sai Baba [Sāī Bābā] tradition; miracles such as the manifestation of sacred ash (*vibhūti*) and objects such as watches are an important part of Sai Baba's relationships with his followers. See, for example, Murphet 1973. As someone trained in science and logic, Murphet makes his own initial skepticism about Sai Baba central theme of his text.

32. See, for example, Brown 1981.

33. Similarly, Brigitte Cazelles (1991: 2) has argued that medieval European hagiology is a "discourse on mediation."

34. This is especially true for Hindu saints; whereas relics have been a central means of maintaining the saint's presence within the Christian tradition, and gravesites have been important for Muslim *pīr*s, such practices are less commonly a part of the worship of Hindu saints. Some communities do save personal effects of the saint (e.g. sandals) and accord them high honors; other communities entomb their saints in *samādhi*s, which may become places of worship. Often, however, as in the case of Swami Rama Tirtha, the saint's body is consigned to a river (after the Swami drowned, his body was recovered, and then returned to the river), and no relics from the corpse are saved.

35. I do not intend to draw too sharp a distinction between biography and hagiography; many biographies, after all, are somewhat "hagiographical" in their portrayals of their subjects insofar as they may depend upon legends. What I wish to emphasize about hagiography, however, is its central goal of expressing whatever about the saint it was that followers saw as "sacred" in some way. On the term "bios" as a part of both biography and autobiography, see Olney 1978.

36. *Satsaṅg* is a compound noun made up of *sat*, the present participle of the Sanskrit verbal root *as*, "to be" (it therefore literally means "being," but its usage incorporates the sense of goodness or even truth) and *saṅg*, "association" or "interaction," from the Sanskrit verbal root *sañj*, "to cling, connect, adhere, etc."

37. *Satsaṅg* is thus conceptually similar to *darśan* ("sight"), the idea that looking at an image or a holy person involves an auspicious exchange or transfer between the two parties.

38. "Experience" in general, and religious experience in particular, are difficult concepts to define precisely, as Gadamer (1985: 55-63; 310) and others (e.g. Wall 1995) have pointed out. Gadamer (in part following Dilthey) showed that the term "experience" (German

"*erlebnis*") became especially popular in the nineteenth century as autobiographers and biographers sought to establish a connection between life experience and its expression or interpretation in artistic work. Similarly, in the Swami Rama Tirtha hagiographical tradition, hagiographers use their own experiences of the Swami (and those of others) as a basis for their hagiographical works. As used here, the term "experience" does not correspond directly to a specific Hindi or Sanksrit term. *Anubhava* and *anubhūti*, for example, though they are sometimes glossed as "experience," do not encompass the same semantic range. A further complication is the usage of "experience" in the works of recent Hindu apologists such as Sarvepalli Radhakrishnan and Aurobindo, who argued that Hinduism was a religion built upon the authority of "experience" (i.e. the Vedic seers experienced the truth of the Vedas) as contrasted with western religions which they characterized as relying upon dogma and prophecy rather than experience. Halbfass (1988: 378-402) has argued that this reading of Hinduism marks a significant break from the earlier Hindu philosophical tradition, which did not make such claims about experience.

39. In Gadamer's words (1985: 60), "what can be called an experience establishes itself in memory. We mean the lasting experience that an experience has for someone who has had it. . . . What we emphatically call an experience thus means something unforgettable and irreplaceable that is inexhautible in terms of the understanding and determination of its meaning." For further discussions of the use of the term "experience" see Proudfoot 1985, Turner and Bruner 1986, and Sharf 1998.

40. Olsen (1980: 425) argued for a similar approach to assessing Christian hagiographies: "A successful hagiographic work has a controlled narrative structure, makes appropriate use of traditional imagery and themes, and enmeshes its polemical arguments within its narrative structure." Vitz (1991) argues that many of the conventions of hagiography, such as its reliance on anecdotal material, result from its roots in oral tradition.

41. See, for example, Jackson 1991.

Chapter Two

1. I have relied most heavily on Brijnath Sharga's *Life of Swami Rama Tirtha* (*LSRT*) for the chronology of events in Swami Rama Tirtha's life; all references are to the 2nd edition published in 1968. Sharga's account is in many ways the most factually accurate of all the hagiographies (an issue which will be considered at length in chapter three). In this chapter, citations to specific hagiographies are given only when a particular event is reported only in one text, or is the subject of debate among the hagiographers.

2. Swami Rama Tirtha wrote both in Urdu and English, often interspersing Persian, Punjabi, and Sanskrit into his writings as well. His collected works were originally published in the three-volume Urdu collection *Kulliyāt-e-Rām* [*KeR*], now out of print. His writings are now available in a seven-colume English collection entitled *In Woods of God-Realization.* All references to this collection are from the seven editions dating from 1978-1990, hereafter cited as *IWGR* volume number: page number. In some instances, I have corrected minor grammatical and spelling errors in *IWGR*. *IWGR* has been reprinted many times; the Swami Rama Tirtha Pratishthan names each reprint a new "edition" although there are no changes in the text. There is also a multiple-volume Hindi version of *IWGR*.

3. Narayan Swami's work appeared in volume two of *KeR*, and is paginated separately from the rest of the volume (it begins at page 1 after 29 pages of other material).

4. According to some hagiographies, she died within a few days of giving birth to Tirath Ram; according to others, she died sometime during the boy's first two years.

5. For a photograph and further information about Dhanna Ram, see *LSRT*: 10-11.

6. Many of the Swami's hagiographers include quotations from these letters, which were originally written in Urdu. Tirath Ram wrote his first letter to Dhanna Ram in 1886 when he had left Gujranwala to visit his wife's family. The original Urdu text of the eleven hundred-plus letters is no longer in print, but the Swami Rama Tirtha Pratishthan published a selection of about five hundred of the letters transliterated into the Devanāgarī script (with some translations of Urdu words into more Sanskritized Hindi) entitled *Rām-patra: Swāmī Rāmtīrtha Mahārāj, Apne Guru ke prati Cune Hue Patrõ kā Saṅgraha.*

7. Some hagiographies mistakenly identify the college as "Mission College," the name of a school where Tirath Ram later taught.

8. The first hagiographers constructed their accounts of Tirath Ram's student days from his letters to Dhanna Ram; the account here is drawn from those letters as well.

9. See, for example, *LSRT*: 46-47.

10. The Sanatana Dharma Sabha challenged the teachings of the Arya Samaj, which was extremely popular in the Punjab. The Arya Samaj, founded by Swami Dayananda Saraswati, was a movement dedicated to restoring what it considered the true religion of the Vedas. Swami Dayananda argued that all developments in Hinduism from after the time of the war described in the *Mahābhārata* (the vast epic of which the *Bhagavad Gītā* is a portion) were erroneous and to be abandoned. He was particularly opposed to the worship of images, arguing that there was no precedent for such practices in the Vedas. The Sanatana Dharma Sabha chapters, however, fought to preserve image worship as a central part of their religious practice. For an introduction to this period, see Jones 1976 and Jones 1989.

11. See *IWGR* 6: 271-390 for transcriptions of two of Tirath Ram's lectures on Sanatana Dharma in Sialkot. For other lectures from 1898 and 1899, see *IWGR* 6: 37-91.

12. The details of Narayan Das' (later known as Narayan Swami) meeting with Tirath Ram vary in different accounts; he described meeting Tirath Ram in Amritsar in his Urdu account of Swami Rama Tirtha's life (*KeR* 2: 67). Similarly, according to Sharga (*LSRT*: 70), Narayan Das first heard Tirath Ram lecture in Amritsar and later met him in Lahore. According to the *Swāmī Śrīmān Nārāyan kī Jīvan-kathā*, a biography of Narayan Swami, however, it was in Lahore that Narayan Das first met Tirath Ram, his family having recently moved there. See SRTP 1989: 10-11. Presumably, we may trust Narayan Swami's own version of events as reliable.

13. Accounts of several of Tirath Ram's "Casual Talks" before the Sabha may be found in *IWGR* 6:245-270.

14. See *IWGR* 5.

15. Many hagiographies report that Tirath Ram once told the principal of the college that if he were looking for Jesus, then he need look no further than Tirath Ram himself.

16. See *IWGR* 5:348-370 for an English translation of the original Urdu essay, *Sair-e-Kashmīr*. It, along with Swami Rama Tirtha's other essays, was published in the three-volume *Kulliyāt-e-Rām* [*KeR*]; the original Urdu *Sair-e-Kashmīr* has also been republished in paperback form by Ram Tirtha Kendra, Saharanpur (1982).

17. See *KeR* 2:205-206.

18. For a facsimile of the cover of *Alif*, see *LSRT*: 168. On the center of the cover is the vertical slash of the letter *alif*; above it is a line from the Punjabi Sufi poet Bullhe Shah, and above that is a verse from the *Upaniṣads*. Beneath the *alif*, there is a short Persian verse. For the original Urdu essays, see *KeR*.

19. Tirath Ram's wife and children are shadowy figures in the hagiographical tradition; some hagiographies do not mention Tirath Ram's children at all. According to some, he had two sons and a daughter who died at a young age; others mention only the two sons.

20. Details of Tirath Ram's vows of renunciation vary; according to Narayan Swami (*KeR* 2: 228) and Sharga (*LSRT*: 188), Tirath Ram initiated himself on the authority of Swami Madhva Tirtha, who had earlier encouraged him to do so, and he changed his name to Swami Rama Tirtha to honor Swami Madhva Tirtha.

21. The Swami's port of arrival is variously reported as Seattle, San Francisco, or New York. The Swami himself said that he first arrived in Seattle.

22. The newspaper clippings eventually ended up in Puran Singh's possession; he reprinted some of them in *SSR*: 254-260. See also *LSRT*: 283-305 for many of the same newspaper articles and letters.

23. No record of this lecture survives.

24. Master Amir Chand was charged with being involved in a Delhi bombing targeting Lord Hardinge in 1912 and was hanged by the British government in 1914. Swami Rama Tirtha's followers maintain that he was innocent of the crime.

25. A more substantial collection of the Swami's Urdu and Persian poetry may be found in the two-volume *Rām-varṣā* (SRTP 1978). For English translations of some of the poems, see Alston 1982.

26. For further information on other organizations established in the Swami's memory, see SRTP 1991: 18-20.

27. The hagiographies described here represent the full range of texts available in the primary repositories for such material: the library of the Swami Rama Tirtha Mission in New Delhi, India (through 1994); the Swami Rama Tirtha Pratishthan in Lucknow, Uttar Pradesh (through 1992); the Jawaharlal Nehru library in New Delhi; the Oriental and India Office collection and the main collection of the British library in London; and university libraries in the United States.

28. Jackson (1992: 717-736) identified an initial phase in which two disciples of Tyagaraja recorded the major events in his life, a second phase in which new stories began to appear, and finally a third phase in which the tellings of Tyagaraja's life began to follow patterns found in tellings of earlier musician-saints' lives.

29. In 1990, N.C. Kansil, an official of the Swami Rama Tirtha Educational Society, was composing yet another Hindi hagiography of Swami Rama Tirtha; however, he was not certain he would complete it, because he feared that Indians were no longer interested in the lessons to be learned from leaders such as Swami Rama Tirtha.

Chapter Three

1. The SRTP issued the first reprinting of *LSRT* in 1968, over thirty years after it was first released, and has not reprinted it since.

2. For accounts of Narayan Swami's life, see SRTP 1965: 1989.

3. For Puran Singh's account of his own life, see Singh 1982.

4. "Gosāī̃ jī ke mastī bhare darśan se jo gahrī coṭ Nārāyan ke dil par lagī, uskā bayān karnā qalam se bāhar hai" ("Gosāī̃ jī" refers to Tirath Ram's status as a Goswāmī Brāhmaṇ).

5. Even the normally circumspect Sharga could find little positive to say about Swami Shivagunacharya. Here, he described Swami Shivagunacharya's behavior when Swami Rama Tirtha first left Lahore: "He treated the other members of the party badly, not sparing even women and children. The manner in which he handled a poor old woman pilgrim to Badrinath, who had joined the party from Hardwar, it is impossible to describe" (*LSRT*: 175-6).

6. According to Singh, Kamalananda, an American admirer of Swami Rama Tirtha who spent some time with Singh's family in India, told him that while in the United States, Swami Rama Tirtha spoke frequently of the sacredness of married life, and seemed to idealize women. Singh took this as a further indication of Swami Rama Tirtha's dissatisfaction with monastic life (*SSR*: 249).

7. Nearly all the hagiographies of Swami Rama Tirtha rely upon the statement that Swami Rama Tirtha's cook (the only one present when the Swami drowned) gave to Narayan Swami. For the original text, see *KeR* 3:301-303, 333-335.

8. For an English translation of this essay, see "The Stamped Deed of Progress" (*IWGR* 5:380-395).

9. There is a facsimile of the original page opposite *KeR* 2:305.

10. See also Din Dayalu's Hindi translation (1982: 232), which reads, "At that time, I thought that Rama was forecasting his own death in this paragraph. But nothing can be said [for certain]. He often wrote in this style. Yes, it is noteworthy that when he thought of death, he thought of it and it came! It is possible that thoughts of '*brahma* is truth, the world is false' which had cast their shadow over him for some time, which we understand to be fatigue, and the sadness of mind and love-intoxication, had given rise to a sense of extreme worldly disgust, which at the time neither I nor anyone else could fully comprehend. As a result, the thought of returning [to life] was far from his mind."

11. Classical Advaita Vedānta philosophy distinguishes among different types of *karma*: *prārabdha karma* (karmic residues which work themselves out during the present lifetime), *sañcita karma* (residues from previous lives which remain latent during the present lifetime) and *sañcīyamāna* or *āgamin karma* (karmic residues accrued in the present lifetime which will mature in subsequent lifetimes). See Potter 1980: 241-267. T.M.P. Mahadevan offered an interpretation of Ramana Maharshi's life that was similar to Sharga's analysis; see Miller (1986: 73).

12. For a study of the biographical controversies surrounding Caitanya's death, see Stewart 1991.

Chapter Four

1. Swami Rama Tirtha's letters are scattered throughout *IWGR*; his notebooks make up the bulk of *IWGR* 7.

2. For the original Urdu, see *KeR* 2:147. Here, I have quoted the English translation in *IWGR* 6:139 (with some minor editing of grammatical infelicities, etc.).

3. This letter prompted Tirath Ram's father to write a rather angry letter to Dhanna Ram chastising him for being a bad influence on his son.

4. Dhanna Ram apparently found Tirath Ram's musings increasingly puzzling; in one letter, Tirath Ram mentioned Dhanna Ram not being able to figure out what his student was thinking anymore (*RP*: 245).

5. Interestingly, however, the names that Tirath Ram gave his sons reflect the shift in his spiritual practice. His first son he named Madan Mohan, an epithet of the god Krishna; his second son, born when he had left Krishna-devotion for Vedānta, he named Brahmananda [Brahmānanda], "the joy of *brahma* (ultimate reality)."

6. Swami Rama Tirtha's description of his experience on Mt. Sumeru is of course a classic example of the hero's journey as described by Otto Rank and Joseph Campbell (among others), although this is not a theme that either he or his hagiographers highlighted.

7. Although he was a staunch advocate of Advaita Vedānta, throughout his life Swami Rama Tirtha spoke often of his love and devotion for "God" (in English) or "Rām" (in Hindi and Urdu).

8. The Hindi word *sādhu* (a term typically used for wandering renunciants) and the Urdu word *faqīrī* (from the Persian *faqr*, literally "poverty"; typically applied to those who undergo austerities of some kind as part of Sufi practice) are translated as "saint" and "saintliness" in the *IWGR* English translation.

9. For the original Urdu, see *KeR* 2:307-329; for an English translation of this essay, see *IWGR* 5:380-395.

10. As with much of his terminology, Swami Rama Tirtha's use of the term "evolution" was imprecise; often, he meant it as a process whereby simple things "evolved" to become more complex, or whereby a diverse group of people or concepts "evolved" towards a unified position (e.g. the notion that all religions are evolving towards Vedānta). For further discussion of Swami Rama Tirtha's views on evolution, see Rinehart 1998.

11. Kṛṣṇadāsa, author of the *Caitanya-caritāmṛta*, a biography of the Bengali saint Caitanya, expressed a similar sentiment: "For I am an insignificant creature, and write only by the grace of Caitanya" [CC III:3:257], quoted in Dimock 1976: 114.

Chapter Five

1. For a study of the changing biographical images of the Bengali saint Caitanya, see Stewart 1985. Stewart showed that the various images of Caitanya's divinity reflect the attempts by different communities to mediate the experience of Caitanya's presence with their understanding of the traditional descents of God.

2. According to the *SRTP ke Baṛhte Caraṇ Smārikā* (1991: 39-40), a brief history of the SRTP, in 1902, when he was a baby, Ayodhia Nath was placed in Swami Rama Tirtha's lap (Nath's father, Mahatma Shanti Prakash, was a devotee of the Swami). The crying baby was quieted by the Swami's gentle recitation of "*oṃ*." In his many writings for the SRTP, Ayodhia Nath himself made no reference to this incident.

3. The god Krishna tells Arjuna that he descends to earth whenever necessary: "For whenever the Law [*dharma*] languishes, Bhārata, and lawlessness [*adharma*] flourishes, I create myself. I take on existence from eon to eon, for the rescue of the good and the destruction of the evil, in order to reestablish the Law" (van Buitenen 1981: 87).

4. Karl J. Weintraub (1975: 826-827) noted a similar tendency in autobiographical writing, which he termed "retrospective interpretation"—the tendency to look back on events and place them within a traditional pattern. Similarly, Heffernan (1988: 23-24) noted that in predominantly oral cultures, stories tend to be reinterpreted in light of present experience, and that tendency is reflected in sacred biography: "The past and the present are in a dialogue within the individual consciousness. Such fluid accessibility between past and present is clearly part of the object of sacred biography; a major premise of that tradition is to

document the continuing presence of past constitutive patterns of behavior as models for the present."

5. For a brief introduction to the Gauḍīya Vaiṣṇava tradition's theology of the *avatār*, see Dimock 1966: 41-63.

6. For a very interesting study of recent usage of the term *avatār* in Hinduism, see Eschmann 1972. Eschmann argued that the contemporary application of the term (which deviates significantly from classical *avatār* theory) has its roots in the apologetics of Rammohun Roy, Keshub Chunder Sen, and other recent Hindu leaders, who first saw the concept of the *avatār* as a problem for the Hindu traditions that required rationalizing, but finally came to view it as a source of strength in the articulation of a universal Hindu tradition that was understood to embrace all religions and all great religious figures.

7. Indeed the current usage of the term in India may well reflect India's encounter with Christian theology during the colonial period, when many Indian thinkers searched for analogs to Christian ideas in the Hindu tradition itself.

8. See, for example, Chaturvedi and Tiwari, *A Practical Hindi-English Dictionary* (1989: 47); they gloss *avatār* only as "incarnation."

9. S.R. Sharma (1921: 3-4) reported that Tirath Ram's maternal grandfather, an astrologer, predicted that either the child or his mother would soon die, and that if the boy lived, he would be a source of great pride to the family. However, none of the other early hagiographers, including Puran Singh, Narayan Swami, and Sharga, reported this or similar tales regarding Tirath Ram's horoscope. Sharma's text apparently did not circulate widely, so whether it is the source for the *RJC*'s story or not is not clear. It is also worth noting that Kedarnath Prabhakar, author of several Urdu texts about Swami Rama Tirtha in the 1980s, mentions that he himself comes from a family of astrologers, yet does not include any reference to Tirath Ram's horoscope in his texts.

10. This tendency to highlight what is relevant to the author is a common explanatory move in much of hermeneutic theory, going back expressly to Dilthey, whose work on biography and autobiography is particularly relevant. The assumption of this connection is that the author can only write about those things which are relevant to and which reflect his or her own experience in the then contemporary world; consequently this has major ramifications for identifying historical changes in the "meaning" of Swami Rama Tirtha, or any other subject of biography or hagiography, to the community promoting the works. See Dilthey 1962. See also Stewart 1985 for an application of this proposition in the analysis of the biographical image as an index to the development of the religious community.

11. According to the letters he wrote as a student, Tirath Ram clearly was not enamored of snakes. However, in an essay from his early days as a renunciant, he did mention lovingly caressing a snake (*IWGR* 5:337).

12. Reflecting some concern for documentation, the author of *RJC* attributes this story to an otherwise unidentified man named Śrī Śivānanda.

13. Some of the early hagiographies mention that one of Tirath Ram's teachers, a Mr. Gilbertson, gave him a watch; perhaps this is part of the inspiration for this story.

14. Several members of the Swami Rama Tirtha Mission told me this story in 1992.

15. The discussion of miracles continues later in the *RJC* with a story about Swami Rama Tirtha commanding a rainstorm to stop so that he could deliver an outdoor lecture. The author makes the same argument that although what Swami Rama Tirtha did might seem to be a miracle, it was in actuality a reflection of his greater understanding of the workings of the world, which gave him the ability to manipulate the world in ways ordinary humans cannot (*RJC*: 41-42). The inspiration for this story is likely a brief anecdote in Sharga's *LSRT*, according to which Swami Rama Tirtha was preparing to deliver a lecture when it was

raining, and stated that the atmosphere ought to be "cheerful" when he spoke. Soon thereafter it stopped raining; Sharga stopped short of claiming that Swami Rama Tirtha directly stopped the rain, whereas the *RJC* explicitly makes that claim (*LSRT*: 226-227).

16. This was also an issue during Swami Rama Tirtha's lifetime, when there were a number of critics of his decision to leave behind his family. See *IWGR* 6:124-126, "Reply of a Letter, Instigating Rama to Return to Domestic Life."

17. The details of this period are somewhat murky, even in the earliest hagiographies, and there are conflicting versions of when, how and why Tirath Ram took vows of renunciation, which may be another reason for the brevity of the *RJC* account.

18. Just as in Swami Rama Tirtha's own description of climbing Mt. Sumeru (discussed in chapter four), the *RJC* presents this story of Swami Rama Tirtha's meditation in a cave in such a way that it follows the typical hero pattern, e.g. Joseph Campbell's separation (Tirath Ram's leaving his home and job), initiation (vows of renunciation), and return (his assumption of a public role).

19. This "name-dropping" technique is common in medieval Indian hagiography as well, where one frequently finds accounts of saints from different regions and even different centuries having profound discussions and debates. For an example of such a debate between Kabir and Raidas [Raidās], see Lorenzen 1996: 169-203.

20. See, for example, *IWGR* 3:347 for a letter that Swami Rama Tirtha wrote (apparently to Narayan Swami) from the United States in which he mentions giving the President a pamphlet.

21. For the two-part lecture "Idealism and Realism Reconciled in the Light of Vedanta," see *IWGR* 3:1-24.

22. In a lecture, Swami Rama Tirtha did once mention that some Christian leaders had tried to spread rumors about him, but were "frustrated and disappointed" (*IWGR* 6:232).

23. Swami Rama Tirtha himself was not entirely clear about his knowledge of German. In a 1905 lecture in Mathura, he mentioned having once travelled on a German ship; only the captain spoke English, and using him as a translator Swami Rama Tirtha conversed with the German passengers (*IWGR* 4:193-194). Later in 1905 in Faizabad, he told an audience that there were five or six hundred Germans on the ship, and that he learned to speak German in eight days through conversing with them (*IWGR* 4:289). Swami Rama Tirtha's own apparent embellishment of his training in the German language recalls the "retrospective dramatization" that Erik H. Erikson (1958: 143) identified in Martin Luther's life.

24. According to Narayan Swami, who was with Swami Rama Tirtha at this time, the encounter with the *paṇḍits* occurred not in Benares, but in Hardwar (*KeR* 2:282). The inspiration for placing this event in Benares may come from the anonymous (1912: 23) *Swami Rama Tirath: A Sketch of His Life and Teachings,* which also reports that the Swami met with *paṇḍits* in Benares; to the best of my knowledge, however, this text was never reprinted and none of the hagiographies makes direct reference to it.

25. Lawrence S. Cunningham (1985: 79-87) has noted a similar tendency to focus on the persona of the saint rather than theology in the accounts of the lives of many Christian saints.

26. See, for example, Lutgendorf 1993. Lutgendorf (1993: 79-101) demonstrates that the biographies of Tulsidas (who, like Swami Rama Tirtha, did not found a sect) became increasingly elaborate over time (the earliest accounts were no more than a few lines), with biographies from the late nineteenth and early twentieth centuries championing Tulsidas as "the single most influential guide of a newly self-conscious and increasingly homogenous mainstream tradition." See also Lorenzen 1991, a study of the legends surrounding the life of Kabir; many of those legends paint a portrait of Kabir designed to suit the purposes of institutions founded in Kabir's memory.

Chapter Six

1. This is especially true of medieval hagiographical collections. For example, in Nabhadas' *Bhaktamāla*, the accounts of a particular devotee may be no more than a few lines; these accounts were expanded in written commentaries and presumably in oral performances as well.

2. Some modern collections focus on the saints of a particular region, such as Khanolkar 1978, which includes accounts of saints from different Hindu sects in Maharashtra as well as accounts of two Muslim saints. Other collections are organized according to the different regions of India, such as Sholapurkar 1992, which covers saints from north, east, central, and south India, and includes accounts of Sufis, Sikhs, Jains, Christians, and saints representing various sectarian Hindu traditions. Others take India as a whole as their primary category, such as Bhattacharya 1982, which includes accounts of the Buddha, Mahavira, St. Thomas, various Śaiva and Vaiṣṇava saints, Sankara, and various Sufis; similarly Hṛday's 1987 Hindi text *Santõ kī Vāṇī* covers a vast range of figures from Swami Rama Tirtha, Swami Vivekananda, and Swami Dayananda Saraswati to the Buddha, Mahavira, Tolstoy, and Sheikh Sādī. Some medieval collections such as the *Bhaktamāl* also include saints of differing theological positions and from different regions. Other collections, such as those recounting the lives of exemplary Buddhists, were often organized around particular virtues (with each subject exemplifying a particular Buddhist virtue).

3. I have been unable to determine the original publication date; all references here are to the second edition.

4. Much of the debate centers on whether Kabir was actually born into a low caste, or whether he was born as a Brāhmaṇ, but adopted by low-caste parents. Some Kabir hagiographies also relate his initiation by the saint Ramanand; this too is contested. See Lorenzen 1991, and Vaudeville 1974: 3-48.

5. The constituent institutions are listed on the inside back cover of most Bharatiya Vidya Bhavan publications.

6. For more on the aims of the Book University, see "Kulapati's Preface" (*TSI*: v-vii).

7. Mahadevan continues with a discussion of the various names used for saints and sages, and argues that the term "saint" is all-inclusive for such figures.

8. Mahadevan wrote a full biography of Ramana Maharshi as well: see Mahadevan 1977.

9. For example, on Jawaharlal Nehru's birthday each year, India's national television network Doordarshan commemorates the day by showing children's films.

10. A similar story is told about devotees of Shiva who point their feet at his *liṅgam*, are challenged, and give the same response as Nanak.

11. Indeed the *RJC*'s version of the Swami's arrival in America is similar. The author correctly places the Swami's arrival in Seattle, and then relates a conversation much like the one in *BMR*: as passengers were gathering their luggage and preparing to disembark, Swami Rama Tirtha sat comfortably on a deck chair, his legs crossed. An American man asked him where he was going, and the Swami replied that he was going to America. The American told him that this was the final port of call, and he would have to disembark. Swami Rama said that he would; the American then asked him if he had any luggage or money, and was shocked when the Swami said he had no money, and no luggage but his own body. He declared that the Swami would starve to death in the United States, and asked if the Swami perhaps had a letter of introduction to any Americans; he did not. The American insisted that the Swami would not survive in a wealthy country which operated on money alone, but Swami Rama could only laugh, insisting that he would be happy wherever he was. The American took pity on him, and asked if he even knew any Americans. The Swami calmly

replied that he knew one—the man with whom he spoke. Then he placed his arm on the American's shoulder. The Swami's touch made the American's hair stand on end, and suddenly it seemed as if he had known the Swami forever. He smiled, invited the Swami home with him, and would look after him for the next year and a half (*RJC*: 55-56).

Chapter Seven

1. The Swami's English poetry may be found in the concluding sections of the first three volumes of *IWGR*. His Urdu poetry has been transliterated into Devanāgarī script for the two-volume *Rām-Varṣā* (1978). When the poems were first published, they were printed in both Urdu and Hindi versions. See Narayan Swami's introduction to volume 1 of *Rām-varṣā*. The text includes not only Swami Rama Tirtha's poems and devotional songs, but also other compositions he had written in his notebooks, such as verses from the *Ādi Granth*, with songs in volume one, and poems in volume two. For English translations of some of the Swami's Urdu and Persian poems, see Alston 1991. Alston's translations do not include a detailed critique of the Swami's poetic style beyond his statements that "if his own Urdu poetry was mainly in a popular style, he could rise, when his theme demanded it, to a more sophisticated mode of expression" and that the "poems can be read for their own intrinsic interest as a restatement in modern terms of the ancient upanishadic wisdom, or they can be used as devotional reading by seekers on a spiritual path" (Alston 1991: 27, 31).

2. Sharma (1921: 106) also remarked that the Swami's "endless repetitions" would "require much pruning."

3. As part of an overall laudatory assessment of the Swami as both an English and Urdu poet in her essay "Kavirmanīṣī Kavihṛday Swāmī Rāmtīrth," Lakshmi Kanta Chawla [Lakṣmī Kāntā Cāwlā](1976: 57) included a Hindi translation of C.F. Andrews' statement that "the outward setting of these poems . . . may often be crude and even grotesque, but the inner spirit may be caught by the sympathetic reader beneath the imperfect vehicle of expression."

4. I have been unable to determine the precise time at which the prediction was included in the first volume of *IWGR*; it did not appear in the first edition published in 1909.

5. Similarly, Raj Kumar Arora (1978: 64-65) asserted that Swami Rama Tirtha's travels to Japan and the United States had shown him that before India could adopt Vedānta, it must attain freedom, and therefore he advocated jail and even the gallows over prayer. This directly contradicts Swami Rama Tirtha's own argument that the only way India could attain freedom was through the adoption of his Practical Vedānta, and that the nationalist movement without Vedānta was doomed to failure.

6. The Hindi phrasing of his version of the prediction suggests that it was translated from English—the vocabulary is Sanskritized (whereas Swami Rama Tirtha himself used predominantly Urdu vocabulary) and the phrasing is somewhat awkward: "Cāhe ek śarīr ke dwārā, cāhe anek ṣarīrõ dwārā kām karte hue Rām pratijñā kartā hai ki bhārat bīsvī̃ śatābdī ke pratham arddh bhāg se pūrv hī punaḥ apne prācīn mahimāmay gaurav ko prāpt kar legā. Āp Rām ke in śabdõ ko noṭ kar lẽ" ["whether working through one body or many, Rama promises that before the end of the first half of the twentieth century, India will reattain its ancient, great glory. Please note these words of Rama"]. A differently worded Hindi version of the prediction appears in the SRTP publication *SRTP ke Baṛhte Caraṇ Smārikā* (1991: 10): Rām cāhe akele yā cāhe anek śarīrõ se kām kare, rām gambhīrāpūrvak vāydā kartā hai ki das varśõ ke bhītar bhārat se andhakār tathā kamzorī dūr kar degā aur bīsvī̃ śatābdī ke pūrvāddh

mẽ bhārat apne purāne gaurav se adhik pratibhāśālī hogā ["whether Rama works alone or through many bodies, he makes this serious pledge that within ten years, he will eliminate India's blindness and weakness, and within the first half of the twentieth century, India will achieve even greater glory than its ancient greatness]."

7. There is yet another version of the prediction in Kedarnath Prabhakar's *Yugsant Rāmtīrth* (1984: 47). According to Prabhakar, the Swami made the prediction during a lecture he gave in Faizabad in the fall of 1905 after spending the summer in Darjeeling. Prabhakar further lists the titles of the lectures that the Swami gave in Faizabad; however, the prediction does not occur in the printed versions of those lectures in *IWGR* 4. Prabhakar's rendering of the prediction is less specific than that cited by the Swami Rama Tirtha Pratishthan: "he said that the time of India's freedom is approaching."

8. Sood (1970: 61) also noted that Tirath Ram failed his B.A. examination the first time he took it because of low marks on the English exam, a fact which other later hagiographers generally omit.

9. See, e.g. Vatsya 1973, Misra 1979: 76-77.

10. It is unclear whether in fact many of the Swami's writings were lost when Amir Chand was arrested. Some later Swami Rama Tirtha Pratishthan publications note that Narayan Swami had to dispose of some of the Swami's notebooks in 1913, but their content is unknown. The earliest editions of *IWGR* note that two essays were not published ("Evils of Capitalism" and "Christianity vs. Churchianity") for fear that they would be deemed problematic by British officials. As of 1992, officials of the Swami Rama Tirtha Pratishthan in Lucknow had no idea what had happened to those essays. See SRTP 1991: 12.

11. This is part of a larger argument with a strong anti-Muslim sentiment and a reading of Indian history that is common among Hindu fundamentalist groups: the notion that Hindus were religiously tolerant, but politically weak and disunified, and this allowed Muslims to take over large portions of the country as part of their "fanatic bigotry." According to this argument, the Mughal empire eventually collapsed due to its own immorality (in Lata's words, they were "locked up in their harems") and Hindus could have reasserted control to stop the British, but were still weak and disunified.

12. This assertion is not part of a complex theological analysis of Swami Rama Tirtha as a saint; rather, his followers treat it as self-evident.

13. The Swami's own writings, of course, provide an opportunity for a kind of direct experience, but that experience is nonetheless influenced by other images of the Swami. Prem Lata and Satish Kumar, for example, when they wrote of their own responses to the Swami's poetry, did so by explicitly contextualizing their remarks within the larger body of commentary on the Swami's works.

14. Wach (1962: 3-4) recognized a similar pattern of development in his study of the master/disciple relationship: "[The disciple] alone possesses the full value of the image, and others are dependent on him for their view of the master. And as he, in order to make known the beloved figure, tries to transmit the features of the master's character to others, so also the other disciples do it, in fact all who surround the master. In them burns the desire to share what they have known by firsthand experience, and they are eager to tell others. But the secret of the master is really the influence of his personality; and only he who has experienced it can evaluate it. So from the beginning the labor of the disciple carries the germ of the tragic necessity that it must fail. Whoever saw the master cannot communicate the experience which he alone had; any talk of it is bound to fail. Each story concerning the master is a legend which has its own action and time. The legend itself changes when it is once established along more universal lines and has received a form that is easily apprehended; as such it reaches those who come after, for whom it becomes tradition and history." For Wach,

if the image of the master became a "legend" along universal lines (rather than an image based on direct experience), then it was a "failure" of sorts. Such changing images, however, are not failures; they simply reflect the fact that images of masters and saints necessarily become detached from the masters and saints as historical figures.

15. For example, speculating on why the biographies of Tyagaraja did not mention war, famine, and the presence of foreigners although they were important in Tyagaraja's lifetime, Jackson (1992: 722) commented, "Perhaps, as some scholars suggest, this is a typically Indian response to history. For Hindus, history does not really exist, being *māyā* and *asat*; it is therefore unworthy of much attention when compared with the timeless reality." However, the ongoing popularity of a figure such as Tyagaraja suggests that part of his power lies in his relevance to people in changing historical contexts. Thus the war and famine of Tyagaraja's own lifetime may no longer be of concern, but surely other aspects of his life are, and that is why people have continued to write about him.

Bibliography

The first section of the bibliography lists materials from the Swami Rama Tirtha hagiographical tradition and hagiographical collections. The second section lists secondary sources. The language of texts not in English is noted after the bibliographic information, and these citations are given with full diacritics. Multiple volume works are listed in volume order rather than chronological order. The Swami Rama Tirtha Pratishthan (SRTP) was originally known as the Swami Rama Tirtha Publication League, and now sometimes publishes Hindi texts using the name "Rama Tirtha Pratishthan"; each citation reproduces the actual name given with the text.

PRIMARY MATERIALS

Hagiographies of Swami Rama Tirtha

Aggarwal, Harikishandas, and Eric Francis. 1974. *Divinity Trail.* Bombay: Tulsi Manas Prakashan.

Arora, Raj Kumar. 1988. *Swami Ram Tirath: His Life and Works.* New Delhi: Rajesh Publications.

Bhāradvāj, Kailāś Nāth. 1976. *Swāmī Rām Tīrth: Jīvan, Darśan aur Sandeś.* Phagwara: Navodaya Sāhitya Saṅgam Prakāśan. Hindi.

Inderjit. 1976. *Swāmī Rāma Tīrtha.* Delhi: Hari Kranti Enterprises. Urdu.

Kumar, Satish. 1977. *Swami Rama Tirtha: Great Mystic Poet of the Modern India.* Lucknow: SRTP.

Miśra, Jayarām. 1979. *Swāmī Rāma Tīrtha: Jīvan aur Darśan.* Allahabad: Lok Bhāratī Prakāśan. Hindi.

Narayan Swami. n.d.. *Untitled* (Urdu life of Swami Rama Tirtha).

Prabhākar, Kedarnāth. 1983. *Rām Bādshāh.* Saharanpur: Rama Tirtha Kendra. Urdu.

———. 1984. *Yugsant Rāmtīrth.* Saharanpur: Rama Tirtha Kendra. Hindi.

Rama Tirtha Pratisthan. 1988. *Swāmī Rām Tīrth kī Saṅkṣipt Jīvanī.* Lucknow: SRTP. Hindi.

———. 1989. *Rām Jīvan Citrāvalī.* Lucknow: SRTP. Hindi.

Sharga, Brijnath. 1968. *Life of Swami Rama Tirtha.* 2nd ed. Lucknow: SRTP.

Sharma, S.R. [1]. 1921. *Swami Rama Tirtha: The Poet-Apostle of Practical Vedanta.* Mangalore: Dharma Prakash Press.

Sharma, S.R. [2]. 1961. *Swami Rama Tirtha.* Bombay: Bharatiya Vidya Bhavan.

Shastri, Hari Prasad. n.d. *Ram Tirtha: Scientist and Mahatma.* London: Shanti Sadan.

Singh, Puran. 1974. *The Story of Swami Rama: The Poet-Monk of India.* Reprint 1924 ed. Lucknow: SRTP.

———. 1982. *Swāmī Rām Jīvankathā*. 4th ed. Lucknow: SRTP. Translated into Hindi by Dīn Dayālu.
Singh, Randhīr. n.d. *Jīvan Swāmī Rām Tīrth*. Hardwar: Randhir Book Sales. Hindi.
Sood, D.R. 1970. *Swami Ram Tirth*. New Delhi: National Book Trust.
———. 1974. *Swāmī Rām Tīrth*. Translated into Urdu by Muhammad Jalandhari. New Delhi: National Book Trust. Urdu.
Sultānpurī, Śaṅkar. 1981. *Swāmi Rām Tīrth (Bālopayogī khaṇḍ kāvya)*. New Delhi: Arya Book Depot. Hindi.
Tara, Pandit Ram Lal. 1943. "The Late Swami Ram Tirath." In *Punjab's Eminent Hindus*, edited byN.B. Sen, 120-126. Lahore: New Book Society.
Taskīn, Śivanāth Rāy Jī. 1974. *Jīvan Caritra Swāmī Rāmtīrth*. Delhi: Chand Book Depot. Hindi and Urdu.
Vatsya, Santarām. 1985. *Swāmī Rām Tīrth*. New Delhi: Subodh Publications. Hindi.

Swami Rama Tirtha's Works

Hindi/Urdu

Swami Rama Tirtha. 1937-1944. *Kullīyāt-e-Rām*. 3 vols. Lucknow: Sri Rama Tirtha Publication League. Urdu.
———. 1960. *Rām-Patra: Swāmī Rāmtīrthjī Mahārāj Apne Guru ke Prati Cune Hue Patrõ kā Saṅgrah*. Lucknow: SRTP. Hindi.
———. 1978. *Rāma-Varṣā: Bhāg Ek*. Lucknow: SRTP. Hindi.
———. 1977. *Rāma-Varṣā: Bhāg Do*. Lucknow: SRTP. Hindi.

English

———. 1913. *In Woods of God-Realization: The Complete Works of Swami Rama Tirtha*. Volumes 11 and 12, *Rama's Note Books*. Lucknow: SRTP.
———. 1971. *In Woods of God-Realization: The Complete Works of Swami Rama Tirtha*. Vol. 10, *Snapshots and Impressions*. Lucknow: SRTP.
———. 1978-1990. *In Woods of God-Realization: The Complete Works of Swami Rama Tirtha*. 7 vols. Lucknow: SRTP.

Hagiographical Collections, Publications of the Swami Rama Tirtha Mission, and Works about Swami Rama Tirtha

Aggarwāl, Hari Kiśandās, ed. 1976. *Swāmī Rāmtīrth Smṛti Granth*. Bombay: Hari Kiṣandās Aggarwāl. Hindi.
Alston, A.J. 1982. *Yoga and the Supreme Bliss: Songs of Enlightenment by Swami Ram Tirtha*. London: Shanti Sadan.
Atreya, Dr. B.L. 1966. *Practical Vedant: The Philosophy of Swami Rama Tirtha*. Lucknow: SRTP.

Bhāradvāj, Kailāśnāth, ed. 1976. *Swāmī Rāmtīrth: Jīvan aur Sandeś*. Phagwara: Navodaya Sāhitya Saṅgam Prakāśan.

Bhattacarya, Vivek. 1982. *Famous Indian Sages: Their Immortal Messages*. New Delhi: Sagar Publications.

Cāwlā, Lakṣmī Kāntā. 1976. "*Kavirmanīṣī Kavihṛday Swāmī Rāmtīrth*." In *Swāmī Rāmtīrth: Jīvan aur Sandeś*, edited by Kailāś Nāth Bhāradvāj. Phagwara: Navodaya Sāhitya Saṅgam Prakāśan.

Dūbe, Śukdev. 1970. *Santõ kī Kahāniyā̃*. Allahabad: Sāhitya Bhavan. Hindi.

Hṛday, Vyathit. 1987. *Santõ kī Vāṇī*. Delhi: Pāṇḍulipi Prakāśan.

Khanolkar, Savitribai. 1978. *Saints of Maharashtra*. Bombay: Bharatiya Vidya Bhavan.

Mahadevan, T.M.P. 1970. *Ramana Maharshi: The Sage of Arunacala*. London: George Allen and Unwin.

———. 1990. *Ten Saints of India*. 5th ed. Bombay: Bharatiya Vidya Bhavan.

Maheshwari, H. 1969. *The Philosophy of Swami Rama Tirtha*. Agra: Shiva Lal Agarwala and Company.

Natesan and Co. n.d. *Ramanand to Ram Tirath: Lives of the Saints of North Indian Including the Sikh Gurus*. Madras: G.A. Natesan and Co.

Pāntharī, Bhagavatī Prasād, ed. 1983. *Swāmī Rām Tīrth Vārṣikāṅk*. Dehradun: Swāmī Rām Smaraṇ Aṅk Samiti. Hindi.

———. 1989. *Swāmī Rām Tīrth Vārṣikāṅk*. Tehri, U.P.: Swāmī Rām Smaraṇ Aṅk Samiti. Hindi.

Shargha, B.N. 1972. *Legacy of Rama*. Lucknow: SRTP.

Rām Rāj. n.d. *Call Divine*. New Delhi: Ram Raj. Hindi and English.

Śaraṇ, Śrī. 1982. *Swāmī Rāmtīrth: Subhāṣit aur Sūktiyā̃*. New Delhi: Arya Book Depot. Hindi.

Sholapurkar, G.R. 1992. *Saints and Sages of India*. Delhi: Bharatiya Vidya Prakashan.

Swami Rama Tirtha Mission. n.d. *Memorandum of Association and Rules and Regulations of Swami Rama Tirtha Mission (regd.)*. Delhi: Swan Press of Lahore.

———. 1977. *Bhajanāvalī*. Delhi: Swami Rama Tirtha Mission.

———. 1991. *Hari Oṃ Vacanāmṛt*. New Delhi: Swami Rama Tirtha Mission. Hindi.

Swami Rama Tirtha Pratisthan. 1965. *Swami Narayana: Some Reminiscences with a Brief Life Sketch*. Lucknow: SRTP.

———. 1989. *Swāmī Śrīmānnārāyaṇ kī Jīvan-kathā aur Saṃsmaraṇ*. Lucknow: SRTP. Hindi.

———. 1991. *Swāmī Rāmtīrth Pratiṣṭhān ke Baṛhte Caraṇ Smārikā: Śrī Nārāyaṇ Swāmī Se Śrī Ayodhyanāth Tak*. Lucknow: SRTP.

Prabhākar, Kedarnāth. 1986. *Ahal-e-Islām kī Nazarīn Swāmī Rām Tīrth*. Deoband: Mahboob Printing Press. Urdu.

Śānti Prakāś, ed. 1933. *Nārāyaṇ Caritra*. Lucknow: SRTP. Urdu.

Swāmī Amar Muni Mahārāj. 1977. *Bhajanāvalī*. Dehradun: Paramādhyakṣa, Swami Rama Tirtha Mission. Hindi.

Talwalkar, Gopinath. 1977. *Some Indian Saints*. New Delhi: National Book Trust.

Vānaprasthī, Prāṇnāth. 1963. *Bhārat ke Mahān Ṛṣi*. Delhi: Rajpal and Sons. Hindi.

OTHER SOURCES

Babb, Lawrence A. 1986. *Redemptive Encounters: Three Modern Styles in the Hindu Tradition*. Berkeley: University of California Press.

Babb, Lawrence A. and Susan S. Wadley, eds. 1997. *Media and the Transformation of Religion in South Asia*. Delhi: Motilal Banarsidass Publishers.

Bassuk, Daniel E. 1987. *Incarnation in Hinduism and Christianity: The Myth of the God-Man*. Atlantic Highlands, NJ: Humanities Press International, Inc.

Bhāradvāj, Bhagavān Śarār. 1978. *Hindī Jīvan Sāhitya: Siddhānt aur Adhyayan*. Allahabad: Parimal Prakashan. Hindi.

Blumenfeld-Kosinski, Renate, and Timea Szell, eds. 1991. *Images of Sainthood in Medieval Europe*. Ithaca: Cornell University Press.

Boyer, Regis. 1981. "An Attempt to Define the Typology of Medieval Hagiography." In *Hagiography and Medieval Literature: A Symposium*, edited by Hans Bekker-Nielsen, Peter Foote, Jorgen Hojgaard Jorgensen, and Tore Nyberg. Odense: Odense University Press.

Brown, Peter. 1971. "The Rise and Function of the Holy Man in Late Antiquity." *The Journal of Roman Studies* LXI: 80-101.

———. 1981. *The Cult of the Saints: Its Rise and Function in Latin Christianity*. Chicago: University of Chicago Press.

———. 1987. "The Saint as Exemplar in Late Antiquity." In *Saints and Virtues*, edited by John Stratton Hawley, 3-14. Berkeley: University of California Press.

Bruner, Edward M. 1986. "Experience and Its Expressions." In *The Anthropology of Experience*, edited by Victor W. Turner and Edward M. Bruner, 3-30. Urbana and Chicago: University of Illinois Press.

Callewaert, Winand M. 1988. *The Hindī Biography of Dādū Dayāl*. Delhi: Motilal Banarsidass.

Callewaert, Winand and Rupert Snell, eds. 1996. *According to Tradition: Hagiographical Writing in India*. Wiesbaden: Otto Harrassowitz.

Campbell, Joseph. 1968. *The Hero with a Thousand Faces*. 2nd ed. Princeton: Princeton University Press.

Chaturvedi, Mahendra, and Bhola Nath Tiwari, eds. 1989. *A Practical Hindi-English Dictionary*. 17th. ed. New Delhi: National Publishing House.

Cohn, Robert. 1987. "Sainthood." In *The Encyclopedia of Religion*, 13: 1-6. New York: Macmillan Publishing Company.

Coon, Lynda L. 1997. *Sacred Fictions: Holy Women and Hagiography in Late Antiquity*. Philadelphia: University of Pennsylvania Press.

Cox, Patricia. 1983. *Biography in Late Antiquity: A Quest for the Holy Man*. Berkeley: University of California Press.

Cunningham, Lawrence. 1985. "Hagiography and Imagination." *Studies in the Literary Imagination* 18, 1: 79-87.

de Certeau, Michel. 1988. "A Variant: Hagio-graphical Edification." In *The Writing of History*, 269-283. Translated from the French by Tom Conley. New York: Columbia University Press.

Dehejia, Vidya. 1988. *Slaves of the Lord: The Path of the Tamil Saints*. Delhi: Munshiram Manoharlal.

Delehaye, Hippolyte. 1907. *The Legends of the Saints: An Introduction to Hagiography*. Translated from the French by V.M. Crawford. London: Longmans, Green and Co.

Dilthey, Wilhelm. 1962. *Pattern and Meaning in History: Thoughts on History and Society*. Edited with an Introduction by H. P. Rickman. New York: Harper Torchbooks.

Dimock, Edward C. 1976. "Religious Biography in India: The 'Nectar of the Acts' of Caitanya." In *The Biographical Process: Studies in the History and Psychology of Religion*, edited by Frank E. Reynolds and Donald Capps, 109-117. The Hague: Mouton.

Erikson, Erik H. 1958. *Young Man Luther: A Study in Psychoanalysis and History*. New York: W.W. Norton and Company.

Eschmann, Anncharlott. 1972. "Der Avatāragedanke im Hinduismus des Neunzehnten und Zwanzigsten Jahrhunderts." *Numen*, 19, 1 (April): 229-40.

Feldhaus, Anne. 1984. *The Deeds of God in Ṛddhipur*. New York: Oxford University Press.

Finnegan, Ruth. 1977. *Oral Poety: Its Nature, Significance, and Social Context*. Cambridge: Cambridge University Press.

Foley, John Miles. 1988. *The Theory of Oral Composition*. Bloomington and Indianapolis: Indiana University Press.

Gadamer, Hans-Georg. 1985. *Truth and Method*. New York: Crossroad Publishing Company.

Geary, Patrick. 1996. "Saints, Scholars, and Society: The Elusive Goal." In *Saints: Studies in Hagiography*, edited by Sandro Sticca, 1-22. Binghamton, NY: Medieval and Renaissance Texts and Studies.

Granoff, Phyllis. 1985. "Scholars and Wonder-Workers: Some Remarks on the Role of the Supernatural in Philosophical Contests in Vedānta Hagiographies." *Journal of the American Oriental Society* 105, 3: 459-469.

———. 1988a. "Jain Biographies of Nagarjuna: Notes on the Composing of a Biography in Medieval India." In *Monks and Magicians: Religious Biographies in Asia*, edited by Phyllis Granoff and Koichi Shinohara, 45-66. Oakville: Mosaic Press.

———. 1988b. "The Biographies of Arya Khapatacarya: A Preliminary Investigation into the Transmission and Adaptation of Biographical Legends." In *Monks and Magicians: Religious Biographies in Asia*, edited by Phyllis Granoff and Koichi Shinohara, 67-98. Oakville: Mosaic Press.

Grierson, George A. 1909. "Gleanings from the Bhakta-mala." *Journal of the Royal Asiatic Society*: 607-644.

———. 1910. "Gleanings from the Bhakta-mala" (continued). *Journal of the Royal Asiatic Society*: 87-109.

Halbfass, Wilhelm. 1988. *India and Europe: An Essay in Understanding*. Albany: State University of New York Press.

Haq, Abdul. 1993. *Urdu-English Dictionary*. New Delhi: Star Publications.

Hawley, John S. 1979. "The Early *Sūr Sāgar* and the Growth of the Sūr Tradition." *Journal of the American Oriental Society*, 99, 1: 64-72.

———. 1987. (ed.) *Saints and Virtues*. Berkeley: University of California Press.

———. 1988. "Author and Authority in the Bhakti Poetry of North India." *Journal of Asian Studies* 47, 2: 269-290.

———. 1993. "Why Sūrdās Went Blind." *Journal of Vaiṣṇava Studies* 1, 2: 62-78.

Head, Thomas. 1990. *Hagiography and the Cult of Saints: The Diocese of Orleans, 800-1200*. Cambridge: Cambridge University Press.

Heffernan, Thomas J. 1988. *Sacred Biography: Saints and their Biographers in the Middle Ages*. Oxford: Oxford University Press.

Hudson, Dennis. 1993. "Āṇṭāḷ Āḻvār: A Developing Hagiography." *Journal of Vaiṣṇava Studies* 1, 2:27-61.

Hughes, H. Maldwyn. 1994. "Experience (Religious)." In *Encyclopedia of Religion and Ethics* 5: 630-635, edited by James Hastings. Reprint 1926 ed. Edinburgh: T & T Clark.

Iser, Wolfgang. 1978. *The Act of Reading: A Theory of Aesthetic Response*. Baltimore: The Johns Hopkins University Press.

Jackson, William J. 1991. *Tyāgarāja: Life and Lyrics*. Madras: Oxford University Press.

———. 1992. "A Life Becomes a Legend: Śrī Tyāgarāja as Exemplar." *Journal of the American Academy of Religion* 40, 4: 717-736.

James, William. 1902. The Varieties of Religious Experience: A Study in Human Nature. London: Longmans, Green, and Co.

Jhā, Narendra. 1978. *Bhaktamāla: Pāṭhānuśīlan evaṃ Vivecan*. Patna: Anupam Prakāśan. Hindi.

Jones, Kenneth W. 1976. *Arya Dharm: Hindu Consciousness in 19th-Century Punjab*. Berkeley: University of California Press.

———. 1989. *Socio-religous Reform Movements in British India*. Cambridge: Cambridge University Press.

Juergensmeyer, Mark. 1987. "Saint Gandhi." In *Saints and Virtues*, edited by John Stratton Hawley, 187-203. Berkeley: University of California Press.

Keyes, C.F. 1982. "Charisma: From Social Life to Sacred Biography." In *Charisma and Sacred Biography*, edited by Michael Williams. Journal of the American Academy of Religion Studies, vol. 48, 3 & 4: 1-22.

Kieckhefer, Richard and George D. Bond, eds. 1988. *Sainthood: Its Manifestations in World Religions*. Berkeley: University of California Press.

LaFleur, William R. 1987. "Biography." In *The Encyclopedia of Religion* 2: 220-224, edited by Mircea Eliade. New York: Macmillan Publishing Company.

Lawrence, Bruce. 1982. "The Chistīya of Sultanate India: A Case Study in Biographical Complexities in South Asian Islam." In *Charisma and Sacred Biography*, edited by Michael Williams. Journal of the American Academy of Religion Studies, vol. 48, 3 & 4: 47-67.

———. 1993. "Biography and the 17th Century Qādirīya of North India." In *Islam and Indian Regions*, edited by Anna Libera Dallapiccola and Stephanie Zingel-Ave Lallemant, 399-415. Stuttgart: Franz Steiner Verlag.

Lord, Albert Bates. 1978. *The Singer of Tales*. Reprint 1960 ed. New York: Atheneum.

Lorenzen, David. 1976. "The Life of Śaṅkarācārya." In *The Biographical Process: Studies in the History and Psychology of Religion*, edited by Frank E. Reynolds and Donald Capps, 87-107. The Hague: Mouton.

———. 1981. "The Kabīr Panth: Heretics to Hindus." In *Religious Change and Cultural Domination*, edited by David N. Lorenzen. Mexico City: El Colegio de Mexico.

———. 1987. "The Social Ideologies of Hagiography: Sankara, Tukaram, and Kabir." In *Religion and Society in Maharashtra*, edited by Milton Israel and N.K. Wagle, 92-114. Toronto: University of Toronto Centre for South Asian Studies.

———. 1991. *Kabir Legends and Ananta-Das's 'Kabir-Parachai'*. Albany: State University of New York Press.

———. 1995. "The Lives of Nirguṇī Saints." In *Bhakti Religion in North India: Community Identity and Political Action*, edited by David Lorenzen, 181-211. Albany: State University of New York Press.

Lutgendorf, Philip. 1991. *The Life of a Text: Performing the Rāmcaritmānas of Tulsidas*. Berkeley: University of California Press.

———. 1993. "The Quest for the Legendary Tulsīdās." *Journal of Vaiṣṇava Studies* 1, 2: 79-101.

Marshall, Donald G. 1993. *Contemporary Critical Theory*. New York: The Modern Language Association of America.

McLeod, W.H. 1968. *Gurū Nānak and the Sikh Religion*. Oxford: Oxford University Press.

Miller, David. 1986. "Karma, Rebirth, and the Contemporary Guru." In *Karma and Rebirth: Post Classical Developments*, edited by Ronald W. Neufeldt, 61-81. Albany: State University of New York Press

Monier-Williams, Sir Monier. 1981. *A Sanskrit-English Dictionary*. Reprint 1899 ed. Delhi: Motilal Banarsidass.

Murphet, Howard. 1976. *Sai Baba: Man of Miracles*. New York: Samuel Weiser, Inc.

Olney, James. 1978. "Autos - Bios - Graphein: The Study of Autobiographical Literature." *South Atlantic Quarterly* 77: 113-123.

Olsen, Alexandra Hennessey. 1980. "'De Historiis Sanctorum': A Generic Study of Hagiography." *Genre* 13 (Winter 1980): 407-429.

Ong, Walter J. 1982. *Orality and Literacy: The Technologizing of the Word*. London and New York: Routledge.

Platts, John T. 1983. *A Dictionary of Urdu, Classical Hindi, and English*. Reprint 1911 ed. Lahore: Sang-e-meel Publications.

Potter, Karl H. 1980. "The Karma Theory and Its Interpretation in Some Indian Philosophical Systems." In *Karma and Rebirth in Classical Indian Traditions*, edited by Wendy Doniger O'Flaherty, 241-267. Berkeley: University of California Press.

Prasād, Kālikā, Rājvallabh Sahāy, and M. Śrīvāstav, eds. 1984. *Bṛhat Hindī Kośa*. Varanasi: Jñānamaṇḍal Limited.

Propp, Vladimir. 1975. *Morphology of the Folktale*. Austin: University of Texas Press.

Proudfoot, Wayne. 1985. *Religious Experience*. Berkeley: University of California Press.

Ramanujan, A.K. 1982. "On Women Saints." In *The Divine Consort*, edited by John S. Hawley and Donna M. Wulff, 316-324. Berkeley: Berkeley Religious Studies Series.

Ray, Reginald A. 1992. *Buddhist Saints in India: A Study in Buddhist Values and Orientations*. New York: Oxford University Press.

Reynolds, Frank E. and Donald Capps, eds. 1976. *The Biographical Process: Studies in the History and Psychology of Religion*. The Hague: Mouton.

Rinehart, Robin. 1996. "From *Sanātana Dharma* to Secularism: Hindu Identity in the Thought of Swami Rama Tirtha and the Swami Rama Tirtha Mission." *Religion* 26: 237-247.

———. 1998. "A Message without an Audience: Swami Rama Tirtha's Practical Vedanta." *International Journal of Hindu Studies*, 2, 2 (Aug. 1998): 189-225.

———. "The Portable Bullhe Shah: Biography, Categorization, and Authorship in the Study of Punjabi Sufi Poetry." *Numen*. In press.

———. "Hagiography." In *Encyclopedia of Women and World Religion*, edited by Serinity Young. New York: Macmillan. In press.

Rolland, Romain. 1931. *The Life of Vivekananda and the Universal Gospel*. Calcutta: Advaita Ashram.

Śarma, Kailāścandra. 1983. *Bhaktamāl aur Hindī Kāvya Mẽ uskī Paramparā*. Rohtak: Manthan Publications. Hindi.

Segal, Robert A., ed. 1990. *In Quest of the Hero*. Princeton: Princeton University Press.

Sen, S.P., ed. 1979. *Historical Biography in Indian Literature*. Calcutta: Institute of Historical Studies.

Shackle, Christopher, and Rupert Snell, eds. 1992. *The Indian Narrative: Perspectives and Patterns*. Wiesbaden: Otto Harrassowitz.

Sharf, Robert H. 1998. "Experience." In *Critical Terms for Religious Studies*, edited by Mark C. Taylor, 94-116. Chicago and London: University of Chicago Press.

Sil, Narasingha P. 1991. *Rāmakṛṣṇa Paramahaṃsa: A Psychological Profile*. Leiden: E. J. Brill.

Singh, Puran. 1982. *On Paths of Life*. Patiala: Publication Bureau, Punjabi University.

Snell, Rupert. 1996. "Introduction." In *According to Tradition: Hagiographical Writing in India*, edited by Winand Callewaert and Rupert Snell. Wiesbaden: Otto Harrassowitz.

Stewart, Tony K. 1985. "The Biographical Images of Kṛṣṇa Caitanya: A Study in the Perception of Divinity." Ph.D. Dissertation. The University of Chicago.

———. 1991. "When Biographical Narratives Disagree: The Death of Kṛṣṇa Caitanya." *Numen* 38, 2: 231-260.

———. 1997. "When Rāhu Devours the Moon: The Myth of the Birth of Kṛṣṇa Caitanya." *International Journal of Hindu Studies*, 1, 2: 221-64.

Sticca, Sandro, ed. 1996. *Saints: Studies in Hagiography*. Binghamton, NY: Medieval and Renaissance Texts and Studies.

Swami Nikhilananda. 1953. *Vivekananda: A Biography*. Calcutta: Advaita Ashram.

Swami Tapasyananda. 1986. *Sankara-Dig-Vijaya: The Traditional Life of Sri Sankaracarya*. Madras: Sri Ramakrishna Math.

Tulpule, S.G. 1992. "Tukārām: The Making of a Saint." In *Devotional Literature in South Asia: Current Research, 1985-1988*, edited by R.S. McGregor, 148-152. Cambridge: Cambridge University Press.

Turner, Victor W. 1986. "Dewey, Dilthey, and Drama: An Essay in the Anthropology of Experience." In *The Anthropology of Experience*, edited by Victor W. Turner and Edward M. Bruner, 33-44. Urbana and Chicago: University of Illinois Press.

Vail, Lise F. 1985. "Founders, Swamis, and Devotees: Becoming Divine in North Karnataka." In *Gods of Flesh, Gods of Stone: The Embodiment of Divinity in India*, edited by Joanne Punzo Waghorne and Norman Cutler, 123-140. Chambersburg, PA: Anima Press.

van Buitenen, J.A.B. 1981. *The Bhagavadgītā in the Mahābhārata*. Chicago: University of Chicago Press.

Vauchez, André. 1981. *La Sainteté en Occident aux Dernières Siècles du Moyen âge: D'après Les Procès de Canonisation et Les Documents Hagiographiques*. Rome: Ecole Française de Rome.

Vaudeville, Charlotte. 1974. *Kabīr*. Oxford: Clarendon Press.

Wach, Joachim. 1944. *Sociology of Religion*. Chicago: University of Chicago Press.

———. 1962. "Master and Disciple: Two Religio-sociological Studies." Translated from the German by Susanne Heigel-Wach and Fred Streng. *Journal of Religion* 42, 1: 1-21.

Wall. George. 1995. *Religious Experience and Religious Belief*. Lanham, MD: University Press of America.

Weinstein, Donald, and Rudolph M. Bell. 1982. *Saints and Society: The Two Worlds of Christendom, 100-1700*. Chicago: University of Chicago Press.

Weintraub, Karl J. 1975. "Autobiography and Historical Consciousness." *Critical Inquiry* 1, 4: 821-848.

White, Charles S. J. 1972. "The Sāī Bābā Movement: Approaches to the Study of Indian Saints." *Journal of Asian Studies*, 31: 862-878.

———. 1974. "Swami Muktānanda and the Enlightenment Through Śakti-Pāt." *History of Religions*, 13, 4: 306-322.

———. 1981. "Hindu Holy Persons." In *Abingdon Dictionary of Living Religions*, 300-303. Nashville: Abingdon.

———. 1988. "Indian Developments: Sainthood in Hinduism." In *Sainthood: Its Manifestation in World Religions*, edited by Richard Kieckhefer and George D. Bond, 98-139. Berkeley: University of California Press.

Wilson, Stephen, ed. 1983. *Saints and Their Cults: Studies in Religious Sociology, Folklore and History*. Cambridge: Cambridge University Press.

Williams, Michael A., ed. 1982. *Charisma and Sacred Biography*. Journal of the American Academy of Religion Thematic Studies 48/3 & 4.

Yadav, K.C., ed. 1987. *The Autobiography of Dayanand Saraswati*. Delhi: Manohar.

Index